Nicholas Patrick Wiseman

Sermons on moral subjects

Nicholas Patrick Wiseman

Sermons on moral subjects

ISBN/EAN: 9783744744720

Printed in Europe, USA, Canada, Australia, Japan

Cover: Foto ©Lupo / pixelio.de

More available books at **www.hansebooks.com**

SERMONS

ON

MORAL SUBJECTS.

BY HIS EMINENCE

CARDINAL WISEMAN

DUBLIN:
JAMES DUFFY, 15, WELLINGTON-QUAY;
AND
22, PATERNOSTER-ROW, LONDON.
1864.

[The right of translation is reserved.]

CONTENTS.

SERMON		PAGE
I.	On the Love of the World,	1
II.	On Scandal,	18
III.	Difficulty of Salvation of the Rich,	36
IV.	On Detraction,	58
V.	On Repentance,	77
VI.	On the Fast of Lent,	92
VII.	On Confession,	111
VIII.	On the Unprofitable Servant,	128
IX.	On Unworthy Communion,	148
X.	On Delay of Repentance,	163
XI.	On the Small Number of the Elect,	180
XII.	On the Hatefulness of Sin,	199
XIII.	On Death,	219
XIV.	An Unprepared Death,	239
XV.	On the Last Judgment,	259
XVI.	On the Character of Faith,	280
XVII.	On Religious Unity,	297
XVIII.	On Charity,	317
XIX.	On the Love of our Neighbour,	334
XX.	On the Celebration of a First Mass,	353
XXI.	On Fickleness and its Remedy,	364
XXII.	On Tribulation,	380
XXIII.	Conclusion of a Course,	400

THE Sermons contained in this volume were delivered from the same pulpit, and under the same circumstances, as those lately published under the title of "Sermons on our Lord and His Blessed Mother." They require, therefore, no Preface, or preliminary remarks, beyond what are prefixed to that Collection; and the reader, it is trusted, will indulgently receive the explanations and apologies given in the one, in extenuation of the faults which he will find in the other.

LONDON, OCTOBER, 1864.

SERMON I.

On the Love of the World.

1 JOHN, ii. 15.

"Love not the world, nor those things which are in the world."

WHAT is it, my brethren, that is so often pointed at and condemned in the Gospel, under the name of the world? Our Divine Redeemer informs His apostles, that the Spirit of Truth, whom He would send down upon them, could not be known by the world; (John, xiv. 17) that the peace which He bestowed upon them was not that which it bestowed. (27.) He forewarns them that the world would hate them as it had first hated Him, (xv. 18) and the prophets before them; (xvii. 14) that it had not even known His eternal Father: (25) and He consequently excludes it from the pathetic prayer which He makes for His apostles. (9.) They, in their turn, were no less careful to caution their followers against the same opposition between their doctrine and the world. St. Paul makes them reflect that it is not the spirit of the world which they have received in Christianity; (1 Cor. ii. 12) that its wisdom is only folly in the eyes of God; (iii. 19) and that his great study was to crucify the world to himself, and himself to the world. (Gal. vi. 14.) And so St. James declares the friendship of the world to be an enemy of God; (iv. 4) while St. John, in the words of my text, draws the consequence from all these truths, by the command not to love it, or the things which it contains.

From all this it is clear, that in this reprobated name are included by far the greater portion of mankind, and that they are so included in consequence of a system of principles which they profess, at variance with the maxims of Christian truth and morality. It is not, therefore, restricted to those only who impugn these maxims, by denying their grounds or their obligation, for the number of these is comparatively small; but it extends to all who, through attachment to the enjoyments of this earth, neglect to profess and to observe them. It claims as its partisans all who, pressing forward to objects of ambition or emolument, are not anxious that the path to them should be through the narrow road of salvation. It counts among its numbers all who, willing to please others on whom they may depend, or for whom they have a regard, fear not to do so by sacrificing their conviction, or infringing on what their conscience dictates to be their duty. In fine, it swells its ranks, beyond calculation, by the thousands who, brought up from infancy with no law but that of fashion, no object but pleasure, and no thought but of mutually obtaining and affording it, flutter through a useless life, totally heedless of any merit or any censure, except that which their companions or masters, in their empty course, may think proper to dispense. All these, you will allow, form a vast proportion of what we even now call the world, though without the odium which the founders of Christianity attached to the name ; since its influence, now, too often extends over the sincere and the virtuous. For it has erected itself into so severe a tribunal, it possesses such formidable means of enforcing its decrees, yet, at the same time, decks itself with such attractions, that many of these are awed, or seduced by its arts, if not into actual abandonment of duty, at least into a frequent attempt to compromise between it and the world.

It is to all these different classes of worshippers that St. John raises his voice, to show them the hollowness of their idol. " Love not the world, nor the things that are in the world." And with reason, my brethren; for in loving the world, you love a tyrant that would impose upon you the most galling slavery ; in loving the world, you love a deceiver that will bring on you nothing but bitter disappointment. The tyranny and deceit of the world should be sufficient motives to keep us from forming any attachment towards it.

Were I to ask you to point out what class of men drag on their lives in the most abject submission and slavery, many of you would, I dare say, seek for them in those very individuals who have *retired* from the world. They have subjected their will to the commands of another ; they have given up their liberty to the obligations of rule and discipline; they have renounced their inclinations, their interests and their passions, in favour of an unvaried and unaspiring life. And yet, in all this, there has been previous reflection and unbiassed choice : the whole of these apparent burthens have been imposed by their own hands, after calculating with certainty, and assuring themselves by trial, not only of their power to bear them, but of the advantages which will repay the attempt. Here the will is previously assured what its direction is ever to be, before it is submitted—it is to be the service of the God whom it loves; here the liberty is subjected only to what is felt necessary by every one for ensuring tranquillity, to a regular undisturbed method of life; here, in fine, every action, every suffering of the future, can be forecast and measured on the scale whereon it is already designed; while yet sufficient choice is left in the selection of occupation, to afford the pleasures of variety. But turn, on the other hand, to those who have devoted their affections to the world, and you find that they are in thraldom to a tyrant that claims full as undisputed a right to their actions, and their wills, and which, moreover, repays their most minute observance with ingratitude, and punishes their slightest deviation with unfeeling rigour. It claims an undisputed sway over every action; for it pretends to regulate every circumstance in life, from public conduct down to domestic arrangement.

Every portion of dress must be copied after fashion, however absurd, or even inconvenient; every dealing with others must be guided by etiquette, however preposterous and unmeaning. Your hours must be measured by custom, though it may be perfectly uncongenial with previous habits or actual circumstances. Your words must be weighed in the most delicate scales, must be measured by the most minute rule, lest they should transgress the appointed standard of condescension or respect. Nothing is left to feeling, or to character,—all is formal and artificial. From our actions, its tyranny extends to our minds. It assumes dominion over our wishes, our inclinations, and our passions. It pretends to prescribe how far you are to bear with your enemy, though your heart may boil against him—whence you must part or quarrel with your friend, though you may really continue to esteem him. And what is the consequence? Why, that in its service, the world exacts sacrifices, which, had they been made for God, would have deserved an eternal reward: it obliges us to subdue or check passions, which, if conquered with purer motives, would have made a perfect Christian. For, how often does interest or established form oblige an individual to bear himself with dissimulating kindness, and esteem, towards those who have injured him, or whom he mortally hates, with an effort far more painful than Christian charity would have exacted in their perfect forgiveness. How often have sums to be wasted in a hecatomb to fashion, where neither profit nor pleasure is reaped, but mere profusion exhibited, a small portion of which bestowed on works of piety might have been highly meritorious. What a command of temper, yet without the merit of meekness; what a restraint upon his most favorite inclinations, yet without the virtue of self-denial; what a guard over his failings, and still without the reward of watchfulness, must he acquire, who wishes to push, by worldly arts, into praise and distinction! Nor does this tyrannous power content itself with imposing all the burthens of virtue, without allowing its merit and reward, but it not unfrequently exacts a sacrifice of our inclinations when they tend to good, and when virtue would be their easiest and most natural choice; it obliges you to deviate from good, and embrace evil, when good would be a pleasure, and the evil a pain.

A forgiving disposition, for instance, which would willingly leave an injury unrevenged, and thus fulfil one of the noblest precepts of philosophy and religion, is taxed by the world as base and cowardly, and has only the choice to repress its virtuous inclinations by violence, and to constrain itself to evil, or be scouted from society. A mind that naturally feels no relish for the foolish or guilty amusements which fill up the life of those around, is condemned as unsocial, and unworthy of its rank, and must force itself, not to enjoy, but to endure them, for fear of risking its prospects or its peace. Indeed, there are not more common remarks, than that some individuals are too upright, and too good, ever to make their way through the world; or that we must be content to take the world as it is, and not as we should wish it. And what is the meaning of these expressions, except that when even virtuously inclined, we must not nourish, but check our tendencies, if we wish to please the world; that natural or habitual honesty and virtue, are drawbacks to our advancement in its favour. Hence our real sentiments are ever fettered; we must approve, or dissent from, what we hear, not according to the dictates of our own minds, but by rules of courtesy or current opinion. We must adopt the ideas of those whom we wish to please, though they may be erroneous, and substitute them for our own; we must watch the passions and the prejudices of the day, and flatter them to insure success; and we shall, perhaps, take to ourselves credit for a great act of fortitude and virtue, if we can hear or see all that we esteem sacred abused, only in silence, without actually joining in the profanation. Thus, while on one side, you have imposed upon you by the world, all that is difficult in virtue, it obliges you to reject, even with pain, whatever would be easy and agreeable in its practice. It might, indeed, be some satisfaction in this total slavery, were the laws which govern us fixed and subject to calculation, or, if they must be arbitrary, could we have a voice in their determination. But, though moving in the world, and directing all our efforts to support it, it is impossible for us ever to discover what power regulates its opinions, what rules guide its fluctuations. All is caprice, all is whim; what is agreeable to-day, is stupid to-morrow: in youth, one line of conduct secures success; as we advance, we must ever vary our step to keep in time with the piping world; (Luke, vii. 32) in age, we must submit to learn a new lesson, or be flung off as antiquated, and insupportable.

And suppose, my brethren, that you do submit, with the most scrupulous punctuality, to this tyranny over your actions and your minds, even against your best interests; what, after all, do you gain but ingratitude. Who was ever satisfied that his attempts to please the world have been ever fully repaid? If you direct them to satisfy all, you aim at an impossibility. Difference of principles in some, ill-nature in many; envy or jealousy on one side, interest on the other, will always bear away a great number to condemn what others may approve. When you wish to be affable, to many you will appear abject; when dignified, you will be pronounced overbearing. Your liberality will be censured by many as profligacy, your moderation as avarice. In fine, every worldly virtue stands so near some fault, that it is impossible to gain the one without appearing, to persons in some particular position, to have only attained the other; and hence it is a vain design to think of winning universal approbation. And if you limit your wishes to the approbation of the few, so many humours, so many passions, so many interests have to be again consulted in even *one* individual, that the chances are infinitely against your obtaining it. How many have here again to complain of cold returns for many an effort to please,—of ungrateful treatment for many a sacrifice even of principle! But with such a poor reward for your services, how severe a vengeance awaits your transgressions. If, having been once attached to the world, you venture to transgress its mandates, or contradict its avowed principles, you incur its resentment, unmitigated by forgiveness,—you bring down its persecutions, unabated by compassion. You become the object of universal criticism or derision; and the least that frequently satisfies its vengeance, is your expulsion or retirement from its society.

My brethren, if your best friend claimed such an influence over you, as to exact a blind submission in whatever concerns you, and in the very sentiments and dispositions of your mind,—if he assumed the right of thwarting them, even where they of themselves led you to your best interests,—if he requited your subjection with ingratitude, and visited your transgressions with severity, how long would he continue to be called your friend? If some fascination had not bound you to him, how quickly would you burst the fetters which he had thrown around you! And can you then love the world, and the things that are in it, while its conduct towards you is equally tyrannical. Living in it, you must, of course, yield to its forms and be regulated by its usages; but there is surely nothing to engage and fix your affections upon it, so as to allow it any ascendancy over your mind. Preserve your independence in that liberty which Christ purchased for you; show yourself superior to its maxims, whenever they are at variance with your principles; despise its practises, when they throw an obstacle between you and your duty. It may frown upon you at first, it may direct its ridicule or its anathemas against you; but if you have strength to resist these, its enmity will soon be turned into admiration, and those poor creatures who have not the courage to imitate your conduct, will envy your independence. It may be true that its tyranny sits lightly upon you at present, in consequence of the flattering promises which it boldly makes of advancement and pleasure. But let not these seduce you into its love; wait not till experience shall have taught you, as it has taught thousands before you, that you can only love a deceiver in loving the world,—a deceiver that can only bring on you a bitter disappointment.

Indeed, my brethren, did the world hold out nothing in compensation for the restraints which it puts upon us, there is no doubt, few or none would choose to submit themselves to its slavery. But it has lures and baits, adapted to every class of persons whom it wishes to gain. To those who have to make their own way to preferment, or eminence, it promises that, by attaching themselves to its service, and following its laws, they will rise rapidly and agreeably; to those who are independent of its favours, it holds out prospects of enjoyments and pleasures, which are in its gift. Experience, however, in general, discovers that these prospects are but delusions, and these enjoyments but vanity. For suppose, my brethren, that our wish on entering life being only how we may advance in the world—in other words, how we may enlarge our means for better procuring its enjoyments, how we may extend our reputation so as to receive its praises—the means which we employ are, to consult the interests and the passions that appear most necessary to favour our views. In this case, how many seeds of disappointment do we sow! For, in the first place, in thus reckoning on the world and its passions, we leave God out of our calculations, on whom alone success and prosperity can depend. We forget that Providence has had designs upon us from our infancy; that He who had known Jeremias, and anointed him as prophet from the womb; that He who had loved Jacob, and determined his successful career before his birth, has no less His views with regard to every individual who comes into the world. He gives to each those abilities and opportunities that will best suit the part which, in His wisdom, He has destined him to act. The order of His heavenly dispensations embraces all. The grand distributions of society, of states, of the rational universe, depend upon the situation of individuals; and if one is out of his place, he goes in opposition to the order designed by God. And can that creature rationally promise himself success, whose views tend to thwart or disarrange this order, by never thinking of the will of his Maker in selecting and prosecuting his course of life? Can he confidently expect to prosper, who never inquires what the designs of God may have been, but has only taken counsel of the world, which he has formally denounced as his enemy? No, my brethren, He has imitated in his conduct that king of Juda, who was placed on the throne by the counsels of men, without the appointment of God; and we may apply to both, with equal justice, the similitude of the prophet in foretelling the success of such conduct. Like that monarch, he may appear at first as a vine set "in a good ground, upon many waters, that it may bear branches, and produce fruit. But thus saith the Lord God. Behold it is planted: shall it prosper then? shall it not be dried up when the burning wind shall touch it, and shall it not wither in the furrows where it grows?" (Ez. xvii. 8, seqq.) In looking forward, then, to the world for our support and advancement, we formally exclude from them the blessing of God, which can alone insure them.

But, beyond all this, we expose ourselves to a thousand chances of disappointment. For what are the grounds on which the world induces us to build our hopes? First, on an exaggerated view, which it ever presents us, of our own capacities. The deception begins from infancy. Whatever little talents we possess are carefully exaggerated to us from that moment, by the fond flattery of parents and friends. Those of our own age, trained to similar ideas as ourselves, keep up within us the same delusion. We enter life at that period when all looks blooming and inviting, when a brisk flow of spirits and a cheerful eye makes us think everything we see to be favoring our wishes. We look around us for the situation most congenial to us, perfectly confident that wherever our choice may fall, our success will be equally complete. It is evident that in such an intemperate state as this we are in want rather of correctives than of additional incentives,—of prudent monitors, to point out our difficulties, rather than of encouragers to precipitate our determinations. And which part does the world act, my brethren? From the elevation to which your fancies have raised you, it indeed opens to you an extended and inviting prospect, which awaits you; but never admonishes you, that this very elevation deceives you, and conceals your difficulties; that what from such a height look like gentle varieties of surface necessary to remove monotony in your career, are in reality rugged and precipitous passes, which you may never surmount; that what appear to you like silent streams that will refresh your course, are in truth boisterous torrents, that will sweep you away before it shall be half finished. It names to you many individuals, who have beaten with success the same track as you have chosen; but it does not show you the peculiar advantage of situation, or support, which they possessed. It exhibits examples of persons of your own age or station, who have gained their wishes; but it does not bid you remark the difference of their character or their genius. Thus the world inflames, indeed, your hopes, but the means of attaining them it does not communicate; it still increases your confidence, but not your powers.

What wonder if, on descending into real life, we find ourselves perplexed and confounded; what wonder that so many fail where their success appeared certain; what wonder that the few who do succeed find that they had miscalculated their means or underrated the opposition they would meet; and that bitter experience, bought by repeated disappointments, has been at last their slow guide, to what at the outset they expected to rush into with easy pleasure? And, if you trust not to yourselves, but to the support of friends, or the patronage of superiors, it requires but little sagacity or experience to affirm, that the chances are infinitely on the side of disappointment.

But you do not depend on the world for your prospects, and consequently are not exposed to its deceits and its treacheries; you are attached to it only on account of the pleasures which it promises, and which it suits so well to every disposition. Alas! my brethren, when you have experienced them, in which of them do you hope to find anything either solid or durable? Not surely in the pleasures of intemperance or debauchery, which degrade so many of its followers, which can only repay you by a wasted constitution and a premature old age. Not certainly in the anxieties and tortures of the gaming-table, which may only requite you with an impaired fortune and a ruined mind. Not even in the giddy and laborious sports of the field, which, when they become a passion, leave scarcely time or capacity for thought. It may be, then, in that constant round of conviviality and gaiety, which is the most innocent of its attractions. But this, after some time, loses its charm of novelty; becomes stale, so as to pass without regret, and be anticipated without eagerness, and ends by being a dull toil rather than a pleasure. And, indeed, my brethren, if you allow that such enjoyments as these are the ties that attach you to the world, you do yourselves an injustice and a dishonour. For you allow that neither in the rational charms of domestic life, nor in your own mind, though well cultivated by education, can you find any resources;

but that you are obliged to be dependent on the caprice of others for your enjoyment of life. Then, how inconstant, how short-lived are all these pleasures! A sudden disgust, a malignant aspersion, a change of views, may drive you in one moment from all the gratifications which the world can bestow, and bring you to discover that you have left your mind a blank, without any substitute for what you have lost; that you have wasted on vain follies the energy and powers which might have procured you substantial and lasting satisfaction and enjoyment. Even if this should never happen, fatigue, or perhaps sorrow, will at last one day break the spirits which now make you relish such fleeting pleasures; infirmities, brought on possibly by a long course of foolish dissipation, may render you unfit for their enjoyment; age will certainly strip you of the attractions of body and mind, which now make you courted, esteemed, and admired. It is then, my brethren, that we shall be glad to pick up and collect the few scattered fragments of good which may have been dispersed through our poor lives, in order to weigh them against our hours, and days, and years of thoughtlessness or dissipation: and God grant that the world may have seduced us to nothing worse than these! It is then that we shall see the worthlessness of those pleasures which have enthralled us to the world. Cool then, and free from the intoxication into which they cast us, we shall remember how often we were gratified by the empty praises heaped upon us; and yet, we may then see that they were only the designing flattery of those who inwardly contemned or derided us. We shall recall how often we were borne away by the counsels of apparently warmest friends, and they proved to be the self-interested suggestions of treacherous deceivers. We shall find that of the numerous promises made to us through life, scarcely one has been fulfilled; that of the benefits and kindnesses we have conferred, hardly one has been repaid or appreciated; that of all the friendships we have formed, almost every one has turned out faithless; that whatever won our affections, faded in an instant; that our hopes have been a dream, our pleasures a shadow, our life a vapour. O God! and is this the happiness which the world promises; and shall we wait till this painful experience has made us feel it, to convince ourselves that, in loving it, we love a deceiver, who will bring upon us nothing but bitter disappointments!

Such, then, my brethren, is the world which the Gospel forbids you to love—a tyrant that claims undisputed sway over your actions and minds, requiting your submission by ingratitude, your transgressions by unfeeling severity—a deceiver that holds out to you prospects of advancement, and hopes of enjoyment, but which will present you with nothing but treacherous disappointment. But, perhaps, you will think I have exaggerated your obligations in telling you that you must not love the world—perhaps I have strained into a duty what is only a counsel of greater perfection. No, my brethren; so far from it, I have not come up to half the obligations which you have taken upon yourselves. Remember that, when presented to the Church to be received into the adoption of the sons of God by the laver of baptism, His minister solemnly asked you what you desired. "Faith," you replied by your sponsors, which might give you everlasting life. But this, my brethren, was no common gift that you asked;

and the Almighty would not grant it without conditions on your part. You were therefore asked, "Dost thou renounce the pomps" of Satan? that is, the shifting pleasures, the dazzling follies, and the pride of the world. Did you then reply: I will love them only while health and youth make them agreeable, and abandon them when their brightness wears away; or, I will take pleasure in them, but so as at the same time to endeavour to observe my duties towards God? No, you answered unequivocally and simply, "I do renounce them." Upon this compact *alone* you were admitted as a Christian; and your name was that day enrolled in the book of life, with this condition annexed. It is by this book that you will be tried at the last day; and on what grounds will you claim from God the fulfilment of His engagement to give you life everlasting, while violated faith and broken vows are all that stand recorded on your part of the covenant?

Take your measures, then, in time. It is not required of you that you should quit your station in life, that you should abandon the world—salvation can be gained in every situation; but live with the world in constant fear of its tyranny and suspicion of its treachery; keep yourself in peace with it, but not in alliance; avoid its enmity, but seek not its friendship: and should its interests clash with those of duty, halt not one moment between God and Baal; should its commands be in opposition to virtue, deliberate not an instant in spurning them; should its practice be at variance with the Gospel, try not to conciliate them. Think not of serving two masters; choose the one who can and will really repay your attachment. Give not your affections to things which perish; make not here a lasting tabernacle; but consider yourself as only using at interest the goods of this world, like the talents of your Master. "This therefore I say, brethren," exclaims St. Paul, "the time is short: it remaineth .... that they who rejoice should be as they who are not rejoicing; and they who buy, as if they were not possessing anything; and they who use this world, as if they used it not: for the figure of this world passeth away." (1 Cor. vii. 29–31.) Yes, my brethren, the figure of this world passeth away, and with it all its cares and anxieties, all its sorrows and misfortunes: it passeth away, and with it all its praises and enjoyments, all its hopes and wishes: it passeth away, and with it all they who move therein, whether they have experienced its evils or its goods, whether they have met its frowns or its smiles. And if all that concerns us thus passes, except God, who alone is great, and eternity, which alone is lasting, what is worth our solicitude in this world, excepting that we serve God, as the Church expresses it in one of her prayers, "that we may so pass through temporal goods as not to lose those which are eternal."

SERMON II.

On Scandal.

Matt. xviii. 7.

"It must needs be that scandals come : but nevertheless, wo to that man by whom the scandal cometh."

By scandal, my brethren, is signified, in the language of Scripture, whatever may cause our neighbour to fall in the way of virtue by offending God. It is a frightful sentence of our Divine Redeemer, when He thus pronounces the commission of this sin to be so easy, and yet its judgment so severe ; when He declares it almost impossible to avoid incurring its guilt, yet denounces it as liable to the most certain and most dreadful punishment. "It must needs be. that scandals come: but nevertheless, wo to that man by whom the scandal cometh." There is, my brethren, a striking resemblance between the manner in which our Saviour speaks of the wretch who was to betray Him, and of those who deliver the meanest member of His dear flock into the hands of the enemy, by seducing him into sin. "The Son of man," says He, "indeed goeth, but wo to that man by whom the Son of man shall be betrayed. It were better for that man if he had not been born." (Matt. xxiv. 24.) We cannot but be struck by the parallel manner in which these two crimes are thus denounced, though the warning against scandal is conveyed in the more severe terms. We can indeed conceive that it would have been better for the traitor Judas never to have opened his eyes to the light of day, or as an "abortion, to have been transferred from the womb to the grave," (Job, iii. 16), rather than to have committed the inexpressible crime of betraying the Lord of glory into the hands of sinners, and "to the will of His enemies." He would thus have escaped the necessity of an almost hopeless repentance, by forfeiting the opportunity of offence. But against him who has betrayed into perdition the least of Christ's inheritance, still more fearful is the sentence. For him He declares it better that he were seized even in the midst of his iniquities, without time for repentance, and plunged into perdition, temporal and eternal, than that by a prolonged existence he should draw upon himself and have to bear the ever accumulating mass of crime and punishment, which this offence, even when apparently light, heaps upon the soul. "He that shall scandalize one of these little ones that believeth in Me, it were better for him that a mill-stone were hanged about his neck, and that he were drowned in the depth of the sea. For it must needs be that scandal come: but nevertheless, wo to that man by whom the scandal cometh." (Matt. xviii. 6.) Nor is it difficult to reconcile this seeming disproportion in the measurement of divine indignation towards crimes of such unequal magnitude.

Our Redeemer Himself has shown, that His solicitude was most lively when His dear disciples were concerned, though never exerted on His own account. When He Himself was betrayed, His only answer was, "I am He;

if therefore you seek Me, let these go their way;" because He would not lose any of those whom His Father had given Him. (John, xviii. 5, 8, 9.) A sin, then, which is denounced in such strong terms of reprobation, at the same time that it is declared to be so universal, must have a peculiar malignity about it, which if clearly explained and feelingly understood, must, at the same time, prove the strongest preservative against its commission. This, my brethren, consists chiefly in two particulars, which I wish to impress strongly upon your attention this day : in the first place, it acts in direct opposition to the intentions of Divine Providence in regard to the salvation of mankind, and most effectually thwarts its best designs to procure it : secondly, it brings upon the soul the frightful responsibility of the crimes of others, to which occasion is given by our conduct.

In this sin there are necessarily infinite varieties, whether we consider the manner of committing it, or the consequent degrees of guilt with which it stamps the soul. There are some men sufficiently depraved even to employ their ingenuity and talents in ruining the morals of others, in instructing them in evil of which they were previously ignorant, or converting them into instruments and associates of their own crimes. This, indeed, is scandal in its blackest and most hateful dye. Others are hardly less guilty, by encouraging or counselling their neighbours in the commission of what they perhaps might of themselves have done, though not so willingly or determinedly, if they had not received this additional stimulus ; or even by simple connivance and silent consent, where duty and opportunity authorized, and imposed on them, to prevent the offence. There is a third more common and more dangerous sin, the seduction and temptation to evil which is held out by irregular or unguarded conduct. Not only the first of these offences rises in opposition to the kind and benevolent designs of God for the salvation of His creatures: they all have the same tendency, though with this unfortunate difference, that the species which appears most *indirectly* to oppose these desires, opposes them the most *effectually*. For one soul that is ruined by the fiendish crime of systematic seduction, tens of thousands are drawn into perdition by the power of bad example.

I need not dwell on the ardour, the constant and unabated affection, with which the goodness of God works for the salvation of His creatures; how the whole exertion of His power in creation, how the whole manifestation of His wisdom in religion, how the whole exhibition of His mercy in the course of Providence—how all these have looked from the beginning to one common object, the salvation of the souls which He stamped with His own image and likeness. I have, upon another occasion, fully dwelt upon these considerations; and it only requires a slight recollection of their principal heads, to comprehend at once the opposition in which the crime of scandal stands to His most earnest intentions. For while, on the one hand, He is zealously employing every art of His varied graces, every power of His numerous attractions, in order to secure salvation, the influence of bad advice, the seduction of evil example, draw in the contrary direction, and tend to render null and ineffectual all the measures of His kindness. What He is endeavouring with pains to cultivate, we are laying waste; what He is striving carefully to erect, we are labouring to throw down. Such is the view taken in the word of God of this crime, by which the evil plot, in design or conduct, the perversion of the good; and corresponding is the wo uttered against them. "Behold the wicked have bent their bow; they have prepared their arrows in the quiver; to shoot in the dark the upright of heart. *They* have *destroyed* the things which *Thou* hast made." The Lord (in His turn) . . . " shall rain snares upon sinners; fire and brimstone and storms of wind shall be the portion of their cup. For the Lord is just." (Ps. x.) And in this judgment of the Almighty, my brethren, hope not that there will be any distinction of persons; think not that the soul of the mean and poor of the world will be demanded with less frightful rigour from your hands, than that of the great or honoured. As the body of both was modelled from the same clay, and will moulder into one common dust, so are the spirits which animate them the children of the same creation, and the co-heirs of the same glory. Their common Father and Creator values both alike, and is equally interested in the salvation of both. It was against him who should scandalize *one of His little ones* that the Son of God pronounced His threat.

If, then, you place yourself in opposition to God when you thus thwart and check His attempts to secure the salvation of His creatures, alas! upon whose side do you then stand? You necessarily join in co-operation with the enemy of that salvation; and what is a still more horrible reflection, you become his most powerful instrument in effecting his plans of ruin and perdition. The enemy of mankind knows too well that his own immediate attempts to corrupt the fidelity, or seduce the virtue, of God's friends, would be too revolting to insure encouragement or success. Any price which he can offer to bribe us into a betrayal of our Lord is generally stamped too clearly with his own hideous image, to be currently and willingly received. It is by artifice alone that he can prevail; and he who was a murderer from the beginning, from the beginning also contrived his plan. He was indeed compelled, in his first temptation, to act in person, and to seduce our weaker parent with the insinuating address of the serpent. But the moment this first step had succeded, he knew that he had secured a more powerful instrument, and he intrusted the temptation and perversion of the man to the winning instigation of the woman. Since then, he has relied upon the same expedient; and has continued weaving, through every age, a chain of bad counsels and of bad example, which goes on from generation to generation, linking together the great mass of mankind under the bondage of his yoke. Compelled himself to go round as the roaring lion, seeking some incautious wanderer whom he may devour, he leaves the great work of corruption to his agents, who, mixing in the society of life, "devise," as it is expressed by David, "iniquities in their hearts, and have the venom of asps under their lips;" who, walking on the same path as ourselves, "have stretched out cords for a snare, and have laid a stumbling-block by the wayside." (Ps. cxxxix.) In fact, my brethren, look into the conduct of those who are plunged in libertinism or irreligion; or if it ever has been your unhappy lot to be entangled in the snares of vice, reflect upon the commencement of your own career, and you will acknowledge that seldom does man run into crime and excess from the mere impulse of passion, without some wretched and treacherous guide that points out the facilities of gratifying them, or some alluring example which makes him cast off the restraints of education and early instruction. So is the beginning of evil described by the wisest of men, under the inspiration of the Holy Ghost. While he assures us, in the first chapter of Proverbs, that the fear of God is the beginning of wisdom, he represents to us the seduction of evil companions as the first step in the precipitate course of destruction: " My son, if sinners shall entice thee, consent not to them." (Prov. i. 10.) Thus, my brethren, by being the cause of other's transgressions, you enter into the service of the enemy of God and man, in order to defeat the counsels of divine goodness; and what must be the lot of such infamous traitors, but to share the fate of their chosen master, and to receive the only recompense which he can bestow for their voluntary service?

But, my brethren, the horrible and satanic character of this crime is generally still further aggravated; for when you cause the ruin or the fall of others, it is generally precisely there where God had placed you to second His efforts for salvation, and to guard against the seductions and temptations of its sworn adversary. For who is it that most generally leads others astray from God and His law? It is the man stricken in years, to whom nature itself directs us to look up as exhibiting in his life the discoveries of reflection and the purchase of experience; he of whom the word of God commanded, " Rise up before the hoary head, and honour the person of the aged man;" (Lev. xix. 32) he under whose semblance the Almighty represented Himself to Daniel as coming to judge the iniquities of the world. Yet, many such as these, still retaining the sap of viciousness in an exhausted frame, become, like the accusers of Susanna, the assailants of youthful innocence ; many such as these, covering under their grey hairs the perfidious spirit of irreligion, like Achitophel, invite the young to throw off the yoke of duty ; or by their discourse lead them to undervalue religion, or despise the force of moral obligations. They were placed on the throne of honour to restrain vice; they use their authority to encourage and advance it. It is the master whose commands the servant is taught to obey and respect, under pain of losing his livelihood and support, to whom God has given a charge, in return for his service, of watching over his salvation : "For if any man has not a care of his own, especially of those of his house, he hath denied the faith, and is worse than an infidel." (1 Tim. v. 8.) Yet it is they who employ them as agents in their intrigues, or allows them to be the witnesses of their excesses, who have no regard to using intemperate or unmeasured language in their presence ; who not only give them the example of a total inattention to religious duty, but would treat the time spent in the service of their common master as a fraud and an injustice practised against them. These were given into their hands, that they might guide and support them in the path of rectitude ; they have taken advantage of the hold they possessed to push them over the precipice of perdition. In fine, it is the parent who too generally gives the first lesson of sin to his children, and leaves them after death a legacy of vicious habits. He teaches them to look up to him for direction and example, and the feelings of nature second his instruction. He accustoms them to consider his conduct as the perfection at which they must aim, and the simple impulse of untutored affection has already impressed the same idea. He teaches with authority from God Himself; and the honour due to him is the first commandment after the worship of the Deity. Yet it is from his example, and that of his society, that his offspring learns false principles of honour, his habits of excess, of love of the world, of untruth, and of inattention to religion.

The parent receives from the Church, at baptism, a child of heaven, to be brought up for God: a few years of his example may change it into a son of Belial and a child of perdition. Good God! and is it not then enough that this abominable crime should stand in the way of Thy kindest intentions and wishes for our salvation, and that it should convert us into allies of our common enemy, but it must almost always be aggravated by a breach of trust, and be committed where we were particularly placed to prevent its intrusion. But the opposition to God's views is not yet complete; it goes as far as possible to render null, in regard to those who are seduced or misled, the redemption of the Son of God. For the attainment of some foolish end, perhaps from no other motive than an unaccountable perversity of will, you lead your friend into perdition, after his salvation had cost the beloved Son of the eternal Father so incalculable a price. Oh, how dearly had He loved that soul!

how fondly had this good Shepherd cherished this little one of His fold! It was His own purchase; and He had prayed the Father, "now that I am no more in the world, and these are in the world, and I come to Thee, Holy Father keep them in Thy name whom thou hast given me." (John, xvii. 11.) "I do not ask that Thou take them away out of the world, but that Thou preserve them from evil." (15.) Alas! my brethren, did our loving Saviour, through the excess of His anxiety for our salvation, forget, when He pronounced this prayer, that even into His fold the wolf would break through, and make dismal havoc among His flock? Did He forget that under the clothing of His own portion, would lurk emissaries of the evil one, many only intent upon killing and destroying them? Did He forget that their very guardians would thus mislead them to destruction? Oh! no; He foresaw too well these dreadful misfortunes, and that no care, no prudence, could prevent them; for, "it needs must be that scandals come: but nevertheless, wo to that man by whom the scandal cometh;" and hence He could only endeavour to diminish them, by pronouncing that solemn threat against their authors.

Such is the first peculiarity of this sin, which renders it so offensive to God; besides this, it draws upon the soul the responsibility of all the crimes and transgressions which it is its essential property to produce. The order of justice requires that all who partake in an offence should also partake of its punishment; but of all the associates in guilt, he who first suggested it must be considered not only as bearing the principal responsibility, but as being the source of all the evil, and, consequently, as drawing upon himself a punishment, much more signal than is reserved for the victims of his malice. This is the character which the giver of scandal bears before God. You may say that you have received no commission to watch over the salvation of your neighbour, and that, consequently, you can have no responsibility in its regard. In vain will you thus answer with Cain : " Am I the keeper of my brother ?" He will answer you, that according to the Scripture, in the Old Law : " He gave to every one a commandment concerning his neighbour ;" (Eccles. xvii. 12,) that, much more in the New, the great commandment of fraternal charity gives to every man an interest in the salvation of all his fellow-creatures, and imposes an obligation of co-operating for it as far as is within his power. The least we can do to comply with this duty is to edify them by our good conduct, and to take care that whenever we are likely to be chosen as counsellors or examples, there may be nothing in our advice or practice which may possibly lead into error or sin. And if, instead of this lowest degree of observance, we act directly contrary to the obligation, is it too much to expect that the " Shepherd of souls " will demand of us, as He did from the pastors of Israel, an account of all that has been lost or torn through our malice or culpable neglect ? The sin, then, of him whom we any how cause to offend, is our sin no less ; and hence it is that by inattention to the responsibility under which we lie for the salvation of those who hear and see us, we may be surprised one day to find ourselves charged with a long indictment of offences which had escaped our notice.

And this is an additional evil peculiar to this sin,

that we may load ourselves with its guilt, even when we have scarcely any reason to apprehend it. Thus you are, perhaps, careful to avoid any irreligious or immoral discourse, but you may have no difficulty in reflecting upon practices connected with religion, in speaking lightly of some observances which you may deem superfluous or ill-timed. But you cannot know to what extent one of your hearers may consider these connected with more important duties, or forming a part of the general system of religion ; you have weakened his respect for the whole ; you have made him consider the entire fabric unsound by depreciating a secondary part ; you have destroyed within his mind that delicate respect for what was sacred ; you have broken down that scrupulous regard for duty which formed the strongest safeguard of religion and virtue in his mind : you have commenced his perversion,—his soul will be demanded at your hand. You would not openly neglect any of the solemn and important practices of religion ; but you, perhaps, may not feel yourself bound to observe that recollection, at the more public functions of the Church, which you practise in your own private devotions. But it may be that many look to that moment to judge whether you really attach that importance to these functions, and entertain that respect for religion, which you always profess. A decision as to our sincerity and the value of our creed may inconsiderately be risked upon the result of this observation ; and your unguarded conduct, though marked by no glaring violation of duty, may have repelled or kept back a precious soul from the knowledge or possession of the truth : you have prevented his salvation,—his soul will be demanded at your hands. In fine, my brethren, we step in general so completely to the last verge of duty and propriety; we live, we speak, we act with so much thoughtlessness, with so little attention to the wishes, the sentiments, the wants of others, that it would be almost a miraculous preservation of Providence, if we did not often transgress the bounds, and come in collision with those feelings of propriety which bind them to their respective obligations.

And yet, while this evil thus proceeds from our habitual inattention to the duty of constant edification, it must necessarily produce a serious responsibility. Will you say that they are trifling causes, and that their effects should only be commensurate with them in importance? Will you say that you are not to be held answerable for the weakness of your neighbours who happen to take scandal, and are led wrong by an action indifferent in your regard? This, my brethren, is indeed a convenient and a courtly doctrine; but, for this very reason, it is not the doctrine of the Apostle. After explaining that the eating of meat offered to an idol was in itself a matter of indifference, he —is careful to urge that the danger of scandal from the practice is sufficient to condemn it, and asserts that he who gives it would have to account for the soul of him who acted against conscience on the force of his example. "But, take heed," says he, "lest this your liberty become a stumbling-block to the weak. And through thy knowledge shall the weak brother perish for whom Christ died? Now, when you sin thus against the brethren, and wound their weak consciences, you sin against Christ. Wherefore, if meat scandalize my brother, I will never cat meat, lest I should scandalize my brother." (1 Cor. viii. 9–13.)

This responsibility, my brethren, is easily contracted; happy if it could be as easily discharged. But here, again, is another frightful feature of this crime; it is almost impossible to free ourselves of the burthen which it thus imposes upon our souls. It cannot be forgiven unless the evils it has caused are to the utmost repaired; and what a work of appalling difficulty this must present. If you have deprived your neighbour of his property, or injured him in his possessions, you have it at least in your power to weigh out an exact equivalent. If you have wronged his reputation, you can at least retract or contradict your calumny, and render all those publicly unjust who continue its propagation. But, alas! what compensation will you give for the loss of an immortal soul which you have precipitated into perdition? What reparation will you make for the robbery of eternal life? In the other cases, the person whom you have injured has been an unwilling victim, and will, therefore, concur with you in effecting this necessary and just satisfaction towards himself: in the present, you have made him consent to his own ruin; you have taught him to feel a pleasure in the injury inflicted, and to be happy in his own destruction. You cannot make the reparation without his concurrence, and that concurrence you have already taught him to refuse. How, then, will you undertake the work? Do you fancy that one good action, performed in the presence of your victim, will prove an equivalent for the bad advice or bad example you on one occasion gave him? Alas! that was enough to seduce and corrupt him; years of virtue and expiation would not obliterate the effect. For your bad example gave impulse and power to evil principles which lurked within him, and you have now not only to contradict *its* impression, but to control *their* force. It was easy to cast the spark into the combustible mass which his mind had formed; it requires much ingenuity, great power, long perseverance, and many resources, to extinguish the conflagration. It cost you but a small effort to push aside the flood-gates which checked the tumultuous torrent of his passions; but will the same hand be able to push back the bounding cataract, behind the barrier which it has made it burst.

No, my brethren, the task is nearly useless; and however you may have repented of your error towards your ruined brother, however you may have tried to repair it, you may, most probably, suffer to the end of your life, or of his, the mortification of seeing him continue in an unchecked and irremediable career of perdition. But the end of this evil is not yet. It is an infection which you have communicated, and it will spread. Your neighbour will taint all with whom he comes in contact, and they will owe their misfortunes to you. The responsibility of all will ultimately lie at your door; and on the day of the Lord, innumerable victims, whose countenances you know not, will rise, clothed in that loathsome and hideous body to which your fault has condemned them, and shriek for double measure of retribution upon you, that besides your own portion of bitterness, you may be condemned to share with each of them the cup of wo which, while on earth, you had mixed for him. Wo in that day to him by whom scandals have come! Before the judgment-seat of man a feeling of pride or honour may arm us to endure punishment even unjustly inflicted, without accusing those who in reality ought more properly to bear it. But, before the tribunal of the Omnipotent Judge, all will be but too happy to lighten themselves of the smallest portion of their lot, by pointing out their seducers and encouragers in evil. The closest ties of friendship and blood will make no difference in the awful challenge. "Thou hast eaten of the tree," said the Almighty to Adam, "whereof I commanded thee that thou shouldst not eat." (Gen. iii. 11.) And what was his answer, but exculpation in its least honourable and most bitter form? "The woman, whom Thou gavest to be my companion, gave me of the tree, and I did eat." (12.) Oh! such will be the answer of all: the ancient friend whom, through the mouth of Solomon, Thou exhortedst me to cherish in my bosom; the husband whom Thou orderedst me, through Thy Apostle, to love as Christ loved His Church; the parent whom Thou commandedst me from the cloud of Sinai to honour, that my days might be long upon the earth;—he gave me the forbidden fruit, and I did eat it. Alas! it will be all a mortal contention among friends; for it is these alone that are generally the cause of each other's ruin. For what a complicated crime, then, will the arraigned demand the transfer of punishment upon his former associate. For a black infidelity, an unnatural treachery, a fiendish malice. "Even the man of my peace, in whom I trusted, who eat my bread, hath greatly supplanted me." (Ps. xl. 10.) "Let death come upon them, and let them go down alive into hell." (liv. 16.) And, my brethren, in this call for sentence, there will join those whose appeal will

c

not rise in vain. "Take heed," says our Saviour, in continuation of the words of my text—"take heed that you despise not one of these little ones: for I say to you, that their angels in heaven always see the face of My Father who is in heaven." (Matt. xviii. 10.)

Those angels, my brethren, to whom He had given a charge over them, to keep them in all their ways, and to bear them up in their hands, "lest they should dash their foot against a stone;" (Ps. xc. 12) they felt a jealous interest in bringing their charge safe to the end of the perilous journey. They were careful to remove every hindrance which the enemy had placed in their way. But, against the insidious designs of false friends, there was no security. Their ill-fated clients had been entangled in their snares, and they have now no resource but to invoke condign punishment upon the unnatural seducers. For God has pronounced: "Thou shalt not place a stumbling-block before the blind; but thou shalt fear the Lord thy God, because I am the Lord." (Lev. xix. 14.) "Cursed be the man that maketh the blind to wander out of his path." (Deut. xxvii. 18.)

Do you wish, my brethren, to avoid the wo uttered against those by whom scandals come? Follow the opposite course: "So let your light shine before men, that they may glorify your Father who is in heaven." (Matt. v.) Aiming always at your own improvement, never lose sight of the good of others; be a mutual encouragement and assistance. "Wherefore," I say once more in the words of St. Paul, "comfort one another and edify one another. . . . And we beseech you, brethren, rebuke the unquiet, comfort the feeble-minded, support the weak, be patient towards all men." (1 Thes. v. 11, 14.) The way that we have to travel together is short, and beset with dangers on every side. Why, then, should we be a source of mutual misery, and at the same time bring evil upon our own souls, by charging them with the guilt of others' crimes? Why make ourselves the declared enemies of God, and place ourselves in opposition to His most benevolent counsels in our behalf? Guard, then, in your conduct against all that can mislead others, and sigh for that happy day when " the Son of man shall send His angels, and they shall gather out of His kingdom all scandals. . . . Then shall the just shine as the sun, in the kingdom of their Father." (Matt. xiii. 41, 43.)

SERMON III.

Difficulty of Salvation of the Rich.

MATT. xi. 4, 5.

"Go and relate to John what you have heard and seen. The blind see, the lame walk . . . . the dead rise again, the poor have the gospel preached unto them."

HAD human feelings suggested to our Divine Redeemer the evidences they might desire of His high commission, assuredly He would have concluded the enumeration of His proofs in a more imposing manner. " Go," He might have said, after rehearsing His marvellous works—" go, and tell him how the great, the rich, and the powerful have begun, and will ever continue, to bear Me testimony; that when twelve years of age, My opinions were listened to with admiration by the haughty doctors of the Temple ; that rulers come in the night to receive My instructions ; (John, iii. 1) that the chiefs of the synagogues worship Me to obtain My succour ; (Matt. xi. 18) that but just now, a Roman centurion openly protested himself unworthy to receive Me under his roof, (Luke, vii. 7, 22.) that rich Pharisees will hold it an honour that I am their guest ; (ib. 36) that Herod himself will be desirous for a long time to see Me, having heard many things of Me. (Luke, xxiii. 8.) Contrasted with this list of attentions and homages, from the powerful and great, how beautifully independent of men and their witnessing, of earth and its support, is the conclusion to His evidence, " and the gospel is preached unto the poor"! And, as He opened His mission, so did He close it with these feelings. "I give thanks," He exclaimed, "to Thee, O Father, Lord of heaven and earth, because Thou hast hid these things from the wise and prudent, and hast revealed them to little ones. Yea, Father: for so hath it seemed good in Thy sight." (Matt. xi. 25, 26.)

Beautiful, however, as this evidence may be, that our Saviour should have been able to appeal to it, is awful and alarming. For, that in preaching His gospel, He should have made a distinction between the rich and the poor, and given the preference to the latter, argues too clearly on which side He placed the probabilities of its doctrines being received, its commandments observed, and its virtues displayed. It argues that His hopes for His religion lay among the more despised and obscure of those who would become His disciples; that while the rich would be among the many to be called, from the poor would be chiefly taken the few chosen unto salvation; for to prefer that the gospel should be preached to the poor, supposes an assurance that it would be best followed by the poor.

There must, therefore, be something in the possession of riches and station, which opposes, or, at least, lessens our fitness for God's service. There must be something in these things which renders our salvation more difficult, and consequently more precarious. And this should seem to depend on two chief points: first, on the obstacles which they oppose to salvation, inasmuch as by riches the dangers of offence are increased, and the remedies thereof diminished; and secondly, in the higher price which the rich are required to pay in its exchange; by the qualifications demanded from them being greater, while the chances of attaining them are less.

The Apostle, writing to his favourite disciple, Timothy, instructs him that "piety with sufficiency is great gain. Because they who would become rich fall into temptation and into the snare of the devil;" (1 Tim. vi. 9) whereby we see what a grievous obstacle the rich have in being open to dangers and temptations more numerous and various, and at the same time more powerful, than those whom Providence has placed in an inferior rank. Their temptations are more varied and more numerous, because they may be said to live in a state of habitual exposure to their attacks. First, their occupations are few, and their leisure long, and it is a leisure procured by the interruption of amusements and pastimes, which leave the mind relaxed, unarmed, unnerved. Languor, listlessness, and empty-mindedness, are the privileged habits of the rich alone. Hours and hours of their time are to be spent while recovering from the fatigue of past pleasures, or anxiously awaiting the hour of fresh dissipation; employment, occupation is to be sought, only in desultory and unimportant actions or conversation, and in throwing the mind open to every trifle that chooses to claim its attention; or, what is worse still, in indulging the vain, unprofitable current of thought which flows spontaneously through it, in pursuing the wandering and bewildered mazes through which their wayward fancy leads them, or in colouring up to a false and bewitching glare the picture which their hopes paint in the air before them. In this manner, for want of sufficient food, the mind's energies are forced to act, and feed, upon its very stuff and substance. Instead of being like " the strong man armed, who keepeth his court, so that those things which he possesseth are in peace," (Luke, xi. 21) all is disorderly, unguarded, unsuspicious. Every thought that passes is gladly harboured, every vain desire that enters is indiscriminately received ; for "as a city," says Solomon, " that lieth open, and is not compassed with walls, so is a man who ruleth not over his own spirit." (Prov. xxv. 28.)

Now our Lord has declared that this is the very state in which temptation will necessarily surprise us. " Watch and pray" are the only means which He has prescribed us to escape temptation ; and, in fact, it is almost impossible that some thought will not arise when one is in that incautious state, which will allure us on, unsuspecting and unresisting, from fancy to fancy, until, like a false meteor, it has plunged us into the corruption and uncleanness from which it took its rise. " For the bewitching enchantment of trifling," says the wise man, "obscureth good things, and the wandering of concupiscence overturneth the innocent mind." (Wisd. iv. 12.)

When from this inactivity you are aroused to exertion, it is only to pass from liability to danger to its actual encounter. It is to attend to the care and embellishment of your person, so to attract more vain if not more dangerous attentions ; to join in festive parties, where, if not your sobriety or temperance, at least the Christian spirit, self-mortification, will be in saddest jeopardy ; to take a prominent part in conversation where your neighbours' characters will be but roughly handled by whosoever wishes to secure any brilliant success; in short, to spend hours, and even entire nights, in amusements and light dalliance, where you are well assured beforehand that God will never once enter your thoughts, but that his enemy, the world, will fill them; where you may calculate with certainty that though you *may* hear and see something to disedify and endanger, you will assuredly see nought that can benefit or improve you. But to these ordinary dangers which beset exclusively the salvation of the rich, we must add many others, from which their inferiors in rank are equally exempt. For them alone the danger of the most opposite vices seems to be reserved: of pride and mean-spiritedness—of prodigality and avarice—of haughtiness in prosperity and impatience under trials. It is among them alone that the poison of infidelity is yet suffered to circulate freely, from lip to lip; against them alone that the arts of systematic perversion are employed by treacherous friends and dissolute companions; it is for vengeance upon them alone that the unpaid earnings of those whom they employ, or the neglected voice of the poor, will ever rise before heaven.

Thus are the dangers of offence which cross the ways of the rich infinitely more numerous than the poor have to encounter; but they are also far more powerful and strong. They are more powerful, because they fall upon minds less able to resist their attacks. Nature itself seems to have framed them of a more sensitive and delicate texture than their poorer neighbours; early and tender care increases this softness of structure both in body and soul; a cultivated education refines the imagination, till keenly alive to stimulating ideas whereof the peasant's rugged mind is incapable; and the romantic tone of our fashionable literature often completes the irritability, fits the mind for false but impassioned feeling, and sends them into an infected world with every pore starting open to inhale its pestilence, and every nerve thrilling to convey it through the frame. Again, they are more powerful, because they fall upon minds unaccustomed to resist. From infancy every wayward whim has been gratified for them; their opinions have seldom been contradicted; their propensities have never been curbed; their necks have never borne the yoke; the law has never dwelt within their hearts. In fine, the temptations are more powerful, because they have close within reach the means of immediate consent. Time is fully at their disposal to plan, to arrange, to fulfil the gratification of their desires; wealth is in their hands to purchase all that their hearts desire; ingenuity and tact to remove difficulties are supplied by their education: advice from friends, co-operation from menials, connivance from superiors, submission from the injured, indulgence from the world—all are at their command; and while a thousand barriers interpose between the wishes and the enjoyments of the poor, in the rich the fear of God alone presents a bar—alas! how frail a bar—between their temptation and their guilt.

Oh! truly, my brethren, he who can remain in innocence among such various and such powerful temptations, must be, in the words of Scripture, a lily among thorns, and must, therefore, anticipate being racked, torn, and defaced by them, even if he preserves himself undefiled. But if he yields, oh! what a dreadful fall; for the sins of the great are fearful indeed; and this is an additional step in the obstacles to their salvation.

All sin, my brethren, is in truth an awful guilt; but the sins of the rich have a triple aggravation, proper to them alone.

First, an aggravation of malice. The law of God in all its bearings has been unfolded to you; its general precepts, its particular obligations, have been taught you from the beginning; you consider yourself adequate, and that justly, to instruct your inferiors in their duty to God and man; you transgress in the face of this clearer and more perfect knowledge of the law and will of God: then draw the necessary consequence. "For," says our Lord, "the servant who knew not (the will of his master), and did things worthy of stripes, shall be beaten with few stripes; but the servant who knew the will of his master, and did not according to his will, shall be beaten with many stripes." (Luke, xii. 47, 48.)

Secondly, an aggravation of ingratitude. The poor, my brethren, comparatively, see little of God's providence, save for the execution of His severe decree that they should eat their bread in the sweat of their brow. The bounties which He bestows upon them are dealt out in measure; they consist in support to bear up against the hardship of their lot, and in an occasional relaxation from the habitual rigour of His dealings with them, rather than in any marked exercise of His liberality in their behalf. If they feel not towards Him that filial affection which would make them dread an offence against

His law, whatever might be its gain, it would seem as if He hardly had intended to exact more from them than the fidelity of servants. If, in the enjoyment of those few blessings with which He sometimes cheers them, they transgress the strict bounds of virtue, it would appear as if the extraordinary nature of their pleasure, and their inexperience in its use, might go far to excuse the fault. But on you He has rained His choicest blessings, like manna from heaven; for you He hath struck the rock, and the waters have gushed out; and it is while feasting upon His bounty that you seek the forbidden meats of Egypt. Of you, as of His chosen people, it may be said: "He hath given them their desire; they have not been defrauded of that which they craved . . . and yet in all these things they have sinned still." (Ps. lxxvii. 29, 32.)

Hear, then, once more, the doom pronounced against all such by the word of God. The Lord "set him upon high land, that he might eat the fruits of the field, that he might suck honey out of the rock, and oil out of the hardest stone. . . The beloved waxed fat, and did kick; he forsook God, who made him, and departed from God his saviour. . . . The Lord saw, and was moved to wrath, because His own sons and daughters provoked Him. And He said: I will hide My face from them, and will consider what their last end shall be: for it is a perverse generation, and unfaithful children. A fire is kindled in My wrath, and shall burn even to the lowest hell." (Deut. xxxii. 13, 22.)

In fine, an aggravation of scandal. The fire which breaks out in the lowly dwelling of the poor may consume all that he possesses, but will soon be smothered by the ruins of its insulated walls; the infection which appears in the cottage may exterminate its little family, but will hardly issue from its shunned and guarded precincts. It is so with the transgressions and vices of its inmate: they may be communicated through his narrow circle, and may cause its temporal or eternal ruin, but vice will gain little abroad from his sanction or example. For, alas! there is small glory before men for imitating even the virtues of the poor! But of you it is decreed that alone you stand not, neither do you fall. Like the infant Saviour of the world, you may be said to be "placed for the fall and for the resurrection of many in Israel." (Luke ii. 34.) A wide circle of friends, through which you study to preserve an influence and weight; a large train of servants and dependants, over whom you are careful to exercise an authority; a crowd of poorer or less influential persons, whom interest, esteem, or some other tie holds attached to your opinions: to all these you must be a source of good or of evil by almost every action which you perform. Every sin committed by one whose conduct influences that of so many others, receives an aggravation proportioned to the number by whom it may be imitated, or whose virtuous principles it may weaken. And so great is the accidental guilt super-added by it, that it often seems to obliterate in the eyes of the Almighty the crime by which it was caused; and the most heinous transgression becomes merged in the scandal which it begets. When the prophet Nathan was sent to reproach David for his double crime, mark well his conduct. In the name of the Lord, he forgives him his enormous guilt; but after this forgiveness, with suitable punishment, has been granted to his personal and direct offences, a far more severe infliction is reserved for the consequences of his crime. Among others: " Nevertheless, because thou hast given occasion to the enemies of the Lord to blaspheme, for this thing the child that is born to thee shall surely die." (2 Kings, xii. 14.)

Imminent as are the dangers of transgressing to which the great are exposed, heinous as are their offences when committed, there yet remains the finishing stroke to their obstacles to salvation, the difficulty of obtaining forgiveness.

You will, doubtless, tell me that the word of God is full of the most extraordinary and consoling instances of forgiveness, bestowed upon sinners distinguished at once for their rank and for the enormity of their crimes. I acknowledge it, my brethren; and they are these very examples which lead me best to measure the hard terms upon which this forgiveness has to be attained. I there see a Zacheus, grown rich in a profession of extortion and injustice, in one instant become the host and friend of the Son of God. But it is not till after he has distributed one-half of all his possessions to the poor, and from the remainder restored four-fold to all whom he had injured, that he heard the consoling words: " This day is salvation come into this house." (Luke, xix. 8, 9.) I see a Magdalen, who had obtained throughout Jerusalem a criminal reputation, in one moment assured by the ever-forgiving Jesus that her sins were remitted to her. But I see her for this purpose compelled to keep no terms with the best usages of society, not hesitating for a moment to break through the most approved points of good breeding, but, with a holy effrontery, intruding herself into the dining-hall of the rich, and there braving, before she can obtain forgiveness, the supercilious scorn of the Pharisee, the scandalized murmurs of the disciples, and the probable loathing of the spotless Son of God. I see her for this purpose sacrificing at once all the means and instruments of her sins; lavishing her precious ointment to honour her good Physician; prostrating her body on the dust before the servants who surround her to crave His kind forgiveness; pouring forth her tears as a fountain to bathe the feet of her Saviour; dishevelling her beautiful hair in order to wipe them; then disappearing for ever from the scene of her guilt, save when once more she followed His bloody footsteps to Calvary, to do public penance at the foot of His ignominious cross. In fine, I behold David the king pardoned for the enormous crimes of adultery and murder, upon his first expression of sorrow; but, oh! what a weight of punishment sanctions his forgiveness, too. The fruit of his crime cut off in its cradle; (2 Reg. xii. 19) the virtue of his family blighted by the incest of one of his sons, and its peace ruined by the fratricide of another; (xiii.) the crown unnaturally torn from his grey hairs, his meek head loaded with the curses, and his royal person assailed by the stones of Semei; (xvii.) his bed infamously defiled, (xvi. 22) his beloved son in arms as a traitor, slain as a parricide, and buried beneath a criminal's heap. (xviii.) Such are the conditions on which he obtained pardon; and as if he feared that he had not yet endured enough, he tells us that himself added to their rigour: that he eat his ashes with his bread, and that he mingled his drink with weeping! And do these examples, then, encourage us to expect an easy forgiveness? or do they not rather point out to us great and awful difficulties in procuring the pardon of sin, when committed in an exalted situation?

And, in fact, my brethren, it must be obvious, not only that the enormity of the offence, as above exposed, must render its absolution more subject to hard conditions, but that the more distinguished the situation of the culprit, the less he is likely to be touched by the ordinary means of conversion. For, what are the means most likely to affect him? The counsel and exhortation of friends? But these are most ordinarily the corruptors of his innocence, or the partakers of his guilt. If any virtuous man have still retained his friendship for him, his counsel, which could not prevent his fall, will hardly produce his resurrection. The remorse of conscience? But *he* has a thousand means of drowning its voice or of assuaging its sting, and every day tends to weaken its influence amidst the facilities of crime. The judgments of God exercised upon others? But the prosperity which surrounds him and his friends effectually assures him that they will not visit him. The word of God preached to call him to repentance? But if *he* deigns to hear it, it can only be when stripped of its harshness and severity. For now, the bitter yet salutary truths of repentance must be honeyed over with human art to render them palatable; and the word of the Lord, sharper than a two-edged sword, must have its edge turned and its point blunted before its ministers can presume to strike. The Son of God assures us, too, that His word, falling among riches, is only as the seed cast upon thorny ground: "and the care of this world, and the deceitfulness of riches, choke up the word, and it becometh fruitless." (Matt. xiii. 22.)

To this inefficiency of the ordinary means of operating conversion, we may add the difficulties of making those reparations which the sins of the wealthy so frequently require, the difficulty of securing perseverance amidst a recurrence of the same dangers, the obstacles of pride and shame in making a public change of life. But if you deem the estimate which I have made of the chances of forgiveness exaggerated and severe, let us recur to the testimony of one whose judgment was founded on experience. It is that of a rich man, of whom no greater evil has been recorded than that he led a life consistent with his rank, and conformably to that of others in his station; merely that he was clothed in purple and fine linen, that he feasted sumptuously every day, and that he suffered not his pleasures to be disturbed by the reflection, that thousands of his fellow-creatures were starving while he was indulging in every luxury; but that one poor beggar demanded alms in vain from the servants at his gate. For leading *this* life he is plunged in eternal torments, and there devises the means whereby he may save his five brethren, yet on earth, from sharing his painful lot. He, too, had experienced the remorses of conscience whenever he passed the poor leper at his door; he, too, had been frequently admonished by friends and counsellors to alter his course of life; he, too, had doubtless heard the priests and ministers of God denounce that the wicked should perish for ever—perhaps had heard the dreadful threats of the Baptist against unrepenting sinners, or the woes of the Son of God uttered against those who had their consolation here: in fine, he had, undoubtedly, read the holy Scriptures, and all the menaces they contain. Yet, on none of these means of conversion, which had been tried on himself, did he place the slightest hope for his wealthy brothers. No; one, only one expedient seemed to him to remain whereby their conversion could be possibly attained—the preaching of one risen from the dead! "Father," he exclaims, "I beseech thee that thou wouldst send him to my father's house . . . . . that he may testify unto them, lest they also come to this place of torments. And Abraham said: They have Moses and the prophets; let them hear them. But he said: No, Father Abraham; but if one went to them from the dead, then will they do penance." (Luke, xvi. 27–30.)

Could a more frightful picture have been imagined to represent the awful difficulty, I might almost say hopelessness, of repentance and forgiveness in the wealthy sinner? Yes, my brethren, and it is given in the reply of Abraham, which allows no efficacy even to the *only* means of salvation which the experience of the prisoner had led him to devise, when the most ordinary calls have been made in vain: "If they hear not Moses and the prophets, neither will they believe if one rise again from the dead." (31.)

Were I to pause here, my brethren, I fear the difficulty of salvation to the rich would be painfully clear, as demonstrated in the obstacles which oppose them: there yet remains to consider the second source of this difficulty, in the high price required from them to obtain it. The qualifications demanded from them are greater, and the means of attaining them more scanty. This is the case whether we consider their duties or their virtues.

It is one advantage of poverty, viewed in order to eternal salvation, that its duties are sternly defined. A rugged hand, that of necessity, has traced a marked decisive path which it must pursue, every deviation from which bears with it its own punishment; and this path is fortunately that of duty. From morning till evening, the support of himself and his family compels the poor labourer to toil; the quality of his hard-earned meal precludes all danger of excess; his mind, necessarily occupied, leaves no room for dissipating thoughts. God demands not from him long prayers, nor deep inquiring into the mysteries of faith; and when he has each day complied with its monotonous occupations, commenced and closed by devotion, in a spirit of resignation to the will of God; when he has frequented His worship, and partaken of His holy Sacraments at the proper seasons; he may be said to have complied with the most prominent obligations of his state. In whatever duty he may be bound towards others, there is generally a sufficient link of feeling between them to answer its discharge with exactness, and even with love. To those poorer than himself he extends, willingly, compassion, and affords his best assistance, because he can enter into their sufferings by the comparison of his own; to his masters he will be attached and respectful, because he is indebted to them for the past and dependant on them for the future; to his little family he is truly affectionate and fond; they provide for his comforts, they solace his few domestic hours, they anticipate his love.

All is exactly contrary in the rich; he has to fulfil duties almost completely undefined, and to discharge them without the compulsive motives which impel the poor man to the fulfilment of his. When he begins to calculate the positive obligations of his state, he finds it hard to determine or to estimate them. Scarcely any occupation presents itself which it seems more necessary to discharge at one moment than at another: and yet he cannot reasonably persuade himself that the whole of his life was placed at his own disposal, to be spent busily or inactively as might seem best to himself. Time, for instance, is a gift, and a valuable gift, for which he is to be responsible to God. He will be demanded to give an account of every single moment, just as rigidly as the religious man whose duties are prescribed by hours and by minutes. He is bound, therefore, to fill it all up in a manner that may satisfy this account to be rendered to a severe Judge; and yet it is left entirely in the hands of his own responsibility, and of his own contrivance, in what manner to occupy it for such a purpose. I may even go further: this time being left completely to his own discretion, is manifestly a liberality on the part of God; and he himself considers his lot on that account more blest than that of the poor. The necessary consequence is, that a higher equivalent will be justly demanded for it; and if God is contented to accept from the poor the discharge of a few necessary duties, He will require from those to whom He has been more bountiful, something more elevated and more perfect still. Again, the poor man is limited by positive necessities in his obligation to prayer; but to him who has no fixed and regular succession of duties, there is no measure defined, but what his disinclination to fervour, or want of the sense he should feel of his necessities, may suggest to him as sufficient. Now, the precept to pray always, and faint not, was addressed to all; and though not to be urged to its literal discharge, it must be evident that its pressure is more severe where we have to determine for ourselves how far we may fulfil it, still being held responsible for the limitations we may define. While thus the uncertainty of his obligations, together with their responsibility, makes them more difficult to the rich, he wants those ties which bind him to their discharge. How numerous are his relative duties to society, to his dependants, to the poor! But between him and these various classes there is little connexion which can ensure their observance.

To his duty to society he is only held by convenience or fashion, and they will certainly never induce him to act for its spiritual improvement; to his dependants he is only united by a feeling of mutual necessity, and this includes not to human eyes the salvation of their souls; to notice the poor he is simply moved by his own love of ease, or the proprieties of his station : and how distant are their dictates from the zealous, active, glowing charity which is demanded from the Christian! Thus, while his duties are more multiplied, the facilities for discharging them are diminished. It is the same with the virtues he is expected to possess.

Two considerations will justify this truth. The first is, that in riches those virtues are no less demanded, whose proper seat is poverty and obscurity. Humility, the virtue of the lowly, of the contemned, of the despised, is even more necessary in the palace than in the cottage; yet, in the latter, it seems to be growing on the very walls, it springs spontaneously from the very ground; while, in the former, it has to be cultivated with painful care, amidst the attentions paid to rank, the flattery of inferiors, the suggestions of pride. Mortification, which appears to be only the offspring and sanctifier of indigence, is the still more necessary curb of abundance; but, then, to the former, it is only a movement of the will, consecrating a necessary want; to the latter, it is a difficult exertion, imposing involuntary restraint. Patience was sent to be the comforter of the distressed, but it must no less be the badge of the wealthy Christian; but, then, to the former it has become an habitual feeling; the latter must put it on under a galling contrast with former comfort and ease.

It might be some compensation, if at least there were some virtues which might be said to be more exclusively the property of the rich; but this is my second observation, that even those virtues for which riches give an apparent advantage, *can* be, and generally *are*, as fully discharged by the poor. Charity, the queen of virtues, and the beloved of the Most High, is the quality which seems most decidedly in the exclusive reach of the wealthy. It is precisely with regard to it that our Blessed Redeemer has decided the point, and decided it, as might have been anticipated, on the side of His favourite poor. " Looking on, He saw the rich men cast their gifts into the treasury. And He saw also a certain poor widow casting in two copper mites. And He said : Verily I say to you, that this poor widow hath cast in more than they all." (Luke, xxi. 1-3.)

To conclude this argument, I have only to observe, that Jesus Christ is the model of all our virtues, and that He practised them in all their brightest perfection. Now, it was in a state of poverty that He proposed His example; and difficult as it must be to imitate His virtue at all, how infinitely must that difficulty be increased, when it has to be transferred to a different state, and when the poor, the meek, the humble, and mortified Jesus of Nazareth has to be copied in the purple and fine linen of the rich man, feasting sumptuously every day!

My brethren, you will think, perhaps, that I have urged too far the truths which I have undertaken to inculcate. You will, perhaps, flatter yourselves that, in spite of all these speculative obstacles, the salvation of the rich may be practically achieved with ease; so that the rich man, living in the spirit of the world and of his station, may yet be happily saved. It is painful, my brethren, to plead on the side of rigour, however just; and I willingly place the issue in your own hands, to be decided according to your own judgments.

Suppose, then, for a moment, that I had reversed the course of argument which I have this day pursued; that I had informed you that the gospel assures us that a life of ease and consolation here below is the natural road to eternal reward; that the table of the rich is a sufficient school for Christian mortification; that in the crowded scenes of society it is easy to preserve recollection of thought and fervour of heart; that a crown of roses was the befitting attire in which to follow the footsteps of a crucified Master! had I proclaimed such flattering doctrines, I ask, would you have received them with consolation or with horror? Would you have approved, or would you not have fled from me as a betrayer of my trust, a profaner of God's word, a deceiver and destroyer of souls? Then, let me ask, will that bear to be practised, which will not bear to be taught; will those doctrines save the flock, which it would condemn the pastor to teach; or do you think that what if spoken would profane the pulpit of God, reduced to action will justify before His tribunal?

Again, my brethren, nothing can be more clearly enforced in the gospel than that the way of salvation is steep and rugged, that the course of the true Christian is one of toil and struggle. When, therefore, you lead the ordinary life of those in your station, let me ask, do you feel that you are in the midst of these painful combats, scarcely crowned with a hard-earned victory—of these laborious exertions, leading to scarcely a visible success; or do you, on the contrary, feel your life to be tolerably pleasant and undisturbed? As easy is it to judge between the two, as to decide in the midst of a rapid current, whether you are straining every nerve to slowly advance your bark against its course, or whether, resting on your oars, you allow yourselves to glide smoothly and unresistingly with the stream. And if you discover, as you must do, that the latter is your case, on what hope do you rely that this state is the arduous, the painful, the only path of salvation?

Once more, my brethren, I will appeal to your own judgment, and then I release your attention. If you have hitherto lived as the generality do in your situation of life, let me ask you have you reposed your hopes of salvation upon your past actions, or upon some undefined prospect of future exertion—some idea that a period of retirement from the gaieties of the world would leave a sober interval for the great preparation—some promise to yourself that old age or your last illness would afford leisure for a more gradual and less rude detachment from the world, than the hand of death is likely to make, if it snatch you now. And, while thus acknowledging to yourself that, speculatively, salvation was not to be purchased by living the life of the rich, did it never occur to you that, while the past is consolidated into a weight of responsibility, the future is but an airy vision, like the distant lake which seems to allure the fainting traveller in the sandy desert, which he may pursue, but may not reach, which he may reach, but will surely not enjoy? And if this consideration, too, came over your reflection, what more could be wanting to satisfy you that your state is practically unfavourable to salvation, when your own mind confesses to you that you must one day quit it to secure that salvation, and, at the same time, you know not whether that day will ever be at your command?

But if, my brethren, all this convinces you not that I have kept within the bounds of justice, let me appeal to the awful words of the Son of God: "It is easier for a camel to pass through the eye of a needle, than for a rich man to enter into the kingdom of heaven." Naught that I have said can equal the severity of this sentence, coupled with its explanation. For, while it treats the salvation of the poor as in the ordinary course of grace, it appeals to the omnipotence of God as the only ground on which the salvation of the rich is to be explained: "With men this is impossible, but with God *all things* are possible." (Matt. xix. 24, 29.)

Are you, then, my brethren, to despair of salvation? God forbid. But you must enter into the narrow road which leads to life; you must use this world, according to the command of the Apostle, as if you used it not; "for the fashion of this world passeth away." (1 Cor. vii. 31.) You must in riches put on the spirit of poverty, in prosperity bear the cross of Christ; and whatever you may exteriorly appear to men, inwardly before God you must be as stripped of riches, and rank, and influence, as if you possessed not anything in this world. In a few words, you must follow the precepts of St. Paul, that you may receive the reward which he promises, when he says: "Charge the rich of this world not to be high-minded, nor to hope in uncertain riches, but in the living God. To do good, to be rich in good works, to distribute readily, to communicate to others, to lay up in store for themselves a good foundation against the time to come, that they may attain true life." (1 Tim. vi. 17-19.)

SERMON IV.

On Detraction.

Lev. xix. 13, 16.

"Thou shalt not calumniate thy neighbour; . . . . . thou shalt not be a detractor nor a whisperer among the people."

THERE is, my brethren, generally speaking, a marked difference between the offences of those who have abandoned, and of those who cleave to, the service of God and the observance of His law. The transgressions of the former are distinguished by the coolness with which they are premeditated, the deliberation with which they are committed, and the remorselessness whereby they are followed. The latters' failings are generally the effect of surprise and inadvertency, and are sure to be succeeded by sorrow and repentance. There is, however, one class of offences, and it is that condemned in my text, in which, unfortunately, both the friends and enemies of God too much resemble each other; so that had we to judge of the prevalence of virtue or vice in the world by the warmth or coldness of charity shown to the reputation of our neighbours, I fear that our judgment would have to be very severe and indiscriminate, and that we should feel obliged to draw the conclusion suggested in the gospel, that "iniquity must have abounded, since the charity of so many hath grown cold." (Matt. xxiv. 12.)

In sooth, the failings of the tongue are the last which the zealous to walk in the path of virtue overcome; so that St. James, taking it for granted that he who has subdued that unruly member, must have previously freed himself of every other fault, hesitates not to declare, that "whoever offendeth not in words, he is a perfect man." (iii. 2.) Hence it was that, even when the disciples had only one heart and one soul, and were distinguished from the rest of men by their mutual love, these were the imperfections which, like a worm growing with the blossom wherein it is folded up, threatened to canker the first promise of Christianity, and ruin the hopes of its zealous husbandman. "For I fear," says St. Paul, writing to one of his earliest and dearest flocks—" I fear lest when I come, I shall not find you such as I would ; .... but perhaps contentions, envyings, *detractions, whisperings*, be among you." (2 Cor. xii. 20.) If thus he wrote in such times as those, what would he have said in our days, when the most blameless innocence is not protected from the wanton attacks of malice or levity; when the most trivial transgression affords matter for exaggerated censure or heartless scoffing; when the most sacred privacy of domestic life is sacrilegiously violated, and the most confidential trusts dishonourably broken, that food may be supplied to the public appetite for scandal, and society may not lack materials for conversation and amusement? So common, in fact, has this sin of detraction become, that its enormity seems scarcely to be measured; and, consequently, there is scarcely any transgression which makes more dreadful havoc among the inheritance of the Lord. "For many," say the holy Scriptures, speaking of these very crimes—"many have fallen by the edge of the sword, but not so many as have perished by their own tongue. Blessed is he that is defended from an evil tongue, that hath not passed into the wrath thereof, and that hath not drawn the yoke thereof, and hath not been bound in its bands. For its yoke is a yoke of iron, and its bands are bands of brass. The death thereof is a most evil death, and hell is preferable to it." (Ecclus. xxviii. 22, seqq.)

This class of sins, my brethren, may be subdivided into various species, each bearing a different gradation of guilt. Thus, by *calumny*, we invent and propagate, to our neighbour's prejudice, what we know to be false; *detraction* contents itself with revealing and publishing his real but hidden failings. To these many others might be added; as that envious diminution of others' fair reputation by mysterious hints and half-suppressed difficulties of assent to it—those cold and limited expressions of approbation, which leave to be surmised secret and deep feelings of an opposite character; in short, all those little and common arts by which the jealous or malicious know so well how to tarnish the good name of whomsoever they dislike.

But though each of these methods has its peculiar character of guilt, and its special motives for being avoided, yet do they all together form one great class among the most common failings of the world—a class distinguished by its violation of justice and charity, and as such condemned in general terms by the word of God. And if we wish to take in the whole evil of these offences, methinks we may best do it by considering, first, its baleful influence on society, and then its difficulty of pardon before God.

There is a feeling, my brethren, absolutely necessary, that society may afford the advantages which it is appointed to administer : that is, a feeling of mutual esteem and confidence, among those who compose it. It has pleased the Almighty so to create and dispose us, that we stand in hourly need of one another's assistance. Our faculties are too limited to comprehend or do all things ; we must communicate our respective qualities or acquirements, to meet the necessary demands daily made upon us. The youth must share his vigour and activity with the aged, and receive in return the lessons of his experience. The ignorant partakes with the learned of the fruits of his application, and contributes, in return, towards his support and his comforts. Advice and correction, encouragement and consolation, and a thousand other aids necessary to the enjoyment of life, lie not within ourselves, but require the interested or benevolent interposition of those around us. In order to obtain this primary advantage of society, a feeling of mutual esteem and confidence is absolutely indispensable among its members. If we cannot depend upon the good will, the sincerity, the ability of others, it is impossible that we should profit by their counsel or assistance.

How happy and delightful would society be, could we consider each neighbour according to the true spirit of Christianity, as a brother upon whose affection at least we may rely in our difficulties, our sorrows, or our doubts, without danger of his wilfully leading us astray, or refusing us his aid ! As, therefore, everything which tends to promote such good feelings, tends, at the same time, to increase the utility and pleasures of social life; so whatever goes to diminish them, necessarily works against the common interests of us all. And what can possibly tend more completely to diminish them, than the practice of detraction and evil-speaking, which directly aims at overturning the good opinion we have of one another?

My brethren, as it is impossible for the detractor to entertain any trust or esteem for the individual of whom he judges so ill, so it is equally impossible for him to communicate the motives of his bad opinion, without, at the same time, communicating the distrust and dislike which it begets in his own mind. What a dreadful havoc, then, must such a one make among the best, the most amiable dispositions of the sound heart! But a few moments before his conversation, your friend or neighbour's character held in your mind an untainted and proud distinction. In his abilities and goodness you felt that you had an additional resource, of which you would not be gladly deprived. Perhaps even the image of his virtues and gifts filled the principal niche in your domestic affections, and around it you had hung a thousand votive records of admiration, of obligations, and of promises of perpetual attachment. Towards it you looked as the proudest ornament of your circle; in its features you thought you beheld the perfect model of human excellence; to its pedestal you purposed to fly as a refuge from every danger; around it you clung as an oracle in every perplexity. But let the detractor insinuate himself for a few moments into your confidence, and direct his malicious criticism against this object of your esteem: as he proceeds, the virtuous features which you had so much admired become distorted in your eyes; the memorial of your gratitude fade in your sight; and before his poisonous breath has yet finished pouring its venom into your ear, you have, perhaps, dashed into pieces the idol and centre of your affections; you have trampled on your contracts of unfailing friendship: and then you find in their stead a ruin and a blank, amidst which your heart stands stripped of what hitherto furnished it support and consolation. Oh! what a cruel triumph indeed is this over all that is pleasing, all that is desirable in life! And yet, who does not remember many instances of long intimacies irretrievably interrupted, of loving friendships for ever broken insunder, of enmity and feud substituted for kindness and affection, in consequence of a false report, a malicious whisper, or a mysterious hint? "He that concealeth a transgression," says Solomon, "seeketh friendships; he that repeateth it again, separateth friends." (Prov. xvii. 9.)

Even if the nature of faults reported be not such as to produce these serious effects, it is impossible that some diminution of esteem and confidence should not result, from hearing new imperfections imputed to our neighbours. Happy, however, would it be if the evils of this odious vice stopped here! Happy would it be if its mischief passed away, like most other crimes, in the action which committed it! For this is its foul, but distinguishing feature, that the moment you have let it escape you, you have no further control over its consequences, which may run to a frightful extent: no penetration can measure the degree of impression which your story may make; no caution can limit the dissemination which it may receive; no prudence calculate the extent of exaggeration which it may reach. No; you know not what impression your story may shake—know not what importance your hearers may attach to circumstances which to you have appeared trifling. There may have been in the breasts of some, suspicions or apprehensions already lurking, which only wanted a spark to be enkindled into a blaze; and your statement may have fully supplied this. They may view certain faults in a more serious light than you are accustomed to do, and may judge that as a crime which you have indicted as an error. In short, they may misunderstand from dullness, they may misjudge from prepossession, they may condemn rashly from misguided goodness. In the next place, seldom does a report unfavourable to another's character travel no farther than its first relation: for seldom is the advice of revealed wisdom followed, "Hast thou heard a word against thy neighbour? let it die within thee." (Eccles. xix. 10.) On the contrary, the defamatory story is generally thought too good an anecdote not to be repeated, and flies through a thousand willing mouths round the whole circle of the injured person's acquaintance, everywhere chilling kindness, and withering his pleasures and his hopes. In addition to this, at every repetition the tale receives an accession of circumstance and of aggravation; by passing through so many hands, its extenuations are gradually worn off, its point becomes more keen and its edge more cutting; till its poor innocent victim finds himself, he knows not why, an object of general dislike, and suspicion; or even if the original charge was founded on truth, its object acquires at last the merit of being the martyr of calumny and falsehood, into which the real facts have been long and completely distorted. Thus, then, my brethren, does the detractor loosen among many more than hear him, and much more seriously than he calculates, those bonds which keep us together in society for our mutual advantage; thus does this hateful bane of all social and domestic happiness separate and estrange those to whom mutual confidence and esteem had been hitherto a source of assistance and of pleasure. After having thus, by one act, caused so much odious mischief, I know not whether it should be reckoned an additional misfortune, or a consolation, that his crime extends still further in its consequences, by causing them to recoil upon himself. For if he has scattered mistrust and disesteem among others, he has certainly heaped them in fuller measure upon his own head. "The detractor," says Solomon, "is the abomination of men." (Prov. xxiv. 9.) And, indeed, can you think that, while you are detracting from your neighbour's reputation, however willingly, however agreeably your accounts may be listened to, do you think you are advancing yourself one degree in the regard of those who hear you? Will they form a higher estimate of your generosity, by seeing you capable of insulting an absent wretch, who has no means of defending himself; of your good faith, by hearing you betray secret failings which you can hardly be revealing without a breach of trust; of your worth as a man, finding you capable of sporting with what is dearest to every individual of your species, his character and his feelings? On the contrary, you will become yourself an object of dread and suspicion; you will be esteemed a creature whose confidence is perilous, whose friendship is a curse, whose tokens of affection are treacherous as those of Joab's to Abner; one who embraces his friend the closer, in order to strike his dagger the more deeply into his side. "If a serpent," says the wise man, " bite in silence, *he* is nothing better that backbiteth secretly;" (Eccles. x. 11) and both are equally odious.

It may, perhaps, appear that these consequences which I have attributed to the crime of detraction, are merely speculative, and produce no practical influence on society. But this is far from being the case. For why is every one who values his character obliged to be so much upon his guard, lest his most trivial failings should be known, though they are almost necessary to human nature; why obliged often to cloak them in hypocrisy, thus substituting crime for frailty, except that his confidence in the justice and good faith of those around him have been so shaken by experience, that he cannot entrust them with a view of his real character? Why is the most virtuous female forced to avoid a thousand circumstances, not only innocent, but, perhaps, even virtuous, except that she well knows that the most harmless action may be perverted by calumny into a ground of suspicion? Who amongst us ever dares to open a secret to his nearest friend without first carefully sounding him, and then fortifying his communications with a thousand promises of fidelity? And why is this, but that calumny and detraction are so common, that in trusting others we feel as if we were only giving them a means of injuring us. Who is not anxious to know the judgment which his friends have passed upon his performances, and does not tremble when he hears that his character has been the subject of conversation or discussion among his most intimate acquaintance. And why is this, but that misrepresentation is so general, that we dread to see our reputation in the hands of a third person, however well-disposed, and would willingly forego the chance of his having praised us, in order to escape the far more numerous and fearful risks of his having said something to our disparagement.

Thus, my dear brethren, is this vice in direct opposition to that mutual esteem and confidence which is absolutely necessary for the peace, the advantage, and the enjoyments of society. To say this much, is no less than to prove that it is odious to that God who founded this state for man, to that God whose law ever inculcated peace, charity, and good will. The earthly considerations against this vice thus link themselves with those which religion proposes, and then leave her to insist on its still more dangerous consequences, by showing it to be a crime most difficult of forgiveness from the justice of God. There are two circumstances which tend to render sins of this class peculiarly hard to be forgiven—the difficulty of having a sufficient repentance, and the necessity of making a full reparation. It has been a kind and beneficent disposition of Divine Providence, to stamp crime in general with such an odious character, that the moment the excitement which suggests it has passed over, the soul feels uneasy and tortured, till she has got rid of so foul a blot. There is a restlessness about the mind, there is a heaviness upon the heart, there is a picture of guilt which is constant, and moves before the eyes of the offender, the hateful features of which he cannot remove from his detestation, though he feels that they are only the reflection of his own true image. Thus, while the Almighty in His justice has made "the sting of sin to be death," He has preserved the order popularly attributed to His providence, by placing in sin itself the strongest antidote against the mortality of its wound. In addition to this, we may observe, that in general the more enormous the guilt, the more lively is the horror which it excites, and, consequently, so much the stronger are the inducements to real and feeling repentance which it suggests.

While every other crime thus "lies at the door," and bears fearful testimony to our souls, the sin of detraction has exactly an opposite effect. Committed without any paroxysm of passion, but with all the polished urbanity and gentle calmness of ordinary social intercourse, it recurs not to our thoughts marked by any of those excitements of the mind, of those violations of outward propriety, or any of those neglects of clear defined obligations, which distinguish our usual offences, stamp them on our memory in regret, and seem almost essential to constitute a great violation of the divine law. Quite on the contrary; the recollection of what we have done only recalls hours of quiet enjoyment and friendly companionship. The crime is mingled with associations of the most agreeable character, and most extenuating tendency; committed, possibly, with virtuous friends, who, doubtless, would have rebuked us had we transgressed; perhaps of interested persons, who, we fancy, must have interfered had we offended. Our conversation was listened to as engaging; our anecdote was pronounced most amusing: not one misgiving of conscience arose while we were thus delighting all around us; not one painful remembrance checks our satisfaction: we sleep without disquietude; we pray without self-reproach.

Such are the fair features with which this sin presents itself to your conscience; and yet it is a sin of the blackest dye. You have been guilty of a breach of charity, odious in the extreme to God, and you *must* repent of it if you hope forgiveness ; but still it stands before the tribunal of your conscience only as a successful discharge of the social duties, which charity itself commands. You have defiled your soul with an injustice so crying, that no other sin against a fellow-man, except, perhaps, that of murder, is reprobated in such harsh terms in the word of God; and you cannot wash it out but by tears of sincere repentance and detestation : and yet you cannot make it assume before your mind any but a light, gay, and flattering aspect, in which you can discover nothing that is hateful. What wonder, then, my brethren, that sins of detraction should be so seldom repented of as they ought? But this difficulty of repentance is still further aggravated, by our being seldom able to view the sin in its full malignity; because we seldom see the extent of its consequences. Could we measure to its full the evil which we have caused by one detracting discourse, we might, perhaps, stand aghast, and feel remorse at what we have done ; but, unfortunately, we seldom do more than wantonly light the train, and remain ourselves too distant to see the ruin which the final explosion makes in the hopes, the fortunes, or the heart of our injured brother. We measure our criminality only by our individual action ; we make no calculation of its remoter consequences : that was but momentary, trivial, and thoughtless, and we never think of charging ourselves with its fatal and lasting effects.

You see, my brethren, what danger there is of never properly recovering from this dreadful crime ; for you see how easy it is totally to overlook it, when collecting your offences, to repent of them before God ; and how difficult to work up your mind into that abhorrence and detestation of it, which is the ground of all repentance. Hence arises the first obstacle to obtaining forgiveness for it ; a second, and much more formidable one, springs from the necessity of making full reparation to the person whom you have injured. The diminution of your neighbour's reputation is a crime of injustice. His good name is the fruit of his toil, the result of his exertions. It is a capital accumulated by constant attention to propriety of conduct, which brings him in many advantages, and is always capable of further increase. He is entitled to its undisturbed enjoyment as much as he is to that of his material property, until he has publicly violated those obligations towards the society which bestows it, the neglect of which at once strips him of its possession. Whoever, therefore, unless that has happened, deprives him of this right, or infringes upon its enjoyment, is guilty of an injustice ; and according to the law of nature and of God, must make reparation for the injury to the extent of his power, if he hopes to obtain forgiveness. He must retract, if necessary, what he has said, in case it was false ; he must destroy or diminish, as far as possible, the bad impressions he has made, if his relation was unfortunately correct; he must bear honourable testimony to the injured character of his neighbour; he must make handsome reparation to his wounded feelings; he must, in short, reinstate him in the rank which he previously held in the esteem of his friends and of the world. But to all this reparation, how many obstacles arise both from our own feelings and from external circumstances! From our own feelings, because while so unsparing to others, we are as tender to ourselves; because when balancing between the neglect of another's reputation and the destruction or diminution of our own, it is not difficult to guess which scale will generally preponderate. The injury which we have inflicted on another can seldom be repaired except by transferring it to ourselves, his wounds can scarcely be healed but by ours; we must, like the unjust accusers of Susanna, bear the punishment which we have called down upon another. In doing this, we manifest to those who have hitherto thought us gentle and inoffensive, that we have been most unfeeling and cruel; to those who have ever valued us as generous and just, that we are in reality insidious and false. It requires, my brethren, an extraordinary degree of courage, or rather of humility, not only to encounter reproach, but to seek it. Many who could, perhaps, stand persecution and insult, would hardly have strength of mind to undergo this self-degradation, especially as in doing so they would not even have the consolation or the pride of feeling that they suffered only from oppression: conscience would whisper that it is the merited punishment of injustice.

But let us suppose for a moment, that you had summoned virtue sufficient to carry you to this dreadful task, how many obstacles would you meet to its full discharge! In a thousand cases, you will find that your poison has worked too deep for your antidote to reach it; that cheerfully and attentively as your tale of scandal was drunk in, your excuses and reparations are received but with little interest or notice. Trusting, like Judas, that there might be moderation or justice in human enmity, you have betrayed the character of your friend into its hands. The cruel and unexpected treatment which he receives, makes you, indeed, repent of your treachery; but when you seek to repair it by declaring that you have sinned against innocent blood, and are guiltless of the farther consequences, you may expect to receive the same answer as the betrayer: "What is that to us? look thou to it." (Matt. xxvii. 4.) For most are willing to think that they incur no fault by the propagation of scandal, but lay it all at the door of its original author. Hence it follows, that reckoning the story public property, they have given it general currency without scruple; and guilty as they have been, and obliged as they are to co-operate in repairing the mischief they have increased, yet their neglect generally throws the whole burthen upon the unfortunate source of the evil. What difficulties, then, must start at every step, what numerous misrepresentations to correct, what different interests to conciliate, how various dispositions to regain! Yet the undertaking must be attempted; there is no hope of pardon without it. You may pray for hours, you may fast for years, you may weep, you may confess your sin again and again; but as long as its injurious effects remain, at least as far as possible, unrepaired, it cries to heaven for vengeance, like the unpaid wages of the labourer, like the blood of the murdered, like every other sin of injustice.

This is, indeed, a dreadful feature of this sin. It cannot be forgiven without full repentance and full reparation; and yet it presents in its very nature the most dangerous obstacles to both. These two difficulties are fearfully increased on further consideration. For, first, the sin itself is one which peculiarly steels the justice of the Almighty against the offender. "Judgment without mercy" He has pronounced to be the lot of "him who hath not shown mercy." You are to expect from Him that same measure with which you have dealt out your compassion to others; you must anticipate the same treatment from your Master which you have used towards your fellow-servant. In the second place, as no influence prevails with him like the intercession of those whom we have benefited, so has He declared Himself the avenger of the injured and oppressed, and pronounced that their cry against those who have wronged them shall ever reach His throne. Remember that He would not forgive the calumniators of Job, unless their injured friend offered up sacrifice on their behalf. Yes, my brethren, if the prayer of malediction can pierce to the Fountain of all blessings, and move Him also to curse one of His creatures, it is when wrung from the bitterness of soul of those whose character has been blasted. "Accuse not a servant to his master," says the word of God—"accuse not a servant to his master, lest he curse thee, and thou fall." (Prov. xxx. 10.) Look at the conduct of the meek and gentle Jeremias. He endured persecution, captivity, and bonds, with resignation and patience; his prayers were even offered up for those who inflicted them. But no sooner did they plot more trying mischief—no sooner did they say, " Come, let us invent devices against Jeremias .... come, and let us strike him with the tongue," than his patience gave way to indignation, and he uttered that dreadful and prophetic curse upon his oppressors : "Give heed to me, O Lord! and hear the voice of my adversaries. .... Thou, O Lord! knowest all their counsel against me unto death : forgive them not their iniquity, and let not their sin be blotted out from Thy sight: let them be overthrown before Thy eyes ; in the time of Thy wrath do Thou destroy them." (Jer. xviii.) Even if the patience of victims should exceed that of the prophet, and should no curse upon their calumniators escape them, still every sigh which they heave is a tacit prayer, that puts their cause and its avengement into the hands of God. Nor will He neglect any cause which He undertakes. He will not suffer the injuries which you have inflicted to sleep ; He will, in the end, visit them upon you; perhaps, even in this world they may be sent to haunt and torment you during life, and to present you with gall and vinegar in the agonies of death. But, at all events, they will work against you as Jeremias prayed they should ; they will make your sin hard to be forgiven, and prevent its being blotted out from the sight of God; that so, in the time of His final wrath, He may destroy you.

An offence, then, which acts in direct opposition to the common interests of society, by destroying mutual confidence and esteem among its members, one for which it is difficult to obtain forgiveness, on account of the obstacles it presents to sincere repentance, and to satisfying the obligation of reparation which it imposes—such is the common vice of detraction. It would seem, then, that all who value their happiness, either in this world or the next, should enter into a combination to banish from among them this common pest. There is only one means of doing this—encourage not the detractor in his conversation. Let your answers, let your manners and your countenance, show him that you take no interest in his scandal, and that you value not his powers of entertainment, his talents or his wit, however brilliant, while prostituted to so vile and odious a purpose. "The north wind," says the Book of Proverbs, (xxiv. 23) " driveth away rain, so doth a sad countenance a backbiting tongue."

In proportion as character, situation, or rank, authorise you to claim greater attentions, should your weight be exerted to crush this evil, and your influence employed to check, if necessary, even by direct interference, the common practice of mingling this poison with the most innocent recreation. Yes, my brethren, this is the honourable respect which you should feel proud of commanding by character, that in your presence calumny should be dumb, detraction should falter, misrepresentation blush. This is the real chivalry of which a Christian gentleman should boast; that, while under his protection, the reputation of the absent and the weak is safe from attack or insult, and that by his interposition every attempt to wound the feelings of others, will be instantly repelled. This is the true pride of Christian nobility, when its scutcheon is flung over the innocent and defenceless as a *shield of good will;* within whose shadow virtue is sacred and human weakness respected, innocence is safe, and frailty compassionated. Such was the boast of David, in recounting his merits as a good and a great sovereign: "The perverse heart did not cleave to me, and the malignant that turned aside from me I did not know. The man that in private detracted his neighbour, him did I persecute." (Ps. c. 4, 5.) In this manner did the great St. Augustine cause to be inscribed over his table two verses, commanding all those to keep far from it who gnawed the reputation of their absent brethren. Oh! did this spirit animate all in the higher ranks of life, we might, perhaps, hope to see one day restored, through their influence, those happy feelings of charity, which made the early Christians distinguished by the Pagans themselves, as having only one heart and one soul, and which form one of the principal features of the Church of the Lamb in heaven.

SERMON V.

On Repentance.

MATT. iii. 1, 2.

"Now in those days came John the Baptist preaching in the desert of Judea. And saying: Do penance; for the kingdom of heaven is at hand."

EVERY step which preceded the dissolution of the Jewish polity and the foundation of the Christian religion, must have been watched with peculiar interest by the zealous Israelite, and must be equally important to us.

It was the time when the seal was just going to be put to the grounds of his belief and his hopes; it was the time when a new light of truth and morals was dawning upon us. Disciplined in the providence and promises of his God, the pious Jew saw, in every fact which appeared most afflicting, the germs of that glorious renovation, which was to take place in the withered stock of David. Notwithstanding the magnificent improvements of Herod, he still sighed with his ancestors to see his Temple so inferior to the one which had existed before the captivity: but the sigh was the source of consolation. It assured him that the prophetic communication was not yet fulfilled—that "the glory of the second house should be greater than the first;" and he looked forward in hope to the Desired of all nations, who was to shed such additional lustre over the sacred edifice.

Judea, which once ruled from the Euphrates to the borders of Egypt, and but a few years before was victorious over all the power of the Syrian monarchy, now sat weeping under her palm-tree, for the dominion of a stranger; and had seen, with indignation, the Roman eagles fluttering in triumph over her sacred walls. But this only gave her new assurance; the sceptre was at length departing from Juda, and its departure marked the moment when the Great Deliverer was to appear.

The voice of prophecy had ceased, and the nation had been left in the dark about the will of God: the cessation was the harbinger of the expected period, when a fuller manifestation of divine wisdom was to be made. One event—one prophet more the Jew only expected; this was the coming of Elias, who was immediately to precede the promised Messias. His coming was to be for the purpose of pointing out, rather than of foretelling Him; he was to prepare His people to give Him a worthy reception. With all these expectations, we may fancy the Israelite anxiously waiting for his appearance— ready to rise at the first note of his rallying call, and determined to obey whatever it might command.

At this moment, an extraordinary personage does appear—a Nazarite, like Elias, uncontaminated by the world, clothed like him with skins, and feeding on the produce of the wilderness. From the desert of the Jordan his voice penetrates through all the country: "Prepare ye; the kingdom of heaven is at hand." His appearance, this proclamation, point him out as the person so desired; and crowds go, consequently, from every part, to put themselves under his direction. But far different from their worldly anticipations is the preparation which he commands for the reception of the great King. "Do penance," he exclaims, "for the kingdom of heaven is at hand. For now the axe is laid to the root of the trees. Every tree, therefore, that yieldeth not good fruit, shall be cut down, and cast into the fire." The Pharisees themselves, attracted by his mission, go from Jerusalem to receive his instructions and baptism. Undaunted by their power, and unsoothed by their submission, John changes not his theme: "Ye brood of vipers, . . . bring forth worthy fruits of penance." Repentance, then, from all sin was the great preparation for receiving the benefits of redemption; the preaching of it sealed up the sacred volume of prophecy, and closed the grand phenomena which announced the coming of a new and perfect revelation. To it all these phenomena naturally turned the attention of the religious Israelite, and they tended to give it most signal importance. Then, if the benefits of redemption have not been diminished in value, and if equal dispositions are yet required for participating in them, this great doctrine, my brethren, has lost none of its importance. Such, certainly, is the view of the Church, who now calls upon us to rise from sin, that we may be prepared to commemorate the great mysteries of redemption; and for this purpose, so frequently brings before us, during Advent, the preaching of the Baptist.

But when I reflect, O my God! on the character with which *he* was invested; that a minister foretold by prophecy, conceived amidst miracles, sanctified in the womb, and born into the arms of Thy Mother; that a minister brought up in the wilderness, in seclusion from all that could taint and all that could allure; that a minister, in fine, pure and spotless in Thine eyes, was alone chosen by Thee to announce this great lesson;—oh! then it is that I feel my unfitness for the grave duty imposed upon me, and that my heart turns towards Thee, to implore Thy strength on my mind, and Thy grace upon my lips, while I endeavour to proclaim to Thy faithful people the dreadful evil of sin, and the remedy which Thou hast prepared for it in repentance!

No object, my brethren, can be more noble or more beautiful than the soul rising from the laver of regeneration. It is restored to the original innocence from which it had been torn in the fall of our first parents. Its Creator, looking down with a benignant eye, sees reflected upon it, without a wrinkle or stain, the bright image of Himself, which He stamped upon man in His creation; the eternal Son fosters it as the fruit of His redemption, adopted as a child of His own Father by the application of His sacred blood; and the Holy Spirit who descended with His graces upon the waters of baptism, has poured on it the fulness of His choicest gifts, and selected it for His dwelling. In this manner, the strictest connexion and friendship is formed between the Almighty and His favourite creature; the angels consider him as the object of divine affection, little inferior to themselves, but crowned with honour and glory; and cheerfully undertake the commission given them, of bearing him up in their hands, and guarding him in all his ways. In proportion as the faculties open and expand, additional blessings and tokens of affection are bestowed. For, when the senses begin to enjoy the beauties of nature, every new gratification is a fresh pledge of the divine goodness towards His creature; as the mind receives its first instructions, every new acquirement is a fresh obligation bestowed by this great benefactor. And when we now begin to have unfolded in our tender minds the great truths of our religion, when we begin to feel the benefits of redemption, to look back upon all that has been done for us, and to cast forward our view upon all that is prepared for us, with what ties of gratitude and of love may we not be supposed to feel ourselves bound.

But the tokens of divine favour end not here. We are at length admitted to the sacred table, and sign, by this last act of familiar intercourse, the covenant of eternal friendship with our God. He may now, with the prophet, ask the soul, what more He can do for her, after having not only sanctified her but communicated Himself to her? Still, every day He showers new blessings and new graces, and endears Himself to her by fresh communications. In this state the happy soul reposes on His bosom with confidence, and looks with the loving eye of a child into the countenance of her heavenly Parent, secure there from all danger and from all suspicion. Every action is full of merit, and laid up to receive its reward; every trial is for her improvement and advancement, and for the increase of her future recompense. But, oh! my brethren, if from this happy state she fall into one mortal transgression, how instantly does it all vanish; and what is still worse, how wretchedly it is replaced! In proportion as the soul was dear to her Creator, she is now become equally loathsome; the print of original innocence, which shone so bright upon her, is now converted into a sore—the stamp of reprobation branded upon her by the blighting curse of her former friend. The sacred blood of redemption, on which she has trampled, cries out in a tone more piercing than that of Abel's, against her ingratitude and baseness. The Holy Spirit abandons her, and leaves her to be the dwelling of remorse and despair. She has now leagued herself with new associates; she has given her right hand to the enemy of God and of her salvation; she must now accustom herself to reckon him her friend, and must be content to share with him her present enjoyments and her future prospects. Whichever way she turns, nothing but objects of reproach and condemnation meet her. On one side, every breath which she inhales, is a new obligation to the Author of her being, and a new accusation of her ingratitude towards Him. And if on the other, misfortunes fall upon on her, they are longer trials of her virtue—storms sent to wean her from the world, and draw her looks towards heaven—but tempests of fire, like those of Sodom, showered down for vengeance and destruction.

In vain the sinner looks back for those good works which he had wrought in the days of his innocence; they are blotted from the divine mind. "If the just man," says the Lord, by the prophet Ezechiel—" if the just man turn himself away from his justice, shall he live? All his justice which he hath done shall not be remembered; in the prevarication, by which he hath prevaricated, and in his sin, which he hath committed, in them he shall die." (xviii. 24.) He may think with satisfaction of the love which his heart once bore towards his Saviour, and of the hardships which he has undergone in His service. Vain thought! they are remembered no more. He may still flatter himself that hours of prayer and years of piety cannot have been counterbalanced by one moment of frailty. Vain hopes! they are remembered no more, while that uneffaced stain calls every moment for punishment upon his head. He may endeavour to trust, that at least the goodness of God is more powerful than his wickedness; that His former friendship cannot have been totally in one instant broken; that pledges of former affection cannot so easily have been thrown away. Vain consolation! "If this man," says He, by his prophet, of the last King of Juda—" if this man were the signet on My right hand, yet would I pluck him off, and cast him from Me." Such is the abandonment, such the rejection of the poor sinner.

And, oh! that my tongue were not too feeble to paint the prospects which meet his view, if he has ever the courage to dart it beyond this. There he sees an ocean of torment in which he is to be plunged, and an eternity of duration through which he is to struggle in it. He sees that he is to be cast for ever into the company of the wicked and their infernal seducers; to be repining, and consoled with insult; entreating, and answered by scorn; thirsting to death for one drop of water on his tongue, and refreshed with ever-renovated flame. He sees that he is to be for ever—for ever withering under the curse of an angry Judge, without hopes of decay; that he is to writhe for ever under all the accumulated mass of suffering under which Omnipotence can bury him, without even the envied, consoling prospect of being ground into annihilation beneath its overwhelming weight. This, my brethren, is the present state, and these the future views, of all who are unhappily involved in sin. While any reflection remains, it must prove to him a source of bitterness, whichever way he turns for relief; conscience, like the angel with the drawn sword, stands in the path, and precludes all attainment of his object. A remedy for this dreadful state is felt necessary, and none seems to remain, except that of multiplying the offence that the mind may be dead to its effects, and of plunging deeper into crime that the struggle with it may be felt the less.

Poor wretch! do you then really think that you will gather consolation from the very thorns that torment and tear you; that you will extract balm to heal, from the very poison which corrodes, your heart? You may endeavour to intoxicate yourself with pleasure into a stupid insensibility, but the instant you raise your eyes, but for one moment, from the draught, they will meet, like Baltassar, the fatal hand recording upon every object the sentence of your reprobation. You may obtain calms, but expect not peace. And then, old age will come, when the heart will be palled with satiety, and the soul will be fatigued with perpetual fiction. The principle of self-trial *will*, at length, break through the delusions with which we may have stifled it, and conscience—conscience—in the pensive moments of the day, and in the repose of the night, will, must, at length, haunt the sinner, and persecute him like a fury into a grave, uncheered by even the last good which deserts man, shunned even by hope.

Well, then, my friends, to the evils of sin, must we add

the worst of evils, that they are irremediable. If sin, as we have seen, deprives the soul of such beauty and happiness, and plunges it into the abyss of defilement, ingratitude, and misery; if alleviation or respite cannot be expected even in this life from its sting; if, in fine, it incurs the anger of God to such a degree that this will be exerted to punish it with the utmost rigour for an endless eternity;—surely, no remedy can be deemed too painful for such a disorder, no commutation too severe for so terrible a retribution.

But no, no. A medicine exists, so efficacious as to produce instant cure, and yet so easy in its application that it can be said to consist in no more than consciousness of wanting it. *Repentance* will, in a moment, heal all the wounds of the sinner, and restore his soul to its original beauty. It will cancel all the evil that stands recorded against him, and revive all the former good works which he has obliterated by his transgression. It will revoke the sentence of reprobation already registered against him in the just decrees of the Almighty Judge, and reinstate him in all the rights of redemption, in the grace and friendship of God here, and the title to eternal happiness with Him hereafter. " As I live saith the Lord God, I desire not the death of the wicked, but that the wicked turn from his way, and live. Turn ye, turn ye from your evil ways : and why will you die, O house of Israel? .... The wickedness of the wicked shall not hurt him, in what day soever he shall turn from his wickedness. None of the sins which he hath committed shall be imputed to him : he hath done judgment and justice, he shall surely live." (Ezec. xxxiii). No sooner had David acknowledged with sorrow his transgression, "I have sinned against the Lord," than his sin was forgiven. Manasses, oppressed with misfortune, in punishment of his crimes, turned in humble repentance to the God of his father, and was instantly received into mercy. Are your souls, my brethren, defiled with iniquity of a deeper dye than that of Magdalen? One fervent flood of tears washed it perfectly away. Have you been guilty of treachery blacker than that of Peter? Go, and weep bitterly, confessing your guilt, and you will be once more, like him, the friend of the Bridegroom. And, my brethren, such is the goodness of our God, that though the impiety of transgression is so much increased in the New Law, the efficacy of repentance has been ever augmented, instead of diminished, by being elevated into a sacrament.

"Whose sins *you* shall forgive," says our Saviour to the pastors of His Church, " they are forgiven." " Whatever *you* shall loose on *earth*, shall be loosed also in *heaven*." This commission not only naturally and necessarily implies, that the sinner, wishing to be forgiven, must present himself to the pastor, who has received its authority, but it gives an assurance that when *he* has pronounced a sentence of forgiveness on earth, that sentence of forgiveness is ratified in heaven. Nor is this all; for the establishment of such a power not only makes Christian repentance more efficacious, but renders it proportionably more easy.

And, indeed, my brethren, contrast the evil with the remedy. If it seem severe that one act of delinquency should counterbalance years of previous piety, we have to calculate that in that one act are compounded all the horrors of ingratitude, treason, and contempt of the Deity;

we must reflect that we disobediently transgress the commands which a Sovereign, a Benefactor, a Father had imposed under the pain of his perpetual indignation, and that at the moment of transgression we were fully aware of the penalty which we incurred. But, on the other hand, if we consider that a poor helpless wretch, unable of himself to perform a meritorious act, by one simple effort of his mind, accompanied by compliance with an easy external condition, can fling off a load of guilt which could not have been expiated by an eternity of torment, can obtain as full, as equal a right to an eternity of reward, as the recluse who has spent a guiltless life in labouring to attain it,—oh! we must indeed acknowledge, that there is no proportion between the offence and its remedy, in the facility with which this acts. And what is this effort of the mind, this so much dreaded repentance? Why, it really consists in little more than in knowing the offence. For, is it possible to view sin as it really is, to reflect for a moment on the dreadful state into which it plunges us, and on the miserable rewards which await it, without being penetrated with horror of its enormity? And can we really see our souls involved in such a state without an anxious wish to be liberated, a sincere sorrow for having fallen into it, and a firm determination never again to incur it? Now these are the principal ingredients of true repentance, and only require the higher motive of divine love, to which they naturally lead, in order to be ennobled into a perfect virtue.

Still, however efficacious, and easy, repentance may appear, thus described, I well know that experience seems at variance with this view. How many attempt to rise from their sins, and yet after one or two ineffectual struggles relapse into their former state? But, to the number of these, oppose the illustrious penitents of holy writ whom I have just enumerated, recall to mind the long series of sinners, who, by one bold effort have separated themselves for ever from their iniquity, and are now enrolled in the catalogue of the saints. The ministers of God well know how frequently such powerful operations of grace even now occur; how often years of crime are expiated by one fervent and solid conversion, how frequently the most inveterate habits of vice are transformed into a steady course of virtue by a few bitter moments of tears. The difficulty, my brethren, is chiefly in imagination; we see terrors in the humble confession of our sins, and in breaking through our former habits. But remember, on the other hand, the real evils which threaten your neglect. Is the confession of sin to one minister of God, whose lips are sealed against discovery, to be put into comparison with the terrible disclosure which will one day take place before all mankind; when those who now partake with you in offence will curse and accuse you, those who are now hostile to you will revile, deride, and scorn you, those who now love and esteem will weep and blush for you? And then, if it will cost you some guard over your mind to prevent a relapse, there will be compensations for it which you can hardly at present calculate; there will be true and grounded peace of mind, not proceeding from an artificial, constrained absence of reflection, but from the conviction that you are in friendship and favour with a Being whose love is as sincere as His goodness is infinite, who has hitherto spared nothing which could conduce to your happiness, and who has set no limits to what He still intends to bestow. In these apparent difficulties, however, we must look up to a higher assistance than our own frail energies. We must raise our eyes towards Him who calls us, and beg of Him to effect within us the change which He requires; we must expect from Him alone the strength necessary to sustain us after it is made.

And do you think, my brethren, that there is the slightest danger of His refusing it? Look at your Saviour yielding His last breath with the last drop of His sacred blood drained out by unexampled suffering. Why does He undergo all this? It is, He tells you, that He may save the lost sheep of the house of Israel; it is that He may redeem you from sin, and purchase for you the graces necessary to salvation. And thus He only closes a public life nearly entirely spent in calling not the just but sinners to repentance. Can that hand which streams with the blood of your redemption, be raised to dash a repenting sinner from His feet: can those lips which made their last effort in praying for pardon upon the most cruel enemies, pronounce a sentence of reprobation upon a returning child: can that heart which was even laid open to make the sacrifice of propitiation and mercy more complete, close unfeelingly, and be steeled against the fervent desires of one who wishes to partake of its fruits? No, no, my brethren; every wound in that body, on the contrary, pleads for forgiveness and grace upon poor sinners, and in its turn invites them to detest the guilt which has inflicted it. This was the executioner that lacerated that sacred flesh, this was the only drop that infused bitterness into the cup of suffering and anguish, which that pure soul prayed might pass away. Well might He wish it to pass away, for He sank under the idea of even putting on the *dreadful character of sinner*. But no, well did He consent to drink it, for thus alone He purchased an *efficacious* and *easy remedy* for this abominable evil, by giving its virtue to Christian repentance.

No season can be more favourable for applying this remedy than the present; when the whole Church, in sackcloth and ashes, prostrates herself before the throne of divine clemency, and implores forgiveness for repenting sinners; when she calls to them, through the voice of her minister, "that it is now the hour to rise from sleep, for now our salvation is nearer than we believed. That the night is passed, and the day is at hand; and that we must cast off the works of darkness, and put on the armour of light." (Rom. xiii. 11, 12.) Obey, then, this call: awake, sinner, from your slumber, and arise! but awake and arise like Sampson, bursting by your first effort through all the bonds which your enemies have straitened round you. And if your first attempt has failed, be not discouraged; rise with renewed energy once more; but beware, that weakly reiterated efforts are but convulsive struggles, each of which, if ineffectual, will only weaken you for the succeeding attempt, till you sink at length, unresisting, into a fatal helplessness. All the Church is sighing for your success; all the blessed are anxious to enjoy on your account a satisfaction beyond that which ninety-nine just are capable of causing them. On, then—

on in the holy combat; your strength is in God, and your prize is heaven! Encouraged by these reflections, lose no time in shaking off the monster which hangs upon your breast, sucking out your life-blood; that we may all meet at the approaching solemnity, united round the altar of the Lamb, by the same bond of grace and divine love, which I pray God may one day unite us all around His throne.

SERMON VI.

On the Fast of Lent.

MATT. iv. 1, 2.

"Then Jesus was led by the Spirit into the desert, to be tempted by the devil. And when he had fasted forty days and forty nights, he was afterwards hungry."

MANY actions in our Saviour's life may justly appear more brilliant than those recorded in this Sunday's Gospel—many situations wherein He was placed seem more in harmony with His sublime character and mission than the secluded fast observed by Him in the wilderness; and yet not one is attributed, in the gospel, to the superior guidance noticed in my text. His instructions, however eloquent, pathetic, and sublime, are recorded as being the simple outpourings of His untaught wisdom; His prayer and contemplation are mentioned as if they were the natural fruits of a holy and devoutly-tempered mind; His splendid miracles are detailed as if they were the production of His own power and benevolence. But when He has to undertake a long and severe course of austerity, this is represented to us as resulting from a peculiar inspiration; when He has to fast forty days and forty nights, struggling against the suggestions of the tempter, then is Jesus led forth by the Spirit of God into the desert.

And why, my brethren, is this high agency called in, upon an occasion comparatively so undeserving of its exercise? It is that, whereas His conduct is a model proposed to our imitation, we needed every inducement and recommendation to make us practise that portion thereof against which our habits, our feelings, our very nature most rebels. It is that, whereas every other virtue, however painful, hath some sensible advantage to attach, or at least to reconcile, us to its practice; while patience soothes pain which cannot be avoided, resignation calms sorrow which cannot be removed, meekness blunts injuries which cannot be averted; the precept which commands us to inflict pain, and sorrow, and injury upon ourselves, seems devoid of every compensation, and must look forward to that distant and, alas! to human feelings, least valued of compensations, invisible merit before God. And fortunate would it be were this advantage, at least, allowed it undisputed and undisturbed. But our inclinations seldom end with tempting us to neglect our duties: they generally proceed to deny their obligation. Even that distant ray of consolation and hope, which can alone support the repenting sinner in the practice of austerity and mortification, even that prospect of future merit, which can alone encourage the Church's obedient son to undertake, after his Redeemer's example, the course of fasting whereon we have just entered,—even these only encouragements that we can hold out, are so frequently made a subject of dispute or doubt, that few, save those whom the Spirit of God hath led with Jesus into retirement, can say that they derive from them support and resolution. And yet I have truly said they are the *only* encouragements we can hold out; for I know not how to excite you to the observance of this practice, save by representing to you, in the strongest light, the spiritual advantages resulting from its faithful discharge, particularly at this season. For, after it shall have appeared that the practice of fasting has been ever enjoined and recommended by the word of God, a brief reflection will convince us that its advantages can never be so well attained as by the exact observance of the Lenten fast.

It is not my intention to convince you how the practice of fasting has been always recommended even without any reference to religious duty; how the very philosophers of antiquity observed it as an aid to contemplation; how it has been praised as a virtue and as a victory over nature in heroes and sages; how experience has proved its practice conducive to health, to mental vigour, and to habits of moderation; nor yet, how the ancient fathers of the desert considered it necessary to support them in their watchings, and assist them in their commerce with heaven. For, my brethren, I do not mean to address you as the advocate of abstemiousness, or the commender of temperance, but as one inculcating to you a duty of penance and mortification enjoined in every page of the sacred writings, as the most proper expiation for sin, as the securest safeguard for virtue, as the most efficacious appeal to the mercy of the Almighty. But, then, the fasting which has to attain their objects must be such as God has chosen, performed, not in sullen submission to a command, but with cheerful obedience to the call of His Church, accompanied by a feeling of internal humiliation and contrition; it must be a fast in which not merely the appetite is restrained, but every other sort of indulgence and dissipation is renounced; a fast not merely from the prohibited gratification of bodily sense, but a fast from sin and all iniquity, from all uncharitableness and evil desires; a fast, in fine, accompanied by prayer, more fervent; by attention to religious practices, more assiduous; by works of mercy, more copious; by alms, more liberal, than we practise at other seasons. " Is not this the fast which I have chosen?" says the Lord of Hosts, " loose the bands of wickedness, and break asunder every burthen. Deal thy bread to the hungry, and bring the needy and harbourless into thy house." (Is. lviii. 6, 7.)

Now, fasting performed with this spirit and conditions, has always been prescribed in the word of God, and proposed by the example of His servants, as the most efficacious means of expiating sin. Need I remind you of the prophet Samuel, gathering "all Israel to Masphath," that they might fast all day and cry out, " We have sinned against the Lord"? (1 Kings, vii. 5, 6) of David, who assures us, that after his sin " he humbled his soul in fasting (Ps. xxxiv. 13), until his knees became faint, in consequence of his rigours"? (ib. cviii. 24) of Daniel, who "set his face to the Lord his God, to pray and make supplication with fasting, and sackcloth, and ashes," making confession and exclaiming: " O Lord God, great and terrible! . . . we have sinned, we have committed iniquity, we have done wickedly, and have revolted"? (Dan. ix. 3, seq.) of Nehemias, in fine, who " fasted and prayed before the face of the God of heaven," and confessed the " sins of the house of Israel, and that he and his father's house had sinned"? (2 Esd. i. 4, 6.) Need I recall to your minds, that through His prophet, the Almighty proposed, as the best and most efficacious means of obtaining forgiveness, that the offender should turn to Him in fasting, and weeping, and mourning, saying: "Who knoweth but He will return and forgive?" (Joel, ii. 12, 14) that by a solemn fast of three days, the reprobate inhabitants of Nineveh effaced the decree of extermination which He had pronounced against them?

Surely, you will not say, that all this happened under the law of bondage, and that the law of Christ has freed us from this harsh and painful atonement. No, my brethren, He taught us that the evil spirit was not to be cast out but by fasting and prayer; (Matt. xvii. 21) He taught us to avoid the hypocrisy of the Pharisees in their fast, and prescribed rules for its meritorious practice; but by these explanations He only confirmed its obligation. And, in truth, is it aught but just that he who sorrows for sin, should exhibit before God and man some symbol of his grief, and some pledge of its sincerity? When a worldly affliction strikes us, our natural feeling is that it should impress upon us some marks, at least, of outward sorrow; mourning weeds must be put on, a downcast countenance must be assumed; our own sense of propriety banishes us from all places of public amusement, and we deny ourselves a thousand gratifications allowed at other times. But if our grief is really seated in the heart, oh! then it does not require a sense of public decency to impose these restraints. Then do our usual amusements afford no pleasure; we shun society which could intrude upon our more sacred feelings of sorrow, we shrink in unaffected disgust from all that may jar with the plaintive music of inward grief: "For as vinegar upon nitre, so is a song unto a heavy heart." (Prov. xxvi. 20.) And if man thus always attests his internal suffering, when the fibres by which his heart clings round the world are but slightly wrung, is it too much to expect that when he stirs up within his soul that real, that deep, that overpowering anguish, which forms the sorrow exacted by God for his crimes—is it too much to expect that he will then also abandon, at least for a time, the giddy maze of enjoyment and gratification, which he himself acknowledges incompatible with real sorrow? But in this case the reasons are still stronger.

It is by these very gratifications that our offences are generally committed or encouraged. It is by our indulgence that our passions are inflamed, and our desires made rebellious. It is by the ties and relations which our conviviality forms, that we are kept in that distracted and dissipated state which banishes God from our souls, and disqualifies us for the discharge of duty. And if the sinner wishes to implore forgiveness of these offences, is it from amidst the dangers that cause them that his cry should be heard? Is it while leading the life of the rich man, clad in purple and fine linen, and feasting sumptuously, that we are to strike our breasts, as the publican, and say, Lord, be merciful to me a sinner? No, my brethren, these are two characters placed in irreconcilable contrast by the word of God. There is a gulf between them in this as in the other world. The Israelites who sat down to eat and drink in the desert, only rose to play in idolatry before their golden image; it was Moses, who had fasted forty days in the mountain, that obtained their forgiveness from God. Baltassar, who was feasting with his chiefs, blasphemed the Most High, and suffered a visible and awful doom; Daniel, fasting in his chamber, saw and accelerated the reconciliation of his people.

But I am degrading this holy exercise when I thus treat it as merely a demonstration of inward sorrow: the word of God which I have quoted authorizes me to consider it as an efficacious part of atonement. And, in fact, if divine justice has punishment in store for sin, it must be appeased by seeing that we have taken its part, avenged its claims, and satisfied its demands upon the instrument of our transgressions. Often, even with revengeful, unforgiving man, the conqueror, who had resolved upon severity, has relented, and forgiven, upon seeing the objects of his wrath prostrate themselves before him in humiliation and sorrow, and bearing upon them, as imposed by their own hands, the emblem of that punishment which they acknowledge themselves to have deserved. And when the sinner thus presents himself before God, exhibiting that body which had caused the soul's rebellions against His law, humbled and subdued, and willingly subjected to the command of the spirit, He, too, will receive the victim, thus wounded, as sufficient testimony of our hatred for sin, nor proceed to inflict the heavier strokes of His justice upon its object, already bruised and afflicted. Penitential fasting is, therefore, the surest expiation for sin; it is also the securest safeguard for virtue. And fasting, too, thus considered, though apparently only performed in the flesh, is, in reality, a great, a sublime, interior work. It is the bringing into actual conflict, within ourselves, the great antagonism which forms the basis of revelation after man's fall. We oppose in effectual contest, in our persons, those mighty powers, one whereof, in Adam's fall, wrought all our woe, and the other, in Jesus's victory, secured our redemption: obedience against pride, self-restraint against indulgence, the spirit against the flesh. And we, therein, conquer and extinguish, by the power of God, that seed and root of evil which the disobedience and indulged appetite of the first parent entailed upon his race, and show how we would comport ourselves under similar trial; for we participate as much as may be in the victories of obedience and suffering gained by our second Adam.

In fact, my brethren, this is the nurse of some most important requisites for Christian perfection. For what is its very foundation, but the acquiring a restraint over the troublesome motions of our own minds—the practising that renunciation of our own wills, that denial of ourselves, which is so often enjoined in the gospel; so to attain a complete independence and detachment from the pleasures of the world, which are denounced in Scripture as God's greatest enemy? But is this conquest to be all achieved without striking a blow? Is this state of superiority to be obtained and preserved without ever subjecting our foe? Can we pretend to hold a command over the inferior appetites of our nature, when we never once compel them to obey us? Assuredly not: hence, the greatest holiness has ever been united with the practice of fasting and mortification. Hence, John, the friend of the Bridegroom, led a life of rigorous seclusion, and fasted in the wilderness. Hence did Jesus Himself assure the Jews, that His followers should be distinguished, after His death, by their assiduity in these same practices. Do you even pretend to rival, in the perfection of your virtues, the fervent and generous St. Paul, whose days were wholly spent in preaching the gospel of Christ, whose body was worn by the fatigues of his mission, whose mind dwelt in visions, and extasies to the highest heavens? Yet did he not account the dignity of his apostleship, nor his labours endured for Christ, or the mysterious assurances which he heard in heaven, a sufficient security and protection, without the holy exercise of mortification: "I, therefore, so run, as not to an uncertainty: I so fight, not as one beating the air: but I chastise my body, and bring it into subjection; lest, perhaps, when I have preached to others, I myself should be cast away." (1 Cor. ix. 26, 27.)

But, in the word of God, and the belief of our forefathers, there is still another advantage attributed in this exercise, to believe in which might, in the present state of ideas, subject us to the charge of weakness and superstition. It is, indeed, my brethren, a grievously afflicting thought, that in proposing and inculcating the practice of many Christian exercises, we should have to appeal to the belief and examples of ages past; that we should have to speak of fervent and unabashed religion, as of something which did once exist amongst us, but is now numbered among many other ruins of man's mental greatness. But it was the persuasion of the early Church, in conformity to the inspired pages, that the public and private calamities which oppress us in such frightful succession, are the visitations of divine justice or divine providence, sometimes punishing, sometimes trying the world; and that these calamities may be averted, suspended, or mitigated by the exercise of fasting and penance. When the scourge of God had desolated the land, the prophet Joel, by His command, enjoined the priests to "blow the trumpet in Sion, to sanctify a fast, and call a solemn assembly." "Then the Lord answered, and said to His people: Behold, I will send you corn, and wine, and oil, . . . and I will no more make you a reproach among the nations." (Joel, ii. 15, 19.) The same pious confidence went even further: men hoped by these means to obtain counsel and assistance from God on important occasions. The Israelites held solemn fast before they proceeded in war against the tribe of Benjamin. (Jud. xx. 26.) Esther requested the Jews to fast, to ensure the success of her hazardous undertaking. (Est. iv. 16.) Esdras and his companions fasted and besought the Lord in their difficulties, and it fell out prosperously unto them. (1 Esd. viii. 23.) The apostles fasted whenever they imposed hands in ordination, so to draw the blessing of God upon the heads of His new ministers. (Acts, xiii. 2, 3; xiv. 22.)

But, alas! the sword of the Lord might be stretched over the whole land—its produce blighted, its inhabitants exterminated—yet who would now think of humbling himself before His mighty hand; or, like even the impious King Joram, in similar circumstances, tear his garments in sorrow, and show the sackcloth of penance on his guilty flesh? (4 Reg. vi. 7.) The judgments of God might visit us in our domestic sanctuary, and blight our most tender hopes; but who would now think of averting them by fasting and prayer, as did King David, when the agonies of death seized his child? These advantages, which are attributed to this holy exercise of fasting, in the word of God, are all concentrated with greater efficacy in the good observance of the penitential season upon which we have just entered. I will not insist upon that additional worth which any work of piety acquires by being simultaneously observed through all the Christian world; when entire nations bow their heads and humble their souls in unison, to claim all the blessings which this exercise obtains: because I wish to distinguish this holy time from even those frequent and general fasts which the entire Church observes, through the course of the year. Even beyond these, is the value of Lent observed in the spirit of true penance.

For, in the first place, we thus happily comply with an obligation as ancient as Christianity, with a practice instituted by the apostles themselves, carefully encouraged by religion in its earliest purity, and preserved with jealous attention through succeeding ages, in spite of every other diminution of zeal and fervour. It can scarcely be necessary to lay before you proofs of this assertion: it is admitted by all the learned professors of every variety of Christianity: it has been demonstrated at full length, and with overpowering erudition, by Dr. Beveridge, Bishop of St. Asaph's, two centuries ago, who has triumphantly confuted the objections of some authors against the antiquity and apostolical derivation of Lent. (Codex Canonum, Eccles. Primit. 1679.) He had already been preceded in this task by Dr. Gunning, Bishop of Ely, who, in his work on the paschal fast, after collecting innumerable testimonies from all antiquity, pronounces the Lent to be a "tradition apostolical." (On the Paschal or Lent Fast, 1684, p. 131.) Hence, it ceases to be a matter of wonder that in the third century after Christ, the commencement of its observance was universally attributed to the institution of the apostles, and its motive justly supposed to be the example of our Saviour. "We fast Lent," says St. Jerome, " by apostolical tradition, and the whole world agrees with us in the observance." (Ep. xxvii. ad Marc. tom. iv. p. 64.) "Lent," writes St. Isidore, "is kept over the whole world, by an apostolical institution." (St. Isid. Hisp. Orig. lvi. c. 19.) Hence, also, it can be explained how the same term should be observed with equal exactness and veneration by Christians in every part of the globe, by Greeks and Armenians, Eutychians and Nestorians, some of whom have held no religious intercourse with the others, since the fourth century of the Christian era.

Now, my brethren, what peculiar fruits must we not expect from the observance of a practice which bears so high and noble an origin, and has been preserved for us with all that is venerable and sacred in religious antiquity? For if the other fasts of the year have been left to the discretion of the Church in each age, this boasts the sanction of the inspired apostles and the example of Christ Himself. It is thus under the special patronage and favour of God; by it we are connected with the founders and earliest lights of our faith, in unbroken succession; it is the continuation of a strong cry for mercy from age to age, from year to year, in which all the martyred champions of Christianity, all the zealous asserters and propagators of faith, all the holy pastors of the flock, and all the myriads of the faithful since the apostles' time, have in their day joined, and which they have transmitted to their successors, to be kept up with unceasing fervour. If any prayer can wring mercy from the Almighty.—if heaven is to be borne away by violence and perseverance, surely it must be by the combined assault of the whole world, continued without interruption through the lapse of ages. Surely the Son of God will then once more say that He has compassion on the *multitude*, when it has followed *Him* so perseveringly into the wilderness, and has been so long fasting, in order to remain in His society.

If the origin of this fast gives it peculiar merit, its motives are of no less weight. These are, to commemorate more devoutly the mysteries of our Redeemer's passion, and to prepare for the participation of their fruit at His holy table. If, my brethren, any circumstance can give additional value to a duty which God has commanded, it must be any connexion with that great event from which alone it can derive its efficacy with Him; and if any preparation can fit us for commemorating this, it must be that of humiliation and penance. For, most surely, it would ill become us to pass in one instant from the usual revels and gaieties of the world, to the solemn contemplation of our great and painful redemption: it would be a mockery of our afflicted and suffering Jesus, to follow His blood-stained footsteps with timbrel and song, and stand as mourners under His cross in bridal array. Oh! no; it is sobered, by seclusion from all that can distract, that we should approach this solemn spectacle; it is by the long and serious reflection upon what we had deserved, accompanied by the humiliations and atonements which this season prescribes, that we can expect to appreciate and obtain the blessings purchased for us at so much expense. But, then, at the same time, with what fruit must that solemn fast of expiation be attended, which leads to the most solemn day when our great High Priest entered the sanctuary, bearing, not the blood of oxen nor of goats, but a price of infinite value, for the salvation of the world? What efficacy, in drawing down mercy and compassion, must the recurrence of that season have, when mercy and compassion were purchased, and attached to the practice of penance and mortification? What a solemn—what a sublime appeal to heaven is made, when the whole flock of this High Priest follows Him, their Head, in slow and mournful procession, through all the stages of His passion, bearing on their own persons the marks of their repentance, and the badge of His mortified and self-denying religion?

Again, we are called, at the end of this holy period, to approach the table of the Lord, and partake of His adorable sacrament. " For what cause," says St. Chrysostom, " do we keep the fast of these forty days? That in these days all of us, being perfectly purified together by prayers, and by alms, and by fasting, and by whole nights' watchings, and by tears, and by confession, and by all other things, we may so, according to our power, with a pure conscience, come to the holy mysteries."

It is, indeed, true, that at all times we must prepare ourselves for this most holy rite, with the utmost purity which we can attain; but the act, on this occasion, becomes, if possible, still more solemn, by being the ratification of our adhesion to the Church, which rejects all those members from its bosom who neglect it at that season. It is, then, by keeping ourselves separated from the dangers which usually surprise us, and from the enjoyments which generally distract us, that we must hope to attain that holiness and devotion of heart, which make us worthy to taste the heavenly gift.

These are the more general advantages which accompany this sacred fast. There are others more intimately connected with the wants of each individual. The great purpose of fasting has already been shown to consist in its providing the best remedy for sin, and the surest safeguard for virtue. But it is not a momentary work to attain these objects—they require time and perseverance. The occasional fasts, which we observe in the course of the year, are, indeed, salutary checks, which make us pause in our headlong course, and turn our thoughts upon the necessity of propitiating our offended God, before His judgments overtake us. But, then, they are soon forgotten: they are a transient cultivation, which represses the growth, but tears not up the roots of our perverse inclinations; they are as an impression made upon an elastic surface, deeply marked on its first communication, but gradually and soon fading, till its mark has totally vanished. But during the protracted term of Lent, there is time for a systematic and thorough cure, and change of habit. There is time for effectually breaking off every indulgence which we have found dangerous, for accustoming ourselves to the want of those pleasures which have seduced us. There is time to plant, to nurture, and to mature those habits of temperance, of self-restraint, and of detachment from the world, which we are now obliged, outwardly at least, to observe, and which are so necessary a part of our gospel obligations.

Reflecting upon our past follies with the calmness and impartiality of distant spectators, we may wonder whence arose the satisfaction which they gave us, and look forward to their repetition with dismay rather than with eagerness. Thus, even if we are tempted to try them once more, it is with cooler and more sobered minds; the burning paroxysm of passion has at least been interrupted, and remedies supplied in the interval, to mitigate it on its recurrence. And a yet happier result will proceed from the longer continuance of this fast: it forms some proportion of your year and of your life, on which to rest with consolation and hope. Our days fleet away in frivolity or transgression; and alas! those are, perhaps, the best during which we reflect the least. And yet it is from this tract of vanity and folly that we must be able to select sufficient good, to outweigh all the evil; it is from this mass of general worthlessness that we must pick sufficient gold to overbalance all its dross. What a faint glimmer of light and hope, amidst the darkness of our past lives, will those few scattered days of penance and restraint afford, which alone break the otherwise unvaried dulness of our course! But what a broad stream of glory will cross the dismal prospect, if we can see, year after year, this tenth part of each, duly laid out in expiating the failings of the remainder, and in serving God with fervour and devotion! How consoled shall we feel on finding that we have never failed to bestow upon

God His tithe of the time allotted to our cultivation; and, in like manner, what He values still more, a tithe of our affections, and of our wills. For if one day passed in the courts of the Lord is better than a thousand, believe me, the remembrance of these forty spent in the spirit of the Church, will afford more satisfaction to you, on your last review of life, than tens of thousands passed in the bewildering revels and tinsel show of the Carnival, which introduced them.

In spite of these advantages of the observance of this holy time, you will still, my brethren, pronounce it difficult and painful. Neither will I attempt to remove this impression, or to treat it as an illusion. I wish not to represent to you the thorny path of mortification as covered with flowers, nor to tell you that the victory over your appetites is easy and pleasant. Their merits consist in their difficulties; fasting would cease to be an expiation if it caused no pain, self-denial would be changed into its contrary failing, if conformable to our wishes. This is the foundation of Christian virtue; and I wish to put no other foundation but that which God has placed.

Admitting, then, to the full extent, that I call upon you to practise that from which your nature recoils as disagreeable and painful, I can only exhort you in the words of the apostle: " That you receive not the grace of God in vain. For He saith: In an accepted time have I heard thee; and in the day of salvation have I helped thee. Behold, now is the acceptable time: behold, now is the day of salvation." (2 Cor. vi. 1, 2.)

Remember that you profess to follow a leader whose way was ever rugged, whose life was ever painful, whose badge and standard is the ignominious cross. Choose, then, another banner, select another master, if you seek only indulgence and gratification. Enter upon this course with cheerfulness, for God loves a cheerful giver.

Yes, my brethren, if any one ought to feel downcast and afflicted during this holy season, it is the man whose infirmities prevent him from uniting in the austere and devotional practices of the Church. Seeing himself disabled from joining the sacred ranks of fervent combatants who are fighting the battles of the Lord, he should feel a holy envy at their happier lot, and consider himself degraded by his rejection. He should think himself, like the lepers, separated from the congregation of the saints, as they gather round the tabernacle of the Lord, and obliged to beg for a place in their acceptable intercession. Then would he compensate for his inability to join the holy rigours of his brethren by additional prayers and alms, or by such works of piety and penance as come within his reach. Instead of this, how differently from St. Paul do such as these " willingly glory in their infirmities" at the approach of this time of penance ! Then are weaknesses searched out and discovered in their health and constitution, which never once prevented them from plunging into amusements, and standing out the far greater fatigues of society. Then are motives for relaxation seriously studied and artfully exposed, which had never interfered with any other occupations but those of Lent. But you, my brethren, when you fast, be not as the hypocrites — sad. Endeavour to comply with your obligation to its utmost extent (once more to quote the words of the Epistle), " in watchings, in fastings, in chastity, in knowledge, in sweetness, in the Holy Ghost, in charity unfeigned, in the words of truth, in the power of God, by the armour of justice." (2 Cor. vi. 5, 6, 7.) Then will you, at its term, approach, like Elias after his forty days' fast, God's holy mount, to behold Him, not as heretofore, in the whirlwind and raging fire, but in the gentle whisper of reconciliation and peace. (3 Reg. xix. 12.) Then, like the Son of God, at the expiration of the same period, you, too, will be fed at a celestial banquet, and receive with the bread of angels a pledge of admission to that true home, where forty days of penance will be repaid you by an eternity of bliss.

SERMON VII.

On Confession.

Romans, xiii. 11.

"It is now the hour for us to arise from sleep. For now our salvation is nearer than when we believed."

The season of Lent is peculiarly intended as a remedy against sin. Its fast is meant to check the passions, and prevent their irregular influence over the mind: its instructions and spiritual exercises are directed to excite in us a determination of never more allowing them to regain their control. In order to do this more effectually, and to put the seal to these good resolutions, the Church has expressly enjoined on all to close this holy time by approaching at Easter to the altar of God, and there participating in the sacrament of the H. Eucharist. For what can be more appropriate than, immediately after commemorating the death and passion of the Son of God, to partake of that blessed institution, destined by Him to perpetuate its memory, and to apply to us its fruits? What can be more consistent than to feed on this bread of angels, after having endeavoured, by a course of mortification, to attain the pure and sublime dispositions of these celestial spirits? Still, my brethren, there is one preparation for this holy duty which is absolutely indispensible: as this bread of life is only to be eaten by the pure and undefiled, an absolute freedom from all sin is the first and principal requisite for a good communion. Without this condition, your communion will be nothing better than a sacrilege; and every one must therefore try himself at this season, and so eat of this bread; he must clear his conscience of all guilt, before he presumes to approach the altar of God.

For this purpose the tribunal of penance must be approached, where, upon humble and contrite confession of all our sins, we may receive the absolution of God's minister. This has always been the practice of the Church from the earliest ages; so that, St. Cyprian, in the third century, deplores and censures, as a dreadful abuse crept in during the heathen persecutions, that some had been allowed to approach the holy communion without first confessing their sins, and receiving the absolution of the priest. "It is required," says he, " according to the rule of established discipline, that they come to confession, and that, by the imposition of the hand of the bishop and clergy, they be admitted to communion. But now, in the time of persecution, while the Church is troubled, these sinners are admitted; and no penance performed, no confession made, no hand imposed, they are admitted to the Eucharist, though it be written, 'Whosoever shall eat this bread or drink the chalice of the Lord unworthily, shall be guilty of the body and blood of the Lord.'" (Ep. xvi.)

That a better preparation for a good communion at this

solemn season, may be duly secured, it is the custom in every religious community and every ecclesiastical establishment, through the Catholic world, to devote a few days in the latter part of Lent to retirement and reflection. These are spent in looking over the past, and studying its failings, in order to discover a proper remedy for them, and to frame rules for future conduct; so as to begin with purified minds and renovated vigour a new course of strivings after Christian perfection.

But that the laity may be also urged to take the same pains with this important duty, though their occupations and plan of life may not allow them to devote to its preparation so long a time, it has been no less wisely instituted in this city, that in all the principal churches a course of instructions should be yearly opened, commencing with this Sunday, on the sacred duty of confession. When the wish and spirit of the Church are so clearly marked out, we cannot do better than to follow their direction; and, therefore, I will this day call your attention to this subject, and, as concisely as I can, lay before you, first, the motives which should induce you to perform it well, and then the conditions requisite for its right performance.

The first and principle motive, my brethren, which should render you earnest and anxious to make a good confession, is that, as your religion teaches you, this is the only remedy appointed in the law of Christ for mortal sin. In the Old Law, upon the commission of any crime, it was commanded that the offender should present himself to the priest and confess it to him, and offer up a stated sacrifice in expiation. But, alas! " it was impossible," as St. Paul observes, "that with the blood of oxen and of goats sin should be taken away." (Heb. x. 4.) And hence the forgiveness of the offender depended upon his own exertions; and he might pass all his life in groans and tears, without any real assurance of pardon, and without receiving any external token of divine reconciliation. The law of grace, however, came seasonably for us, to remedy this imperfection, and provide more accessible means of pardon. It was clearly the wise and gracious economy of our heavenly Master, to attach participation in the benefits of His redemption to external rites, which rendered their application more easy than when left entirely to each mind, as under the Old Law.

Thus, He made us partakers of His adoption, by the sacred ceremony of baptism; and He communicates to us the fulness of His mercies and graces, by the holy sacrament of the Eucharist. It would, then, have been something incredible, that an institution for the pardon of sin, and reconciliation with God, should not have been appointed by Him; and that the penitent sinner should have been still left to the same unaided exertions and torturing uncertainty as in the law of Moses, while the greatest of Christ's objects in coming down and dying for us, was to procure and render easy the remission of sins. But we need never fear that the mercies of God towards us, can have been less than we should calculate or wish. Jesus Christ has left just such an institution as might have been anticipated, by communicating to the pastors of His Church that power, which He Himself held, of forgiving sins.

For, He entered the apartment where His apostles

were assembled, and addressed them as follows : " Peace be to you. As the Father hath sent Me, I also send you." Among the powers which He had claimed here upon earth, was that of forgiving sins. He wrought a miracle upon a paralytic, to prove this claim : " That you may know," said He, " that the Son of man hath power on earth to forgive sins." As He communicated, therefore, to His apostles the fulness of power, which He Himself had received from His Father, this was necessarily implied ; but lest any mistake might arise upon so important a point—" When He had said this, He breathed on them ; and He said to them : Receive ye the Holy Ghost : whose sins you shall forgive, they are forgiven them ; and whose sins ye shall retain, they are retained." (John, xx.) To you, my brethren, I need not prove that a power of really forgiving sins was here given, not merely a power of *preaching, baptising,* or *working miracles,* as some have maintained ; both, because these particular powers are given specifically on other occasions, and always in the clearest and most precise terms, not in such ambiguous words as these would, in that case, be ; and also, because the expression to *forgive sins* never once, in the New Testament, either in the other places, where it is used by Christ, or in the epistles, has any other meaning than a real remission of offences against God. But you must be no less aware of another circumstance, that the commission here given is a judicial, discretional one, which empowers the person receiving it, either to grant or to refuse the pardon of the sin. This necessarily supposes a cognizance to be taken of the case, on which he has to pronounce. For if a judge receives a commission, with full delegated authority to pass sentence of condemnation, or acquittal, in all causes, could it, for a moment, be suspected that it was the wish of his sovereign giving that commission, that he should pronounce his sentence, without even knowing the crimes with which the delinquent stood charged? Would it be consistent with the very lowest principles of justice or good sense, to give such a discretionary power, on the supposition that it was to be exercised without any inquiry into the circumstances of guilt, or into the claims which the offender's dispositions might have to mercy, but to depend solely on the caprice or unfounded opinions of the judge? As, then, Christ gave to the pastors of His Church the power of granting or refusing pardon, and as the exercise of this power necessarily and essentially implies an examination of the case on which the sentence is to be pronounced, it is no less a necessary consequence that the offender, who alone can lay it before them, must do so, with all such circumstances as may enable them to form a just decision.

"In this manner," says the learned doctor, St. Jerome, "with us the bishop or priest binds or looses, not them who are merely innocent or guilty; but, having heard, as his duty requires, the various qualities of sin, he understands who should be bound and who loosed." (Comment. in Matt. xvi.) The establishment of this tribunal necessarily implies, that there is no other regular means in the New Law to obtain remission. For, in points depending upon positive institution, the foundation of any means for a definite object, of itself, excludes the efficacy of every other. Thus, when God appointed the priests judges of legal cleanness or defilement in cases of leprosy, every one concludes that their declaration alone was the legitimate release from the legal inconveniences, to which individuals were for that disease subjected. Similarly, the manifestation of our sins to the pastors of God, is a necessary condition for obtaining the forgiveness of them.

You have now only fully to meditate on what an enormous guilt sin is, and what dreadful consequences it brings upon the soul. You must reflect that it is the most odious thing in existence in the eyes of God, and that it will entail upon you, for all eternity, the infinite punishments with which His outraged justice can overwhelm you. If you have any love for yourselves, you must be willing to embrace the only means which can wash you from this guilt, and secure you from this suffering. It is, indeed, a remedy accompanied with difficulty; it costs a humiliation and a pain to submit our secret failings to the view of another person, and be our own accusers to a mortal like ourselves. But is this transient confusion to be put in comparison with that dreadful manifestation which will at last take place before all mankind? " For," observes St. Chrysostom, "he that is ashamed to reveal his sins to a man, and is not ashamed to commit them in the sight of God, nor willing to confess them and do penance, he, at the last day, shall be publicly exposed, not before one or two, but before the whole world." (Orat. de Samarit.) Is this trifling momentary pang to be for one instant weighed in the balance, against the load of evils which will one day overtake those, who are deterred by it from a reconciliation with God? " If still you draw back," exclaims Tertullian, the most ancient Christian writer in the western Church,—

"if still you draw back, let your mind turn to that eternal fire which confession will extinguish; and that you may not hesitate to adopt the remedy, weigh the greatness of future punishment. And as you are not ignorant that against that fire, after the baptismal institution, the aid of confession has been appointed, why are you an enemy to your own salvation?" (De Pœnit. c. xii.)

But this shame, my brethren, the difficulty, which restrains so many from frequenting this tribunal, might have some weight, were it to a stern, unfeeling judge that we are to reveal our faults, and not to one who knows how to have compassion on our weakness, and to assist us in our difficulties; and the consideration of the aid thus given in confession is the second motive which should make you anxious to perform it well. It is impossible for any one with a conscience open to the suggestions of good and evil, to go through life, without his mind being often agitated with inquietude for the past, or solicitude for the future. The thought of our former offences and miseries returns to our mind connected with doubts as to our conduct under them; the experience of our past weakness makes us apprehensive for our future perseverance in good. Sometimes we foresee new temptations; sometimes we are aware that we must again pass through circumstances, under which we have before fallen. Occasionally we see virtues which we ought to attain, but have ever found ourselves baffled in every attempt to reach, and yet without knowing whence our failure has arisen. Often we find it necessary to take some important step, and yet do not clearly see what influence it may have on our minds, or how our future conduct should be regulated under it. We know in all these cases how dangerous, how deceitful, our own judgment may be, when it has to be pronounced upon ourselves; and besides, whoever has experienced any of these discomforts knows equally well, that however he may have endeavoured to soothe them by his own decision, they have perhaps never once yielded to his own skill, but have returned to haunt him again and again. Did our embarrassment regard our property, our health, or our domestic concerns, we should at once know our best resource. We should run to the lawyer, who had devoted his life to the study of jurisprudence, who could tell us what the statutes of our country have prescribed in our case, what redress remains for our grievances, or what arrangement would best suit our circumstances. We should hasten to the physician, who had given his time to study the best remedies, and whom a long experience had enabled to ascertain and prescribe what diet, what course of life, what medicines are best for our disorder or our constitution. In fine, we should fly to a tried and able friend, we should open to him the causes of our uneasiness, we should disburthen before him the load that weighed upon our hearts, we should find relief and consolation in unbosoming ourselves to him, and should repose with confidence upon his decision.

If this be the natural, the most secure way of obtaining comfort and assistance in worldly troubles, must it not be so much more in those where salvation is concerned, and where, consequently, much greater prudence is requisite, much greater learning advisable? And who, my brethren, can be with more propriety your counsellor, your physician, and your friend upon these affairs, than the minister of God, who has devoted his life, from infancy, to prepare for these very offices; who has studied, as a conscientious obligation, the principles of the divine moral law, and the collected experience of ages, upon these important subjects, and who has torn every domestic tie, and given up every worldly prospect, on purpose to minister to God's servants? He knows how to compassionate your frailty, and to apply the remedy with a tender hand; for he has been taught to make himself all to all, to be weak with the weak, that he may gain all to Christ, and to imitate the example of the saints, by his charitable compassion and anxiety to give you his best advice. "Impart," says St. Asterius, an early Father of the Church—" impart your trouble to the priest as to your father; he will be touched with a sense of your misery. Open to him the secret recesses of your heart; show this physician your hidden wounds: he will take care of your honour and your health." Thus it was that St. Ambrose, as is related by his secretary, Paulinus, " as often as any one doing penance confessed his faults to him, wept so as to draw tears from the sinner, seemed to take part in every act of sorrow." (Vit. Ambr. n. 39, p. 10.) He will endeavour to enter into your feelings and dangers, to remove your doubts, to calm your anxieties, to suggest to you motives of confidence, and prescribe the best plan for the future; and instead of being offended or harsh for your past failings, will consider himself as another Ananias in your regard, to whom you have been sent, like Paul, to learn the will of God. These incalculable advantages are, I am sure, motives sufficient to make you anxious to discharge this duty well: but what are the qualities of a good confession?

To treat these at length would require too much time. I will confine myself, therefore, to the two most important requisites for a valid and good confession—a true contrition, and its necessary consequence, a firm determination never more to offend God. You are too well instructed in your religion to require to have inculcated on you, that without these two ingredients, confession is of no value. You may recount your offences to the priest with all sincerity, with every appearance of humility, and he may pronounce over you in the most solemn manner the sentence of absolution; but if you are not really sorry for your sin as an offence against God, and if this sorrow be not so sincere that you are determined never more to offend Him, cost you what it may, your absolution is null, and void of effect. But this is the slightest evil incurred; for the confession is a sacrilege—a profanation of a most holy rite, instituted by God for a most sacred purpose. Instead of retiring from the feet of God's minister, like Magdalen, cleansed from your stains, you have added to them another of the blackest dye, and have plunged still deeper into the abyss of crime. Truly, the latter state of that man is become worse than the former.

True contrition consists in a real inward sorrow for sin, considered as an offence against God. Its motive must be supernatural, or resting on the love of God, whose infinite goodness deserves all our affection, and yet has been outraged by our crimes. It must extend to all our sins: not one must be left without repentance. For, as the cause of our sorrow must not be the specific nature of the crime, but the offence which it has given God, it must be evident that he cannot be really sorry on this motive, who excludes from his sorrow some one sin which has offended God in the same manner as the others.

It must be sovereign; that is, we must hate and detest sin more than any other evil whatsoever; and we must be afflicted that we should have offended the best and most amiable of beings. This contrition for all our sins committed must be ready to stand any test. It must be ready to repair all the damages of sin, to part with whatever has been its unlawful fruit, to restore whatever has been unjustly taken or gained, to make satisfaction for every injury committed, to retract or repair every calumny uttered, to regain all whom our words or actions may have misled; in fine, to make amends for every scandal or evil which has been the consequence of our sins. Whoever is not ready to do all this, so far as in his power, has not, cannot have a real contrition for his sin, but is like the idolater, who protests his detestation of idolatry, and still retains his idol. He is like the judge who declares his regret for having condemned an innocent man, and yet allows him to be conducted to the scaffold. So necessary an ingredient of a true conversion is this readiness to make all possible reparation, that if this be not intended, if you be not resolved to make it, no power upon earth can absolve you from your sins. No dispensation, no fasting, no tears, no charities, though to a thousand times the amount of the injuries done; in fine, nothing in this world can excuse, or be a substitute for, this reparation of the consequences of sin, so long as this reparation is in our power. There is another test which your contrition must be ready to stand, the making of satisfaction to divine justice for the outrage done it by sin.

It is, you well know, the doctrine of holy writ, that even after the guilt of sin is perfectly remitted, there remains due to it a degree of temporal punishment; so much so, that God, after assuring David, by His prophet Nathan, that his sin was forgiven him, still told him that he was to undergo a severe chastisement for it, in the death of his child and the cruel dissensions in his family. But how admirably did David's contrition stand these painful tests! He submitted to all the dreadful trials which afflicted him, with a patience and a resignation truly astonishing; and you have only to peruse his Psalms, to see the humble and ready piety with which he bowed his neck beneath the scourges of divine retribution. Such was the example this glorious penitent has left us. But examples equally striking have been afforded to us in the Christian Church. In its first ages, every great sin was submitted to its pastors, who decided, according to established canons or statutes, the degree of penance to which it was subject. This lasted frequently for ten, twenty, or thirty years—sometimes for the life of the penitent. They were obliged to abstain from every amusement, to wear a dress of mourning, and to fast rigorously. Instead of being present during the divine worship, they remained prostrate in the court of the church, bathed in tears, and begging the prayers of the faithful that passed. Rank, wealth, or power, afforded no protection from this law. St. Ambrose obliged the Emperor Theodosius to submit to eight months' public penance in this form, for a massacre of which he had been guilty. No absolution was granted, without a contrition ready to undergo thus much. By degrees, indeed, this severity was relaxed. During the persecutions, those penitents, who received a recommendation to indulgence from the Confessors, confined for their faith, had a part of their penance remitted to them: those whose extraordinary sorrow and diligence entitled them, like the incestuous Corinthian, mentioned in St. Paul's Epistles, to a similar grace, were also, in part, dispensed. The declining fervour of Christians, in consequence of the troubles of the Church, the difficulty of enforcing such rigid satisfaction amongst growing numbers, still further increased the quantity of dispensations; and, instead of obliging them to these austere acts of penance, the Church, which, from the time of St. Paul, had exercised this discretion, commuted them into lighter practices of prayer, fasting, alms, or any other good works, under the name of indulgences.

But you must see clearly, that if the milder discipline of the Church does not now put your contrition to so heavy a trial, yet it has not any whit diminished its required measure. All the indulgences in the world can only remit to you the *punishment* otherwise exacted of you for your sins; but to obtain the *remission* of them, you must still have a contrition as supernatural in its motive, and as sovereign in its measure, as that which made the early Christians submit with cheerfulness to their severe penance. Our contrition must, therefore, make us ready to undergo whatever the providence of God, or the advice of our director, may prescribe for our satisfaction to divine justice. It must make us discharge, with humble readiness, the penance imposed upon us, and submit with resignation to all the trials and sufferings which the Almighty may destine to fall to our lot.

But the greatest effect and the most assured test of a true contrition, is a resolute purpose never again to offend God. So strictly is this a necessary quality of a good confession, that if a person repeatedly fall into the same sins after having repented of them, it may excite a suspicion that his repentance has not been sincere ; and a priest may be led to refuse him absolution unless he be satisfied that he really is determined to do his best never more to relapse. This determination never more to offend God, must not reside merely in the interior; it must manifest itself in work. It supposes that we are determined never more to put ourselves into dangers which have already proved fatal to our virtue ; that we shall make every sacrifice which may insure our perseverance. It supposes that we are ready to desert our most favourite occupations, to abandon our dearest connexions; in a word, to use the strong figure of Scripture, to pluck out an eye, or cut off a hand, if there be no other way of securing our future steadiness in the path of God's holy law. And in addition to this, it must make us docile, and willing to follow the advice of our director in our future life, and to take all the measures, use all the means in our power, to preserve ourselves from relapsing into our former misery.

You see, then, the immense advantages of approaching with due dispositions, at this holy time, to the sacred tribunal of penance; you are aware of the principal dispositions requisite to make this institution efficacious and beneficial. All that remains then is, that you should courageously undertake this duty, with a determination to discharge it well. The season which we are approaching is the most favourable for your undertaking; everything which you will see or hear, if considered in a good spirit, will bring to your mind the sufferings of your Redeemer, and suggest to you motives for repentance. You will hear Him inviting the impenitent Jerusalem to return to her Lord God; you will see Him forgiving His most inveterate enemies; in fine, you will contemplate Him in spirit, suffering the bitterest torments, and undergoing the most cruel death, on purpose to purchase remission for you. Can you want more moving incitements to shame and sorrow for having offended Him, and to confidence in His mercies? In addition to this, the prayers of all the faithful are united in your favour. At the season of the Paschal solemnity, in remembrance of their deliverance from bondage, the Jewish people had a right to claim the release of a prisoner from their governor. And shall the Church have less influence, when in one general body she addresses her entreaties, not to the heart of a brutal Pilate, but to that of the Father of mercies, in the very time commemorative of her grand deliverance, in favour, not of a hateful, abandoned Barabbas, but of a penitent, returning prodigal son? Sovereigns are often accustomed, on the anniversary of their accession to the throne, to release debtors, to impart forgiveness to offenders, or to distribute liberal charities. And will the King of our souls refuse an humble petition, or spurn a suppliant penitent who casts himself before Him at that season, when He purchased dominion over us at the price of His adorable blood? You have nothing to fear. Fall, with Magdalen, at His feet, acknowledge your crimes and implore His pardon; He will instantly grant it; and you will be, like her, among the first to be visited by His consolations on the day of His resurrection, by seeing, by touching, by feeding on, His adorable Body, and there receiving a sweet pledge of eternal glory.

SERMON VIII.

On the Unprofitable Servant.

Matt. xxv. 30.

"And the unprofitable servant cast ye out into the exterior darkness. There shall be weeping and gnashing of teeth."

The parable, my brethren, from which I have selected the words of my text, is so simple in its import, and disguises its lessons under so thin a veil, that an unembellished narrative of its leading details will enable us to deduce much serious instruction. A certain man is represented as distributing different sums of money among his domestics, driving it to be improved by traffic on his account, desiring his absence in a distant land: "To one he gave five talents, and to another two, and to another one; to each according to his proper ability: and immediately he took his journey." (15.) Upon his return, he assembles them before him, and demands a strict reckoning from each. Two had employed the talents committed to their charge so as to double their amount; and though that amount was in one instance five, and in the other only two, both were greeted with the same approbation, and recompensed in the same measure: "Well done, thou good and faithful servant; because thou hast been faithful over a few things, I will set thee over many things; enter thou into the joy of thy Lord." (21, 23.) Thus far we recognize the justice and beneficence of our bountiful Master, who apportions His recompense, not so much to the success, as to the efforts of His servants, and who gives the same wages to the labourers who enter His vineyard at the first or the last hour, provided they are diligent in the work to which they are appointed.

But the lot of the third servant is singularly awful, and seems to contain a rigour of justice, which we scarcely know how to reconcile with the splendid liberality of the preceding rewards. He restores to his Lord, weight for weight, the talent which he had received, and which he had kept carefully wrapped up to preserve it from injury, and jealously concealed in the ground to save it from risk. The doom, therefore, to which he should have been delivered seems sufficiently obvious: if he had done no evil, still he had merited no reward; and he should have been left, to all appearance, unpromoted, in the humble capacity which he then held, an unmanumitted slave. Instead, however, of this mild treatment, his master commands his talent to be taken from him, and condemns him, in the words of my text, to be cast, not, indeed, as a rebellious, but as an unprofitable servant, into that place of eternal punishment, where there shall be weeping and gnashing of teeth.

The conclusion to be drawn from this severity is very simple; to have neglected the improvement of the talent committed to his care, is imputed to this servant as a grievous crime. But from the gospel, it appears that his offence went further still. He not only neglected himself, to increase his master's deposit, but, by burying it in the earth, he deprived others of the benefits which it was meant to afford them. "Thou oughtest therefore (at least) to have committed my money to the banker, and at my coming I should have received mine own with usury." (27.) If, therefore, by the talents, are signified the means of salvation provided for us by our heavenly Master, it follows that we have a double obligation in their employment. First, our talents must be improved; our means of salvation must always produce an increase, till a reckoning of them is demanded from us; secondly, our talents must not be buried; they must produce advantage and good to those around us. In two words, our virtue must be progressive in ourselves, it must be fruitful in others. Such are the lessons which the punishment of the negligent servant is calculated to teach.

It may be said, in general, that we all enter life with a disposition for good, and a feeling in favour of virtue. Unless corrupted by premature seduction, we are all in effect free from guile, and blessed with upright intentions; an early education has furnished our minds with a code of moral principles which appears to us just; the practice of our parents' first instruction, has recommended to us acts of piety which soon become habitual; and the bias of our minds, as well as the suggestions of our hearts, leads us to an abhorrence of vice, and a determination to stand on the side of virtue. Whatever may be the direction of our subsequent course, we may all be said to start from the same ground. Yet, perhaps, this expression is not strictly correct; since the distinction which subsequently occurs between the follower of the gospel and the servant of the world, is not so much that, turning towards opposite parts, each pursues a different path, but rather that the virtuous man tries to remain stationary at the point which the other abandoned.

For, to retain the character of a virtuous man, before mankind, it is not necessary that his improvement should be traced like his neighbour's progress in vice, from year to year, nor that greater acts of virtue, distinct, indicative, and characteristic of a fresh advance in righteousness before God, should be successively observed in his daily conduct. It suffices, that a steady perseverance should be seen in the same religious practices, albeit these be attended through life by the same faults of temper, of the tongue, or of conduct, which were noticed as prevailing over him in his youth. And within ourselves, we generally feel and act upon the same estimate of a virtuous life. Perhaps no consideration would induce us to omit or curtail a single duty which the usual order of a Christian life, the propriety of our situation, or our own choice, has once imposed upon us: we daily repeat our prayers; we observe most exactly every ordinance of the Church; we are careful to avoid any clear transgression of the law.

But, at the same time, it is too true, that week after week, and year after year, sees us bring the same faults, in undiminished number, to the feet of Christ's minister: the same failings and the same weaknesses are laid before God in our daily supplications, yet never seem removed: we are content to oscillate through all our lives between good and evil, between transgression and repentance, so long as we never decidedly fall over the precipice; every defect which characterized our devotions, our conversations, our virtue in early life, characterizes it till death: and we depart from the world, sanguine that we shall enter into the joy of our Lord, because we have never lessened the measure of virtue with which we undertook His service! And does the parable which I am expounding warrant that this is safe? That early virtue which you have preserved, those pious exercises in which you have persevered, were no stock of your own; they were communicated to you before you, even knew how to appreciate them, by the kindness of God, through the means of a good education; they are the talents which He entrusted to you to trade with; you have been careful that they diminished not; but the question is, wherein are they doubled, wherein are they even increased? For, was it not the consideration of this alone which drew from the master his cheering words of approbation?

Nor can such a demand be reckoned unreasonable or severe. Our own conduct in every other affair, the judgment which we pass upon others, the nature of the means put into our hands, conspire to determine this exaction on the part of God to be just and consistent.

Our conduct in every other affair. Did the all-wise Judge, when He sees this stagnation in our virtue, perceive, at the same time, a corresponding arrest in our advance towards every other species of good, He might suppose that some relaxation had occurred in those springs, which push us forward in pursuit of happiness, and discover a motive for being satisfied with our neglect. But when He looks down on the streams of life which circulate through our cities, and finds them throbbing as yet to every passion, and bounding forward as heretofore to supply, in a thousand varying forms, every general or individual desire, will He be led to conclude, that the energies of life have been paralysed no less in our social existence? When He sees, as now, every avenue leading to influence, power, and distinction, crowded by candidates who press onwards for superiority, ready, in their eagerness, to trample down those who are before them, and using every art to supplant their rivals, will He conclude that the desire to surpass, the passion to reach excellence, has been extinguished amongst us, and that they, too, who started in the race of *human* ambition, have flung down the reins, heedless whether they reach or no the goal for which they started? When He beholds at this season, the merchant anxiously balancing his accounts, minutely calculating whether in the last year his capital has remained an unimproved stock, or produced him a competent return, and standing dismayed, as if on the brink of ruin, if he discover not a notable increase; when, at the same time, He considers the risks by which this has been sought, by perils from the waves, and from the casualties of human life, by risks from the inability, the malice, or the weakness of thousands, whom he must trust; will He be able to conclude that in other concerns besides that of salvation, man is now content ever to remain in the same condition where he commenced life, or that he is easily deterred by trouble from improving the means which he originally commanded?

But, in fact, we are all constantly boasting that the spirit of the age is one of renovation and improvement, and that, too, working in favour of virtue; that the tone of society, as we have grown older, has decidedly become more serious and religious; that the habits and feelings of the world itself have become more propitious to virtuous sentiments, and markedly hostile to open excess; that sound moral principles have been analysed, digested, expounded with sagacity and depth by the philosophy of the age; and that even the lighter literature of the day has become a vehicle of good instruction; and that species of composition which our fathers withheld from their children as poison to their innocence, has now been converted into a charmed cup, administering virtue infused in recreation. While, then, we see all endeavouring to advance, from day to day, in the career which they have chosen; while we, indeed, acknowledge that the moral world can no more suspend its progress towards improvement, than this physical globe can pause for an instant on its axis, is it not truly, must it not be most just, that God should demand a corresponding advance in us, an equal desire to reach perfection in that course which *He* considers alone worthy of a Christian's ambition, and in the increase of those riches which alone have weight in the balance of His sanctuary? Our own conduct, then, and that of the whole world, will rise against the slothful, unprofitable servant, who does not use to advantage the talents of his Master.

Not only our conduct, but our deliberate judgment, in every other case will condemn our inertness as criminal. For, from whoever undertakes any profession, you unrelentingly exact a constant improvement in its exercise. You surely would never encourage the artist whose maturer productions do not excel the rude pencillings of his boyhood; nor would you applaud the author whose disciplined taste produces nothing better than the puerile effusions of his early attempts. So, likewise, in the profession to which you train your children, and in the accomplishments which you bestow upon them; you ever do expect to see sensible progress, and you are disappointed and chagrined if it be not as rapid as you anticipate or desire. Still more from those who serve *you*, you demand additional expertness in proportion as they understand your affairs, and as they become acquainted with your arrangements, your opinions, and your very caprices. Of a truth, then, well may your Master exclaim to you, when you proffer back to Him your unproductive talent: "Out of thy own mouth do I condemn thee, thou wicked servant." From all who depended on *you*, from all who served *you*, you exacted a constant, an unremitting exertion to improve, although their means of serving you, were not your gift; and you punished, you even dismissed as unprofitable to you, all who succeeded not in their efforts to improve, however sincerely attempted: and shall it be by Me alone that this is to be overlooked, and in My service only shall all remain stationary, and no improvement be deemed necessary or reasonable?

But, can it arise from no defect in the nature of the talents committed to us, that they produce so little fruit? My brethren, they are talents infinite in their worth, and capable of increase a hundred and a thousand-fold: talents which have produced these effects in innumerable saints; not only capable, in fine, of giving such results, but naturally tending of themselves to multiply and increase, unless repressed by our wilful and guilty neglect. Those virtuous dispositions which, infused by baptism, were invigorated by early education, of their own nature were calculated to strike a deeper root in proportion as we advanced in reason and reflection, and consequently to produce maturer and more abundant fruit. The daily exercises of prayer which we commenced so early, in virtue of the divine promises, must bring down blessings upon our future undertakings, and consequently prosper whatever we attempt for salvation. If seed such as these produce no increase, it argues some failing in our watchfulness over its growth; or some defect in our cultivation, which absorbs the profit that would arise from it, under proper management. Then, too, the grace of God is heavenly, and momentarily at our command; of itself capable of overthrowing every obstacle in our way, and calculated to make *us* powerful and irresistible in spite of our innate weakness; flowing upon us in varied channels, suited to our different situations and our peculiar dangers and wants. When the slippery, perilous time of youth approached, you were anointed with the holy chrism, emblem and instrument of heavenly strength and vigour infused into your soul, to enable you to meet your coming dangers. When entering into the matrimonial or the ecclesiastical state, a new blessing was invoked upon your engagements, and fresh aids sent down to sweeten and to sanctify even their very burthens. Each of these periods should have marked an epoch in your life, distinguished by increased virtue, and an advance to perfection.

Then, my brethren, you have the more ordinary, but even more efficacious, means of renewing your strength. You have the tribunal wherein the minister of Christ sits to dispense, in His name, not merely medicine for wounds received, but unction for coming conflicts, not only forgiveness for past sins, but grace for future improvement. And in what terms shall I speak of that banquet of grace and of love, that daily food, simply to gaze on which in heaven, renovates each moment the immortality of the angels, to partake of which on earth, associates man with the Giver, and incorporates him with the exhaustless treasure, of redemption and grace? It is a paschal feast, which not only, by the sprinkling of its blood, secures us from the stroke of the destroying angel, merited by our transgressions, but, if partaken of with girded loins, and feet shod in readiness to obey the call of heaven, gives us a sure pledge that the tumultuous waves of passion shall open before us, and that the pursuing array of our enemies shall be destroyed, to our salvation. It is a manna, the food of the strong, not only refreshing us after the toil of our preceding march, but giving vigour to undertake each day another stage towards our promised land. It is the bread of angels, not merely consoling us by the sweetness of its savour, when escaped with Elias from the persecution of our foe, but, renewing our youth as the eagle's, to push forward our journey to the mountain, where we shall see God. Oh! is it possible that we should periodically—perhaps daily—partake of food like this, and yet make no sensible advance in grace; that receiving such additional means of sanctification, we should remain, from year to year, moving, as it were, round one point, receding, indeed, too often from it by transgression, then only anxious to regain it by amendment, but seemingly never able to advance our position a single step!

You will not, surely, screen yourself with the foolish apology, that all are not called to equal perfection, that the higher degrees of humility, mortification, meekness, or patience, are incompatible with your situation in the world, and that you have not in you the germs of that perfection, to which others may aspire, but must be content merely to tread the beaten paths of obvious duty. Alas! alas! how do we deceive ourselves! Were your adversary to raise his voice and proclaim thus much to the world; were he to denounce you as one whom nature and grace have only destined to move in the lower spheres of virtue, as one whose barren heart was incapable of supporting the luxuriancy of full-grown excellence; if your friend were to whisper that he had observed in you no disposition to superior good, no prospect of your ever attaining distinguished virtue; oh! how would you rise in your indignation to strike down the one as a slanderer, and discard the other as a railing hypocrite! In fact, while we plead before God, with mock humility, our inability to reach perfection, our pride flatters us that it is perfectly within our grasp. We fancy that, if the days of persecution were to return, we should be able to display the courage of the martyrs, though at present our faith is cooled almost into indifference; that if the world were to turn upon us, and unjustly condemn us, we could bear its unmerited scorn, with fortitude and patience, while we now start into passion on the slightest provocation. Nay, even in the midst of our habitual lukewarmness, we imagine that a period will come, when we shall be fervent indeed: and, perhaps, we picture to ourselves our last moments, as to be edifying to all around us, by our resignation and calmness, by the tender and affecting piety in which we trust to breathe our last. This plea then will not hold; at least it cannot be urged by us in favour of ourselves; pride itself, as well as religion, forbids us to appeal to our natural imperfection for excuse.

No, my brethren, it is only just that God should demand from us, a constant advance towards perfection; and that the talent which He has committed to our care, should be returned to Him with interest.

It is a law that admits no exception. The degree which each of us will reach may vary: the point at which we must all aim is fixed and unchangeable. "Be ye perfect, as your heavenly Father is perfect." Humble, indeed, must be our imitation of this great model: but the distance at which it is placed is selected on purpose to incite us to unremitting exertions, that so each day may bring us nearer to our standard of perfection. To this law, even the divine Son of God submitted; and He to whom the Father did not give His spirit in measure, but who received of the fulness of His glory, even *He* chose to disclose His perfections gradually with advancing years, so that it might be said that " Jesus increased (at once) in wisdom and age, and grace with God and men." (Luke, ii. 52.)

Our virtue, therefore, my brethren, must be ever progressive, within ourselves: it must be more, it must be fruitful in others. If our talent must be improved, with more reason it must not be hid.

The virtuous man has it in his power to be a means of salvation to many besides himself. He can beat down those obstacles which the world throws in the way of virtue, and he can exert himself directly to induce his neighbours to practise it. In other words, his virtue should be *fearless*, and it should be *active*.

It is unfortunately true, that while vice, which has so many motives to blush and to conceal itself, should daringly move in public, and seek the destruction of thousands, virtue, amiable in so many respects, should court retirement, and avoid every appearance of publicity. Unobtrusiveness is, indeed, one of its beautiful properties, but there is imminent danger of its degenerating into cowardice. It seems to have become a maxim among the good, that they must not expose themselves, without unavoidable necessity, to the enmity of the world; that it is better to overlook many things that are said or done, when there is not nearly a complete certainty that good will result from our interference. Hence it happens that, again and again, a sneer or a sophism is thrown out against religion or morality, in society where there are many sincere followers of both; and it passes unheeded and unexposed, from the desire to preserve peace: that ignorance, or petulance, or malice, indulges in invectives or sarcasms upon the principles, and especially in this city, upon the practices of our thrice-holy religion, and that we stand by, almost afraid of being supposed to profess it, lest we may be expected to rise in its defence. Hence religion is often decried as weak, and as conscious of its weakness. Now, this conduct is manifestly condemned both by reason and the gospel. The proper attitude of virtue is one of authority and command, exacting respect and overawing opposition; and we are unjust in its regard, if we condemn it to such disparaging submission. The virtuous man has been described by a heathen poet (Virgil), as able, by his sole appearance, to disarm an enraged multitude, and oblige them to disperse and slink in shame from before his face.

And yet, with how much greater power than heathen virtue can the Christian's, strengthened by the grace of God, and by the consciousness of holding the noblest cause, abash and confound its enemies, even when conspiring against it? The rebuke which it can give is seconded by a powerful monitor within him who has deserved it, which makes him feel little and humbled before the superior excellence which chides him. Once or twice he may have the hardihood to encounter such a check, but the ascendancy of virtue must be final, and it will not be long before its triumph is complete. Yet, when do we see now old and hardened transgressors fear, as they did before the youthful Aloysius, to utter a word which could offend the most delicate ear? Then, unless rank or signal distinction entitles him to marked respect, when do we find the presence of any person prevent or curb sentiments subversive of moral order, or injurious to religion? When do we perceive that the vein of unedifying conversation runs more sobered, that the empty ebullitions of thoughtlessness are repressed, that the merry tale of scandal is interrupted, that the slanderous jest is softened down, in consequence of the approach of one who is known to be a professed advocate of virtue and religion?

Yes, it is when thus asserting its dignity that religion

assumes its proper station among men. And thus it eventually succeeds in doing the greatest good. While it ensures the tranquillity of its follower without danger of seeing its principles insulted in his presence, it prevents the commission of much transgression, by keeping others, however constrainedly, within the bounds of duty; it imparts an habitual feeling of respect for what is good to the circle within its influence, and finally draws others to admire, and esteem, and practise, what they have found themselves compelled to revere. The gospel not only approves, but prescribes this course. "He," exclaims our blessed Redeemer, "who is not with Me, is against Me." No room is left by these words for the neutrality which we observe. Active co-operation with Him or against Him, are the only courses which it leaves open to the Christian. And this is but reasonable.

For, to witness the undisguised attacks every moment made upon His authority, and to stand by as if it concerned us not, argues surely but little esteem for His cause, or a very mean opinion of its strength. In this manner, therefore, my brethren, must we be fearless and courageous in our pursuit of virtue, no way ashamed of avowing our principles, but, on the contrary, boldly bearing ourselves as persons who have, and feel, an interest in the cause of truth, and never overlooking an occasion where we can with propriety defend its principles. Thus will our virtue be *active*. Not content with producing fruit indirectly in others, by removing obstacles to virtue, we must gladly seize every opportunity of ourselves communicating the means of salvation. How many will daily occur of removing prejudices from the minds of some, by explaining the rites, the doctrines, and the laws of our religion; how many of guiding others to virtue by charitable exhortations, by meek reproofs, by prudent counsel, and more than all, by virtuous example! Oh! how happy that soul which thus moves not alone on its path to heaven; which sends before it many others to prepare a mansion for it, and carries in its train, like its Saviour on His ascension, those whom it has been instrumental, however feebly, in rescuing from perdition!

So will our talent be repaid with accumulated interest; when, besides our own increase, we show it multiplied in the salvation of others. With full justice does God, on His part, demand this two-fold improvement; and let me, in conclusion, simply note the wickedness and folly of a different conduct in us. Its wickedness: for hear the dreadful apology which alone those can make who refuse to attempt it. "Lord," says the unprofitable servant, "I know that thou art a hard man; Thou reapest where Thou hast not sown, and gatherest where Thou hast scattered . . . behold, here Thou hast that which is Thine." (24, 25.) I have ever deemed Thee, in other words, a harsh and tyrannic master: Thou leftest me, as in derision, to gain salvation by means which could not attain it; Thou orderedest me to prepare a harvest, but furnishedest me not with the indispensable means; Thou demandest of me more than Thou hast given—take back Thine own, and do with it according to Thy pleasure.

Fearfully blasphemous as this excuse may be, it is still more foolish: for in refusing to serve God upon this plea, and serving the world, you actually engage yourself to a master of the very character which you reprobate—one who expects to reap where he has not sown, and to gather where he has not scattered; a master who exacts from you, as a loan, abilities and talents which he never bestowed, that he may squander them on himself; who expects from you the employment of a time, one moment of which he cannot arrest, to be wasted in his dissipations; of a health and constitution which he did not frame and could not repair, to be shattered, broken, and lost in his gratification; of a soul which he cannot even comprehend, to be eternally lost for seeking to please him. Oh! this is indeed an exaction of service at once cruel and ungrateful, by a taskmaster like those of Egypt, who extorts from you his stated weight of bricks, yet withholds even the paltry straw with which they are to be tempered.

To sum up and apply all that hath been said: if the improvement of your Master's talents is so clearly your duty and your interest, this is a most proper moment to consider, how far you have hitherto attended to this obligation. Standing on the common limit which separates two of the numbered years of our existence, we may look back upon the lessons of the past, and forward to the prospects of the future; and gather from both the motives they offer to increase your stock of virtue. Never, perhaps, in the memory of man, has a twelvemonth passed in which so many and such striking lessons have been given us, of the mutability of all that is human, and the worthlessness of all that belongs not to heaven. We have seen, as on a sudden, popular feeling, which our forefathers used to liken to the breeze of heaven, from the unsteadiness and irregularity of its actions, become so fixed in its direction, so powerful in its course, that God grant it prove not as destructive in its fury as the periodical whirlwind, which sweeps over the fair regions of the west. We have seen diadems transferred from brow to brow with a rapidity which would have been scarcely decent in the mimic representation of a pageant drama; and with a facility which has changed into a practical lesson, what before seemed only a sententious saying, that a crown of gold is as frail and as fading, as the wreath which is woven from the flowers of the field. Those great changes in nations, which used formerly to break history into long and convenient epochs, have crowded upon us in such number, that they must now be recorded in its current page; and those signal judgments which the Almighty used to reserve, by His prophets, as the rare and terrific exhibition of His power—the crushing of sceptres and the removal of kings—seem now to have been transferred to the dispensation of His ordinary providence.

In the meantime, the Master has returned from His journey to many servants. No less than four sovereigns have been called to account for the multiplied talents entrusted to their charge; and many who, this time twelve months, formed part of this congregation, have had to make their reckoning for the one which they had received. Oh! happy those amongst us, who thus convinced how utter valueless all is, save the one thing necessary, have been endeavouring to improve their store! And if we look forward to the ensuing year, what do we discover but a land of mist and obscurity? All is uncertainty as to our future projects; all is uncertainty as to our sufferings or enjoyments; all is uncertainty even as to our very existence. Alas! who of us are the victims allotted to the next year; who amongst us, after twelve months more, will be held up to the survivors, as the annual examples of the brittleness of human hopes! Will another stand up in my place, and remind you that he who warned you, at the commencement of the year, that all flesh is grass, had, before its close, exemplified and proved the correctness of his lesson? Or shall I have to repeat once more the same truths, only illustrated by fresh examples drawn from among you? Oh! we know it not; but this we do know, that to some of us our Master is now at hand, yea, that He already stands at the door and knocks. Improve, then, the time, the uncertain time, that remains; husband well the talents you have received, increase them to the utmost of your ability; and may you hear the sentence of the diligent servant, "Well done, thou good and faithful servant, enter thou into the joy of thy Lord."

For, if we have just closed one more of our numbered years, we are entering upon another stage of our measured pilgrimage. There was work for us to perform in that which we have just finished, and it is meet that we pause to see if it have been performed; and there have been lessons taught us, and it is just we should consider whether we have learned them. What have you done this year for God and for yourselves, beyond what you had practised before? Can you enumerate any virtue which you have acquired, or any great advance in godliness which you have made? Is your talent, then, still upfolded, and hid, and buried; and is the interest demanded of you to depend upon your future exertions?

If this be so, begin them in earnest, and at once. Oh! could you only say, with truth, I have another year before me, in which to repair past deficiencies, you might feel somewhat at ease, in contemplating the work before you. But the entrance into a new year gives no security for reaching its completion. The next year may mean for you, a few months, a few weeks, even only a few days.

Make those few days profitable as months, or even years. Earnestness, industry, perseverance, will condense into a small space, that which, diluted, requires much room; and secure a reward equal to that which others, less active, have taken years to earn.

SERMON IX.

On Unworthy Communion.

Matt. xxii. 12.

"And he saith to him: Friend, how camest thou in hither, not having on a wedding garment? But he was silent."

WHEN man prepares a banquet, it can only be for a few chosen guests. When God spreads His table, it is for universal refreshment. When the one inviteth to a feast, it is but by friendly request or kind intreaty: the other's bidding is a command, and imposes a duty. When we come into an earthly festival, men have no right to pry beyond our outward vestment, to see that it is seemly and respectful; but the feast of God involves a searching into the reins and heart, a curious investigation of motives and impelling reasons, a minute examination of disposition and interior qualities, a proving of oneself with delicate scrutiny, before presuming to partake. And if we neglect this ourselves, the Master of the feast will come in upon us while we are at meat, and will make the search for us, and interrogate us, saying: "Friend, how camest thou in hither, not having on a wedding garment?" And if we are conscience-stricken, and silent, as we needs must be, He will turn round to His servants, His ministers of wrath, and say:

"Bind his hands and feet, and cast him into the outer darkness; there shall be weeping and gnashing of teeth."

Such, my dear friends, are the lessons of this day's gospel, couched in a most expressive parable. The King of heaven and of earth makes a great feast—a wedding feast for His Son; for, His eternal Son has condescended to espouse His divinity to our servile nature, binding Himself to our humanity by an indissoluble tie. To celebrate this union, He, the eternal "Wisdom, hath built Himself a house, hath prepared a table, and hath mingled His wine." (Prov. ix. 1, 2.) Then He hath sent His servants to call aloud in the city, inviting all to partake of His heavenly banquet, in which He is Himself at once the host and most delicious food—the Giver and the Given. To these divine mysteries all have been invited: first the Jews, and then the Gentiles; the former represented by the rich guests, the latter by the poor and lame from the streets and wayside; all, in short, who have been called to the knowledge of Jesus Christ; to whom, without exception, it hath been said: "Unless ye eat the flesh of the Son of man, ye shall not have life in you." (John, vi. 54.) And this general invitation includes a command. For who is not bound to have life eternal? Who that is called by God, is called to any other thing but this? What commandment is there that ends not in the acquirement of everlasting life? If, therefore, the partaking of this eucharistic banquet be necessary for the attainment of this life, the invitation to it is a command: and woe to whoever shall neglect it! To abstain from Christ's food for a time, is perilous; to refuse it entirely, is fatal.

But, alas! (what a dreadful alternative!) to receive it, unvested with the wedding garment of innocence and grace, is, of all others, the most awful and soul-dooming of crimes. And as it is to this, more than to any other point of instruction, that the parable of our gospel seems directed, I call your attention towards it, and will endeavour, with the help of God's light and grace, to represent to you, if faintly, at least correctly, this terrible sin of an unworthy communion, as a compound of treachery and sacrilege beyond those in every other crime.

Judas was the first unworthy communicant; for he received his Lord, while in league with His enemies to betray Him into their hands; and notwithstanding the new pledge which he received of love, went on in his horrible purpose. All who, after him, receive the divine Sacrament of our Saviour's Body with similar dispositions, that is, with conscious guilt, are partakers of his treachery. But let me not be misunderstood.

You betray not your Lord, if merely cold and faint you approach Him; if, conscious of daily and hourly imperfection, easily distracted in prayer, languid in God's service, subject to smaller transgressions, you seek for nourishment, and warmth, and support, from the living Source of them all. You are as a child, or as one sick; you have a right to that which is milk to babes as well as meat for the strong—to that medicine which strengthens and recovers, as well as confirms and perfects.

You betray not your Lord, if, struggling against the assaults of passion, you feel yourself staggering and miserably weak, nay, wounded and maimed; if, in spite of your determination, your frailty is surprised, and your good resolutions for a moment overthrown, and your virtue impaired; and you still nobly determine to repair immediately the fault, and to fight generously on, and not yield to the foe. You are as the Israelites in battle in the wilderness; you have a double claim to that bread from heaven, that manna which is at once a balm and a food, cure and strength.

You betray not your Lord, even if fallen into the very depths of sin, sunk into the lowest degradation of vice, dead in soul, you rise obedient to God's voice speaking to your troubled heart, and, casting aside the garment of death, breaking through the winding bands of iniquity, you return to life. You are as the young woman whom Jesus raised from the dead in the house of Jairus, and to whom He bid her parents give food and refreshment, to recruit her exhausted state.

But you do betray Him, and that most cruelly, when you have entered into a previous compact with His enemy, when you have sold yourself to him for his slave, and are involved in his evil practices, and yet presume to approach the holy communion. It may be that you have only just fallen into a grievous sin, and feel all its remorse, but shame hath tied your tongue, and you have concealed your guilt from God's minister, and you suffer all the bitterness of repentance without its fruit, reconciliation, and do cruel penance without forgiveness. Or, it may be that, by long habitual guilt, your heart hath become callous, your spirit hath sunk into cold apathy, and you neither take the trouble, nor desire the effects, of repentance, or you go through its conditions with hollow insincerity, and without determination to amend. And so, when the usual periods for approaching the Lord's table come, you scruple not to save appearance by unworthily and wickedly approaching it. In either case, what have you done? The blessed Jesus hath invited you, as a disciple, to His paschal feast, and you, with others, have come. At your right hand is one like Peter, full of ardour and zeal, burning for His honour, ready to share His sufferings, amazed at the condescension which can stoop so low for "a sinful man;" on your left is another, like to John, pure, virginal, in child-like innocence, who stretches forth to receive the pledge of love in simple confidence, in unassuming affection, leaning upon the heaving bosom of his Master; others are around, scarcely less holy, repentant sinners like Matthew, or simple believers like Philip. And whose place do thou occupy at the sacred board? Who is your type among the twelve? Look at that scowling wretch, who, under a studied seriousness, masks a lurking disbelief; who, while he seems intent on the actions and words of his Lord, is absent in thought amidst very different scenes; who, in all outward forms, acts and speaks as a faithful follower, while he is in fact a base and scornful traitor. Can you trace no resemblance between yourself and him? You, too, have been lately dallying with the sworn foe of Jesus, sin; you have received its price, and you have given it a permanent lodging in your heart and body. Your mind is no less made up to go on with your transgressions, after you shall have sat at His table. You speak with Him in your prayer of preparation, or you go over the mockery of an outward form of it, without sincerity, without serious meaning; you are like Judas, in truth a mocker, a scoffer at that sacred rite, a hypocrite in your prayer. And is not this false treachery?

Perhaps, as you proceed, a touching glance of reproach, a feeling word of expostulation, reaches your mind. In those forms of prayer which you recite, however coldly, there may be words whose force you cannot escape. Through them your sorrowing Lord seems to address you, and say: " Behold, one of you shall betray Me," yea, " he that dippeth his hand with Me in the dish ;" or, in the words of the prophet: " Behold, the man of my peace, that eateth my bread, hath greatly supplanted me." (Ps. xl. 10.) Oh! when such words or such looks were addressed to Judas, the traitor's heart perhaps quailed for an instant beneath them; his hand, perhaps, faltered as it took the proffered morsel from his Master's; but he relented not: and dost thou? Dost thou abandon, unhappy wretch, thy villanous purpose; dost thou cast thyself down at thy Saviour's feet, and beg forgiveness, and desist? Or dost thou persevere in the fatal resolution of advancing still to the holy table, and consummating the insult to divine love? And if thou dost, is not this a most unfeeling treachery?

But mark the traitor's purpose. He is, in that preparation for the first Christian Passover, arranging what must ensue. Yes, he has thought again and again what course will be best, in what way the treachery may be most securely accomplished. It shall be by a kiss of affection. He has hit upon this expedient as most likely to secure himself from suspicion, and to attain the quiet, undisturbed possession of his object. He is now resolved —he will betray the Son of man with a kiss! And soon—yes, in a few moments—that very Son of man will stand before thee: and hast thou resolved to meet Him in the semblance of one that loveth Him, with downcast eyes, and hands crossed upon thy bosom, and lips parted, as though chastely to salute thy welcome Lord? And *thus* He is to be delivered over to the enemies that lurk within. And is this other than a most fiendish treachery?

But, lo! the time is come; the awful words have been spoken; the mouth of unfailing truth hath declared His own Body to be there. All are reverently and silently awaiting their turn to partake of the tremendous gift: the first have tasted it, Peter is burning, John is melted into tears; the life-giving portion is proffered to Judas, and he stretches to receive it. Oh! in pity let us hope that he understands not, notwithstanding the words just spoken, what it is! O Son of God! exclaim, if Thou canst, "Father, forgive him, for he knoweth not what he doth!" Yet he seems to receive but as the rest; he does not turn pale, his throat is not scorched, his breast does not throb with anguish; and he makes way for a brother disciple, without his black deed of baseness being ever suspected. And how is it with thee? The same Lord of glory hath uttered the same words of power; and thou knowest it, the same effect hath ensued. It is not bread that hath been held up before thee: thou hast bowed down before it in real or seeming adoration as the sacred Body of Christ; and striking thy breast before Him, thou hast declared thyself unworthy that He should enter under thy roof. But He comes nevertheless; He comes as a friend, He comes as a brother, and thou takest advantage of His condescension and His love, of His eager desire to be united with thee. Thou hasteneth forward to meet Him; thou openest the unclean gates of thy house to admit Him in; and thou closest them upon Him, to leave Him in the company of all that He hateth and abhorreth, while thou mockest Him by muttering some formal words of thanks and congratulation! And is not this a worse than Judas's treachery?

But this is not the worst. Judas, when he so cruelly betrayed his Lord, and outraged Him in His sacrament of love, could not know the extent of his crime. He lived not to see Him scourged and buffetted, and crowned with thorns. He saw not, and heard not, of Calvary. Three long hours of torture and anguish, endured for his sake, he knew nothing of, nor foresaw not, as the consequence of his crime. The love of his Saviour he had experienced in life, but knew not of in death. The Eucharist with him preceded that which gave it efficacy: it was a commemoration of what was to be, rather than of what was. But to thee it is not thus. Thou hast seen Christ suffer and die for thee. Thou knowest that thy wickedness inflicted His cruel blows, and that through love for thee He was nailed, and expired, on a cross. All this He represents to thee in this living banquet; the fruit of all these sufferings He comes now to pour into thy breast; and yet thou dost not relent—thou heedest not all this love, but recklessly turnest this wonder of Almighty power and charity to the means and instrument of offending Him, of insulting and of outraging Him! And is not this—but no, this is a treachery which none upon earth, or in the abyss below, can commit, save a

Christian; and God forbid that I should characterize it by that name!

Such is the infamous treason of an unworthy communicant. He takes advantage of the goodness of his Saviour, and of His most amiable institution, to sin against Him; he insults Him most grossly where He most specially wishes to be loved and honoured; and, to crown all, by his sacrilege he turns into poison His sweetest food, and into death His fountain of life.

A sacrilege, my dear friends, is a violence done to, or a profanation of, any consecrated or holy thing. And the guilt of this crime must be measured by the sacredness of the object, and the character and extent of the profanation. Apply these standards to the crime under our consideration, and see the result. All holiness and consecration proceed from God; it is by dedication to His service that things in themselves common become endowed with sacredness. In the Old Law, whatever belonged to His temple partook of this quality, and became jealously protected by His power. None but Levites might touch the precious vessels of the tabernacle—none but priests pass into the precincts of the sanctuary. When God had permitted the Assyrians to carry away the golden vessels of the Temple, and when His justice had not only remained silent, but seemed to approve the deed, it might, indeed, have been supposed that the permitted desecration had deprived them of their imparted holiness, and delivered them in punishment to their blaspheming plunderers. And yet God watched jealously over His own, and still held them holy; and when, after nearly seventy years, Baltassar ordered these vessels of gold and of silver to be brought forth, and to be profanely used in a drunken revel, and in them praised his idols, "in the same hour there appeared" the handwriting on the wall which pronounced his doom; and that hour of sacrilege was the last of his reign. (Dan. v.) And still more striking and more frequent were the manifestations of divine vengeance on profanations of the ark. When the Philistines placed it in the temple of Dagon, it broke in pieces the beastly idol; and wherever they took it through the country, there broke out plagues and foul diseases, so that they must fain restore it to its proper dwelling. (1 Kings, iv.) And when the Bethsamites saw it coming, and gazed upon it with irreverent eyes, thousands of them were struck with sudden death, as was afterwards Oza, though a Levite, for presuming to touch it, as it seemed to totter, with incautious hand. Yet, what was the ark? A chest of satinwood and gold, wherein were tables written by God's finger. In it was no divinity, no essential holiness, save only that it was the type of Him who was to be the giver of the New Law, the mercy-seat of its sanctuary. If God, then, so resented, as a grievous and unpardonable sacrilege, every, even the smallest, insult—nay, levity itself—towards the symbol, do you think that He will treat with less severity any profanation of that which is the real source of all sanctification, His own Holy of Holies?

And if we come to the New Law, all idea of sacrilege is referable to the presence of the adorable Eucharist, and proportionate to its approaches unto it. The Church is sacred, because in it the divine mysteries are celebrated, and it is a crime to violate it; the altar is still more holy, because upon it the divine Victim is immolated, and its profanation is more heinous; the tabernacle, and holy vessel, which contain the blessed Sacrament, are still more jealously screened from profanation. But if their sacred contents are ignominiously treated, oh! how does the Church humble herself, and mourn over the outrage, and beg of God not to visit the enormous crime upon His people! And why? Because the crime has mounted, step by step, from the outward ornament to the most sacred of things; from the consecrated, by emanation of holiness, to its centre and source, by essential sanctity; from the temple of God to God Himself. A direct, insulting, contemptuous misuse of the blessed Eucharist, is necessarily the deepest and most awful sacrilege which can be committed upon earth. Such is the estimate of this crime, if viewed with reference to its object: what shall we say if we weigh it, by the consideration of its manner?

A sacrilegious communion is never the first sin; it supposes, of course, at least one previous crime to have made the receiver unworthy. But generally it is the crowning act of many enormities; the seal of hardened iniquity set upon a long catalogue of sins. It has almost ever been preceded by habitual vice, which has at length rendered the heart callous against its terrible judgments. Early virtue has been gradually undermined; religious principles have been weakened, and then have ceased to act; the curb has been cast off the mind, and it has roamed lawless after evil thoughts; the law of the will has been withdrawn, and it has freely indulged in unlawful desires; the conceptions of the corrupted heart have, perhaps, ripened into acts, and the living temple, destined for the living God, has been profaned and degraded to the service of sin. Then there has been a long career of duties violated, prayer neglected, vanity indulged, passion unrestrained, irreverence in behaviour, looseness of tongue, of looks, of reading, idleness of mind and body, forgetfulness of God. There have been, too, in general, doubtful repentances and but sickly communions, for sometime preceding, the forerunners of the last more certain catastrophe. The soul of one so involved, has gradually been more and more enslaved by vice and crime; the seven other spirits, worse than the first occupier, have got undisturbed possession, and his breast is, before God, as a den of thieves, the abode of hideous and of hateful things. To these is generally added the preliminary sacrilege of an insincere or an uncontrite confession, which closes down, like the seal upon a sepulchre, the corruptions that are within. It is into contact with this dreadful mass of filthiness and defilement that the Body of the Lord is to be brought. The heart sickens at the idea.

For supposing, my friends, that when Nicodemus and Joseph took down that sacred Body from the cross, they had not, as their feelings naturally impelled them, laid it in a new and clean monument, in which no one had been placed, but had been compelled by the Jews to cast it into the common grave of malefactors, do not the feelings of a Christian recoil with horror from the contemplation of that virginal flesh, born of Mary, and exempted from the law of seeing corruption, flung into the charnel-house, amidst the impure remains and loathsome carcases of the vilest of men: and while one can contemplate it gashed and torn, and pierced and bruised, even while alive, does not one shrink with disgust from imagining the possibility of such contamination? And yet, what would this have been, compared with the frightful descent of the living Christ, with His soul no less than His Divinity united to His body, through that mouth which, in the words of the prophet, is truly an open sepulchre; into the abode of a corruption, and an uncleanness, far beyond what I have described, a living, a stirring, a conscious mass of sin? Oh! the saints have been permitted to see our Lord struggling with horror, against passing the lips of a sacrilegious receiver, and drawing back from stepping over the threshold of such an impure abode! But there He must needs enter in, and for a while remain amidst its disgusting inmates. The Son of God must stay a while, because you will have it so, with the enemies whom He died to overcome: the Holy One must be the companion, because you have doomed Him to it, of the uncleanest spirits: the living God must be shut up, because such is your impious pleasure, with the children of Satan. And this horrible crime is committed by you, under the form and semblance of a solemn religious act—the holiest rite of your service and duty to Him! And you retire after this, and are cheerful and mirthful, and walk with men, yea, with virtuous men, as though nought had befallen you! And you think you shall be happy and prosper, and have length of days, and a peaceful end, and perhaps a place one day in heaven!

Oh! no, no; surely your cruel mockery goes not so far! Surely you have at least made up your mind to the being bound hand and foot and cast into the outer darkness.

Surely you had prepared yourself for eternal weeping and gnashing of teeth! You knew that you were about to eat judgment to yourself, by not discerning the Body of the Lord, by eating of this bread unworthily. And that judgment will soon begin to show itself, in the searing of the conscience, and in the withering of the affections, and in the blighting of hopes, and in the palsy of every power for good. It will show itself in prayer and in study, in activity and in rest, in the present and in the future. It will manifest itself in that root of impenitence which it will now plant, and which, if not speedily plucked up, will grow and deepen, till the fulness of time shall come, and the judgment which hath been eaten and drunk, shall be followed by the cup of divine wrath, swallowed to the dregs, in the final judgment of Him whom you have thus sacrilegiously insulted.

O eternal God! avert from these Thy children so tremendous a judgment, and so frightful a curse! Assemble them often and often, like youthful olives, round Thy table; but in all the number, let there be not one found without Thy wedding garment, without that purity and innocence which best become their age, that inward loveliness in Thine eyes which befits their appearance before men. Impress, on the one hand, in their tender hearts, a love of this sacred feast, a longing after its enjoyment, a relish of its sweetness, a sense of its necessity; and, on the other, a salutary awe of approaching it irreverently, much more unworthily. Teach them to try and prove themselves, and to cleanse their souls of every stain, before they receive the Body of Thy blessed Son; and give them the full richness of consolation and strength, which flows from this source of blessing. And if there be but one amongst us all who has laid upon his soul this terrible guilt, oh! allow him not to plunge into despair, but mercifully raise him from the gulf, and give him strength and courage to bewail and confess his fault, and make him the most fervent of his brethren; and so join us hand in hand, and heart with heart, at Thy fatherly feast—the prodigal returned, with the faithful child—one in charity among ourselves, one in love with Thee, both now and for ever. Amen.

SERMON X.

On Delay of Repentance.

ECCLES. v. 8, 9.

"Delay not to be converted to the Lord, and defer it not from day to day. For His wrath shall come on a sudden, and in the time of vengeance He will destroy thee."

OUR lives, my brethren, are such a series of transgressions and frailties—we are so constantly violating some duty, or committing some fault, that repentance becomes to those, who are anxious for salvation, a work of almost daily necessity; and that which was instituted as an extraordinary remedy, has to be turned into a regular and ordinary duty. Happy, indeed, my brethren, are those who consider it as such, and as such discharge it! happy they who, knowing that, whilst in this frail tabernacle of the flesh, the "just man shall fall seven times," (Prov. xxv. 16) tire not, and become not discouraged in the never-failing work of repentance! But woe to him who, darkened in understanding, thinks himself free from evil; who, going on without attention or care through those numerous dangers which the just, though on their guard, can hardly pass without offence, never finds anything wherewith to reproach himself, or to make him think repentance necessary for him! Woe to him who, obdurate of heart, sees, indeed, much in his past actions that requires repentance, much in his present conduct which calls for amendment, and yet neglects to turn at once, the instant he reflects upon it, from what he dares not approve, and blot out, by an efficacious conversion to God, whatever merits the condemnation of his own conscience! Small, indeed, we may hope, is the number of those who can coolly look upon the enormity of sin, and yet intend not at some time or other to abandon it; who, having received a Christian education, and being consequently convinced of the punishment that awaits the wicked, go on in their path with the cool resolution of finally throwing themselves over the precipice, in which it terminates, without ever turning aside to escape the hands of the living God. Few, indeed, are those—and those few must be rather demons than men—who sin with the determination of doing so always; who intend not only to live the life, but to die the death, of the wicked.

On the contrary, most sinners seek enjoyment in evil, with an intention of escaping, by some means or other, from its punishments. They flatter themselves that, on some future occasion, they will be able to undertake the work of conversion with greater facilities than at present; and that, however ill they may be now spending their lives, they will, at least, close them in the friendship of God. This, my brethren, is the mischievous delusion which blinds, misleads, and ruins the greater portion of mankind; a delusion the more dangerous, that it rests on two most specious grounds: on an apparent confidence in the goodness and mercies of God, and upon a proud presumption of our own powers. But false and vain are these two motives for delaying this important duty; for I trust to convince you, that, by delay of our conversion, instead of its becoming easier on these two grounds, the difficulties against it go on daily increasing, first, on the part of God, and secondly, on the part of the sinner himself.

We have been ever accustomed to hear and to speak of the infinity of God's mercies, and of the power of His grace. We have been taught that when He touches the mountains, they instantly smoke; that when He strikes the rock, springs of living water immediately gush from it; that when He moves the heart, it dissolves in a moment, and yields to His obedience. Such powerful grace has not as yet been granted to us; and as the Almighty loves not the death of the sinner, but that he be converted and live, and gives him all the necessary means for this purpose, we flatter ourselves that our day is not yet come, that our graces are still in store; and we are resolved, as soon as the moment of our visitation arrives, to follow the divine call. But what do we expect these future graces to be? Not surely a voice from heaven, such as converted St. Paul from error, and St. Augustine from vice; not an angel from God, such as was employed to conduct Cornelius to the truth; not, in fine, even a prophet like Nathan, to come with a special mission from the Almighty, to denounce to us the grievousness and the punishment of our sins. No, my brethren, the ordinary grace to which alone we can look, is the horror of sin which God excites in our minds; and this He ordinarily does by the hearing or reading of His word; sometimes, in a more dreadful way, by His judgments.

On every delay in conversion, grace becomes less powerful, and the ordinary means of conveying it less efficacious. Your early sins probably cost you pain and regret. It perhaps required the powerful concurrence of bad example and persuasion, of dangerous opportunities and unguarded surprise, to seduce you. You felt sorrow after their commission; you made, perhaps, efforts to recover. But as you advanced, have you found that it has required stronger and stronger temptations to induce you to offend God, that the sting of remorse has been more acute, and that your efforts to rise have been more effectual, in proportion as you have increased the number of your offences? Yet such is the only ground on which you could have a right to calculate, that in progress of time your mind will become more softened towards repentance, that a few years more of guilt will make easier to your heart a horror for offence. Only apply your expectations to other circumstances of life, and see how delusive they are.

In any profession or practice which requires a certain degree of callousness and unfeelingness, would you allow that any chance remained of those who exercise it becoming, in course of time, more tender and more alive to the sufferings they inflict? Does any one ever fancy that the murderer or the robber prepares himself for remorse by the frequent repetition of his crime, and not rather that he blunts his feelings more and more, each time, against repentance and amendment? In like manner, it must happen to every sinner: the longer he continues to offend, the more he hardens his heart against the enormity of his sins, and thus renders it more unfit to receive the grace of conversion. But, unfortunately, while he thus removes furthur and further from himself this first step towards repentance, he also destroys the efficacy of the means which God, in the ordinary course of His providence, uses to conduct him towards it. The word of God, which is generally the means of bringing the sinner to a detestation of sin, is likened in Scripture to a seed, the produce of which depends upon the state of the ground which has to receive it. Certainly it is not by allowing your soul still farther to harden like the highway, that you can hope to render it on some future day more fit for cultivation. It is not by allowing the little soil which remains to be swept from it, by the constant repetition of crime, till it become hard and cold as the rock, that you can expect to prepare it for producing worthy fruits of penance. The more accustomed the mind is to sin, the less impression can the threats and denunciations of the divine law make upon it.

In addition to this, the word of God itself, though more cutting than a two-edged sword, ceases to have the power of penetrating, or of opening any longer a channel of grace to the unrepenting sinner. For he has long since heard the worst; the terrors of God's judgments have repeatedly thundered in his ears; he has shuddered at the nature of sin, and of its consequences: and yet all this has not wrought upon his mind. What more can he expect? Does he hope that stronger motives for detesting sin may yet be discovered, than the consciousness that it is odious to a God who is goodness and mercy itself, and who merits all our love? Does he fancy that some aggravation may yet be discovered in the chastisement with which the Almighty visits it; that the torments prepared for the wicked may be shown to be more intense than the word of God has described them; or that their duration, though eternal, may be proved to be more fearful than he has hitherto been taught? Or is it that he thinks these motives to conversion may, on some future day, be placed before his eyes in a more vivid light than they have yet presented themselves; that they may some day be addressed to his heart in a more feeling manner than they have hitherto approached it? Alas! he looks forward to the skill of man to do that for him which the commands of God have not been able to effect. He hopes that the feeble words of human eloquence may influence him more than the divine authority has been able hitherto to do. But no, my brethren, this hope is, in general, but vain. The word of truth has spoken it in the gospel, "that if they will not believe Moses and the prophets inviting to repentance, neither will they believe if one should come to preach to them from the dead."

Thus does the sinner, the longer he continues in his evil ways, render more and more ineffectual the ordinary means of conversion, by both disqualifying himself for its action, and diminishing its efficacy. His only resource can be in the more terrible calls and mercies of the Lord; he can only look for those dreadful graces which grind and crush the heart into repentance, after it has refused to melt before the softening influences of His Holy Spirit: in other words, he has nothing to look to for his conversion, except the judgments and scourges of God. What a dreadful alternative is this, and what a madness to incur it! To stand against all the kindness and persuasions of a Father, and leave Him no means of bringing about your good, except by His severity and rigour; to resist all the affectionate assistance of a Friend in your disease, till you leave Him no resource for your cure, except a painful and dangerous operation! Nor can we be sure that even these calls to repentance will prove more efficacious than those which have been already neglected. The sinner has probably already felt the hand of God. He has been touched in his goods, in his friends, in his own flesh: and yet has all this produced his conversion? He has, perhaps, seen the companions of his crimes fall victims of God's justice; he has himself been the object of His visitations by accidents or sickness: have all these caused anything more than a transient remorse, which soon died away? And if these trials have failed in working his conversion, what hopes are there that they will have a stronger effect in future? No, my friends, even the most awful invitations to repentance have sometimes proved abortive.

Look at the thieves crucified with Christ. Had they been dismissed with Barabbas, they would have, perhaps, joined the mob in calling for our Saviour's crucifixion, and rejoiced in His execution. But, hardened in guilt, the Almighty reserved for them a strong, though painful call. His wrath overtakes them, and subjects them to the merited punishment of their crimes; but places before them, in their dreadful tortures, the innocent Lamb of God, bleeding and expiring for their redemption. Oh! if ever the goodness of God made a strong and a last effort to save a hardened sinner, it was on this occasion. And yet, alas! though one yields to the severity of His judgments, the other scoffs at even this attempt;

blasphemes amidst his acute sufferings the Redeemer that proffers him His mercy, and dies as he had lived, hardened and impenitent. Still you may say, that though the delay of repentance thus renders more and more ineffectual the ordinary modes which the Almighty employs for the conversion of the sinner, who will presume to limit the resources of His power and mercy, and to say that He who holds in His hand the hearts of princes, and turns them whithersoever He wills, has not a thousand hidden means by which He can work, in an instant, conversion in the oldest offender.

True, but what motive is the unrepenting sinner suggesting to God to bring into action these extraordinary favours? Is it by despising the proffered bounties of the God who "is not to be mocked," (Gal. v. 6) that he intends to found a claim for more efficacious graces in future? Very different is the doctrine of St. Paul— "Dost thou contemn the riches of His goodness, and patience, and long suffering? But according to thy hardness and impenitent heart, thou layest up to thyself wrath, against the day of wrath." (Rom. ii. 4, 5.) Or is it by the marked insult of which he is guilty towards His divine majesty, by delaying conversion till a more advanced age, that he hopes to propitiate Him? For what can be more insulting than to tell God, that as yet vice presents too many attractions not to be preferred before Him; that when the tongue has grown too dull for the scandals and loose conversation of the world, it will have sufficient strength to be spent upon His praises; that when the mind will have lost its vigour and energy, the intervals of its dotage will be quite enough to meditate on His commandments; that, in fine, it will be time for repentance when infirmity and indulgence shall have sufficiently weakened the body, to entitle it to claim exemption from the rigours of penance? Yet such are the replies made, if not in words, at least in conduct, by every sinner who hears the voice of the Lord calling him to repentance, and yet delays to undertake it. Truly, and with ten-fold indignation, may He address them in His words to the priests of the Israelites:—"If you offer the blind for sacrifice, is it not evil? And if you offer the lame and the sick, is it not evil? Offer it to thy prince, if he will be pleased with it, or if he will regard thy face, saith the Lord of hosts... I have no pleasure in you: I will not receive a gift from your hand." (Mal. i. 8–10.)

Delay of repentance, then, instead of trusting to God's mercies, has nothing to hope from them, because it makes the soul more and more unfit for His grace; it renders void the ordinary means of conveying it; it leaves no resource but in His chastisement, which may also prove ineffectual; and it proposes to claim extraordinary favours, in exchange only for the most insulting conduct. On the other hand, innumerable obstacles on the part of the sinner himself, render conversion more and more difficult after every delay. The present moment always seems the most unfavourable for undertaking anything to which we are of ourselves disinclined. But if we look back upon it after it is past, it always appears that we could have done it better then, than in the period which has succeeded. With regard to every habit, this is really the case; for, while we magnify the difficulties that oppose our immediately breaking them off, we shall find always that these difficulties do, in reality, increase by time, so that, at any subsequent epoch, the struggle will, in truth, prove more and more arduous. We are inclined to consider ourselves attached to our failings merely by some advantage which they procure, or by some enjoyment which endears them. We fancy that, in course of time, our ardour will fade away and be extinguished, the ties which bind us will become more feeble, and that, as experience and years will, at the same time, administer more skill and steadiness, we shall find no difficulty in shaking off the sins and habits of our youth.

This view is, however, in a great measure, erroneous. What is most to be feared in evil is, that like everything else to which we become habituated, it enters at last into the composition of our character, and interweaves itself with daily actions; it then becomes necessary almost to our very existence; and the rooting it out is like thwarting the primary feelings of nature, and turning the whole course of our lives into a totally new channel. If a person, for example, indulges in the practice of intemperance, his palate and tongue may become palled and insensible to the flavour which, at the beginning, seduced him into excess; his mind may become tired of the company which, at first, decoyed him into its practice. But his constitution is now habituated to this stimulus; his whole system feels irritated and uneasy without it; and this odious vice, unaccompanied any longer by pleasure, has grown to be almost necessary to the existence of its wretched slave. The same must be said of every other vice, and, still more, of every omission of duty. The time, for instance, which should be given to prayer and public worship, becomes habitually devoted to more agreeable employment, or to necessary business. We must begin our occupations early in the morning, we must prolong our amusements till late, and our day passes without once thinking of God. Our habits thus become formed, and our hours distributed, according to this arrangement; and it is an inconvenience and annoyance to vary its disposition.

Now, it is precisely as we advance in age, that we find an increasing difficulty in altering our habits and course of life, and that a trifling variation more easily irritates us, and causes pain. Yet, in delaying of conversion to God, we anticipate that we are rendering more easy the change of a long series of customs and feelings, that will have become our daily occupation, and an integral part of ourselves. No, my brethren, the habits of his younger years, if suffered to gain strength with his growth, are not so easily to be stripped off by the unrepenting sinner. "His bones," in the energetic expression of Job, " will be filled with the vices of his youth;" (xx. 11) and well will it be for him, if "they sleep not with him in the dust."

Such is the first increase of difficulty which results from deferring a change of life, that we suffer our offences to become habitual, and harder to be left. But, in the second place, the work of repentance itself, becomes more distressing, the longer we delay it. We must recount our sins before God and His minister, in the bitterness of our souls. What a complicated undertaking, after years and years of varied offences! At first, a few hours of consideration, while the offences were recent, and our memory in vigour, might have sufficed to place before our eyes all our transgressions; and, as yet not hardened by their so frequent repetition, we might have been moved to detest them. One effort would have cleansed us from them; and our happy escape might have been of itself a sufficient motive, to render us more cautious and guarded for the future. But to do this after additional years of guilt, with almost every duty neglected, almost every commandment of God transgressed, every single virtue uncultivated, and every one of these innumerable sins varied in feature and quality, by circumstances of peculiar aggravation; oh! what a task to be undertaken, at a period when the faculties are declining, and losing their energies! It is well if the overwhelming attempt does not overpower the wretched delinquent, and, if unable to retrace the mazes of his own wanderings, he does not abandon himself in despair, with the load of his iniquity, to the justice of his unappeased Judge. And, after all, if he does succeed in taking something like an accurate measure of his guilt, what a weight of reparation awaits him, in order to atone for it! Reparation for injustices, from which, perhaps, his hands may be clean, but which have been done by those whose conduct he was bound to inspect; reparation for the calumnies and detractions, which may, which *must*, have escaped him in the years that he kept no guard over his tongue; detractions that, perhaps, committed a long time before, have wrought an extended and deadly effect, the origin of which is probably forgotten, though their victims are still suffering: in fine, reparation for the scandal and bad example which he has been giving to all around him, to his children and domestics, to his friends and dependents, and which has passed from them to hundreds of others. All, all, must be fully made up, to obtain forgiveness, and the mercy of God.

And can any one flatter himself that he is lessening the work of conversion, by suffering all those dreadful debts to go on accumulating, so as to have to unravel the complicated mysteries of his endless iniquities, and to compensate for years of crime, when their number and extent are multiplied a hundred-fold? Every delay, therefore, increases the difficulties in the necessary conditions of conversion. In the third place, the risks arising from delayed conversion are still further increased by the uncertainty of time. Did we delay this important undertaking to some specific period, when we could be sure of having peculiar facilities, even then we could not calculate against this danger; for we know not how much yet remains of our life. But when we merely defer it to a distant and undefined epoch, without contemplating any thing more than the freeing our present thoughts from so disagreeable a subject, it is blindness itself not to consider that a thousand accidents may carry us off to-morrow, even to-day, much more in that indeterminate period during which we make up our minds to live in enmity with God. You are, perhaps, young, robust, and healthy. Yes, but it is God who holds your life in His hands; and still you coolly calculate upon the length of it which He may grant you, in order to decide how much time you may yet spend in offending Him! Is not this sufficient provocation to induce Him to fling you from Him at once into perdition? You are trying to act a deceitful part with Him. Remember His threat, that "deceitful men shall not live out half their days." (Ps. liv. 24.)

Finally, the obstacles to conversion are infinitely increased by delay, because, being put off from day to day, and death always overtaking us before we expect it, it has at length to be undertaken in the most unfavourable situation, in the last illness, and on the death-bed of a sinner. In fact, my brethren, disguise it as you will, bring what specious pretences you choose, he who delays his conversion to God, in reality looks to that, as the time when he thinks himself sure of its accomplishment. The sinner always makes this his refuge and his hope, though, perhaps, he dares not acknowledge it. All the difficulties to conversion which we have hitherto enumerated, are concentrated in a much more formidable degree in that awful moment : the want of strength and time to review the past, and to repent of it; and, at the same time, to make full reparation for its guilt. To these obstacles will be added the troubles and anxieties for health, for temporal affairs, and for friends ; the far greater weakness of the mind, and the far more rapid decay of the faculties ; and, in fine, the sufferings of the last and agonizing illness.

But, my brethren, this is not all. There is a period, after all, beyond which the patience even of the Lord endureth not ; and that period is, then, too probably come. The Spirit of God, in the words of my text, assures us, that if we delay to be converted to the Lord from day to day, " His wrath shall come on a sudden, and in the day of vengeance He will destroy;" and that day is too certainly arrived. Alas! when the hand of death comes upon the sinner, it is too sure a sign that the earth, wearied of supporting his iniquities, has cried at length to heaven to remove the reproach from off its face ; it is a sign that, not having known, in the day of his visitation, the things that were for his peace, his enemies are at length digging a trench about him, and are encompassing him on every side; it is a sign that the destroying angel, standing over him, has lifted his hand to heaven, and sworn by Him who liveth for ever and ever, that there shall be time no more. (Apoc. x. 6.) Oh! what extraordinary grace must, indeed, be required for the sinner who has despised the commands of God, when enjoined in sweetness and meekness, now on a sudden to esteem and embrace them, when enforced by suffering and trial; for him who has never cared for God when He bestowed on him blessings, now in an instant to love Him, when He has let loose upon him the storms of His vengeance. Instead of this, he will look upon the graces which he has received and despised as so many motives of despair ; he will hear with horror the mercies of the Lord enumerated, which he has outraged so violently as to have at length forced Him to unlock the stores of His revenge ; he will consider his whole life as a contest between his obstinacy and the all-powerful God ; he will view the illness which oppresses him, not as a kind call and invitation to repentance, but as the last effort of a powerful adversary, who, now at length grappling with him, has prostrated him at his feet, and holds his hand over him to avenge himself. With such sentiments as these, he may own his crimes, but he will not repent them ; he may acknowledge his demerits, but cannot attempt to cancel them ; his tears, like those of the dying Antiochus, will be the bitter tears of hopeless despair, the acknowledgments of God's justice, and his submission will be only pronounced in the same spirit as by the apostate Julian, when, casting a handful of blood from his death-wound towards heaven, he exclaimed: "Thou hast conquered at last; O Nazarean, thou hast conquered!"

These, my dear brethren, are some of the difficulties which arise to conversion from delaying it, on the part both of God and of the sinner himself. If, then, you this day hear His voice, harden not your hearts. If there be any here who is as yet involved in the evil habits of vice, let him lose no time, nor delay till another opportunity, what he can so well accomplish at this favourable moment. We are, in fact, just going to enter upon a time of penance and of prayer, the season especially dedicated, by God and His Church, to the work of conversion; and this year, in particular, it is introduced by one of those strong contrasts and lessons, which He sometimes deigns to give. You had promised yourselves to pass these weeks in gaiety and festivity, and you have seen them glide by in solemnity and mourning; you hoped to feast your eyes on pageants and revels, and they have only fallen on the sepulchre and the shroud. It was thus the wish of the Almighty, that instead of passing suddenly from gladness and dissipation, into fasting and penance, you should enter these almost imperceptibly, sobered by the awful picture which He has held up to you of the instability and uncertainty of life; and that the ashes which you will receive upon your foreheads in a few days, should not be placed there merely to wipe off the dissipation of the preceding weeks, but to impress the awful words that accompany them by a striking proof, that no dignity however elevated, no station however necessary, no character however amiable, no virtue however pure, can redeem the dust which embodies them from the sentence pronounced against it, of returning to the dust from which it sprung.* Oh! profit, then, by the opportunity; turn now to the Lord in fasting, in weeping, and in mourning, while He may be easily propitiated; seek Him now when He may easily be found; and one effort alone will cleanse you from your crimes and evil habits, and make you worthy to partake of the table of the Lord at His resurrection, the partner of His joy and the coheir of His glory.

* Alluding to the death of the Sovereign Pontiff.

SERMON XI.

On the Small Number of the Elect.

MATT. xx. 16.

"Many are called, but few are chosen."

The Apostle, my brethren, compares the life of the Christian to a race in which all push forward to obtain an eternal crown; but where, of many who start together, one only obtains the prize. Some soon drop off, wearied with the exertion which attends their efforts; many, perhaps, do not deem the object worthy of the labour and pain necessary for its attainment; few persevere through every opposition, and finally reach the goal at which they have aimed. Such, my brethren, is the illustration given, by this faithful interpreter, of the awful words, which teach, that though many are called by God to the participation of His mercy and His glory, yet few are found worthy to be chosen for their enjoyment. This appalling and unqualified denunciation stands almost alone amidst the mild and gentle doctrines of Christianity, but is alone sufficient to impart a sternness to its features, and to check, with a serious apprehension, that unbounded hope which its promises might otherwise excite. The consequence of this is precisely what we might anticipate. The spirit of the times, anxious to facilitate the work of salvation, and to render it compatible with more agreeable occupations, gratifies itself with blazoning forth the kindness and benevolence of God, and His desire of that salvation, and in concealing or diminishing the difficulties and obstacles which oppose its attainment.

The worldly or irreligious are soothed by the fashionable doctrine, that it is inconsistent with His goodness to reject the creatures whom He loves, or doom them to eternal punishment. The more thinking, too often run into a still wilder fanaticism, and deluding themselves into the belief of some system of instantaneous justification and inammissible grace, become assured that their lot is invariable, and their salvation decreed. But, my brethren, Jesus Christ is the same "yesterday and to-day;" He has pronounced that salvation is an attainment of difficulty ; that of the many who enter the lists, many, very many, must be foiled. Men, then, may speculate on His attributes, or pretend to fathom the mysteries of His justice ; but still His strong and impressive sentence stands twice recorded and unrepealed, that " many are called, but few are chosen."

It is, then, folly to avert our eyes from this dreadful declaration. It is folly, like king Joakim, to efface or destroy the words of threat which have been pronounced against us, while the authority which dictated them is beyond our control. (Jer. xxxvi.) The small number of the elect must, in spite of all our delusions, strike us, whenever we peruse the sacred page ; and the fearful consideration that those who are saved form only a happy exception to the bulk of mankind, must terrify us when we meditate on it. It is true that the mercy and goodness of God are unbounded; but they have a powerful counterbalance in the folly and perverseness of man. Hence, religion exhibits to us an unceasing struggle between the one, ever desiring and promoting our salvation, and the other ever thwarting, and too often successfully, His benevolent designs. These will be the topics of my discourse. The Almighty anxiously desires the salvation of all His creatures; in spite of this, the number of those who are saved must be very small.

The history of man, my brethren, or the life of each particular individual, is equally a record of His unwearied solicitude and anxious endeavours to procure us eternal happiness. All the faculties, with which in the beginning was stored the mind of man, were directed to this purpose: that thirst and capacity for knowledge, which made him dart through creation with a rapidity that proved him destined for a bolder flight, and which at first sight showed him the whole system to which he belonged, centered in a Being infinitely superior to all that he beheld; that eagerness of the affections after whatever promises enjoyment, which yet sickens of each gratification within its reach the moment it has been tasted; that constitution of mind, which will not allow us to remain indifferent in the choice of any proposed object, but forces us to calculate its good and evil, and repays us with pleasure or pain, according to the correctness of our choice;—these magnificent properties of the soul were given to man by his Creator for some very noble end; and what could this end be, if not that he might have a guide, as sure as any instinctive feeling can be, to direct him towards a sublimer possession than the visible creation can propose; to inspire a longing anxiety for its acquisition; and keep him steady in the way which could alone conduct him to it.

The malice of man, opposed to the will of his Maker, though working for his good, soon ruined this gracious plan, and rendered insufficient the means of salvation provided for him. But no, that kind Providence which is so attentive to all his wants, that not even the smallest bird falls from the air without its loss in creation being perceived and repaired, could not be indifferent to the noblest of terrestrial creatures, nor suffer the station which he held as child of heaven to remain a blank. It became, indeed, necessary to devise some means more efficacious for securing to us the happiness which we had rejected; and our sovereign Benefactor failed not to undertake its attainment. For this purpose the splendid fabric of religion arose, every part of which displayed the kind anxiety of its Author for the salvation of His creatures.

Wherefore did His providence watch over one nation, and, through ages of ignorance and vice, preserve within it the spark of truth and virtue, if not that from it might break forth a light of salvation to all the races of the earth? Wherefore did He communicate to man those resources of His wisdom and power, which at the creation He had reserved to Himself, and unfold the veiled mysteries of the future through His servants the prophets, if it were not that authority might be given to those accompanying calls of mercy and kindness, by which He assured the sinner that He willed not his death, but that he should be converted and live; and exhorted the wicked man to abandon his ways, and seek with sincerity of heart the salvation of the Lord? With what view did He deliver into the hands of His weak creatures the keys of life and death, and invest them with the power of varying the laws which He Himself had imposed on Nature? With what view in particular did the Son of God work such a splendid series of miracles, if not to fix the attention and confirm the reliance of all men upon that first, that fundamental doctrine of Christianity, that He was the Saviour of all, so often inculcated by the Apostle; that no distinction of Jew or Gentile, of Greek or barbarian, can exclude any one from redemption, and the earnest desire of the eternal Father for his salvation. These, however, my brethren, are but the more distant manifestation of God's kind intentions in our regard.

He knows how little we are moved by promises of happiness beyond our senses, and He has condescended to meet our weakness: drawing from before our eyes the curtain of His holy sanctuary, and breaking down its wall of separation. He has, in His inspired word, invited us to gaze on the glories to which we should aspire, and allows us, like Moses from the mountain of Nebo, to survey, even while in the wilderness, the land of promise which we are to inherit. And all is shown to us in that blessed city, as would be deemed on earth most glorious and beautiful; golden edifices and jewelled gates, and streams of living crystal, and groves of most excellent and perennial fruits, with the Lamb that was slain for its temple, and the bright eye of God for its luminary. And when we mingle in thought with the happy inhabitants of this holy seat, we find that we are no strangers there, but rather brethren; that much is thought among them, and much done, for us; that the altar which stands in the midst of them, burns for its incense nought but such prayers as we send up from earth; that the golden vials which venerable elders, nearest to the awful throne, pour around its footstool, have no fragrance save from our supplication; that holy martyrs, who cry from beneath the altar for the accomplishment of God's retribution, are soothed to rest by the sweet promise that we, their brethren, necessary for their complete happiness, are hastening to join them, and share their crowns. And why are the eternal gates thus lifted up, and why is this sublime spectacle revealed, if not that we may be induced to take the dove's wings, and fly— fly from this earth, which the waters of bitterness and iniquity yet cover, and bear the olive-branch of our reconciliation to this open ark, where alone our feet may rest? There may we see many orders of blissful spirits, who adore and praise in unceasing harmony, and holy men innumerable, who have lived as angels here below, and have been caught up to join in their songs and raptures of joy.

And if the Almighty sometimes opens to us a different scene; if He exhibits to us the terrible judgments which He has prepared for the punishment of sins, and puts on the stern features of a severe and uncompromising judge; yet is even this only a disguise which His kindness and mercy assume. It is to terrify us from falling into what He knows would cause our misery, and to second His exertions for our salvation, by our own dread of suffering and unhappiness. Yet would all this be nothing, if He provided us not with all the means requisite to attain His proffered good. And, in truth, these means He has supplied abundantly; for every weakness and want of our humanity has been well cared for by Him. The original stain which infected all our powers has been washed away by the laver of grace and sanctification; our subsequent failings are cancelled and repaired by the holy sacrament of penance. These are all proofs of God's wishes in our favour. For every state on earth a source of grace and assistance has been opened, and in all, the holy table of the Lord is prepared " against all our enemies."

But who requires such general proofs? Not all the splendid testimonials which He has publicly given of this truth, not all the inviting prospects which He has opened to our view, not all the means which He provided for its attainment, can give us half the conviction of this earnest desire, which each of us must derive from the private testimony of his own heart. You alone, besides God, know the extent to which He has carried His mercies in your regard; how He has divested Himself of every attribute but His goodness, to allure you to your own eternal good. You alone can feel how, as you varied your rebellions against Him, He varied no less the calls of His grace, now checking you by the gentle voice of self-reproach, now terrifying you by the threatening denunciations of His word; on one occasion winning you by new favours in the midst of your ingratitude, on another arresting you by some unexpected punishment, which He mildly measured, not by your deserts, but by His love. When you have wandered, you have seen Him, like the good shepherd, tracking you through all your crooked paths, to bear you home upon His shoulders; when sunk down in guilt, and unable to rise, you have found Him at your side, like the good Samaritan, to pour healing into your wounds, and refreshment into your soul; when tired of your separation, you have made an effort to return to Him, He has met you, like the father of the prodigal, by His embraces. Well may He exclaim to you as He did to Jerusalem: "Can a woman forget her infant, so as not to have pity on the son of her womb? and if she should forget, yet will not I forget thee. Behold, I have graven thee in my hands; thy walls are always before my eyes." (Is. xlix. 15, 16.) Oh! yes, my brethren, a painful memorial He has to remind Him, every day of your life, of His interest in your salvation. A bloody record He has always before His eyes of what He paid as the ransom of your evil, and the price of your redemption.

If you need have this proved, I would lead you up the holy mountain where He enthroned His love and crowned it, and gave it to us as an inheritance; but He enthroned it on a cross, and He crowned it with thorns, and He made it purchase that inheritance with much precious blood. Oh! you should sit often and long at the foot of this His throne, between a weeping mother and a scoffing multitude, and mark the springs from which the streams of redemption gush. For, as from the garden of Eden, four rivers flowed and divided themselves over the whole land, bearing everywhere gladness and benediction, so does an equal number of streams pour out blessing and peace from His four painful wounds. And who shall count the smaller sources from which distil innumerable rills of life and grace, from the goring points which encircle His brow, from the mocking blows which have disfigured His features, from the ignominious stripes which have rent and gashed His body? And yet if you count all this, you shall have done but little, unless you can count also the number of His pores; for they all have bled for the same cause, in the garden of olives. And what was this cause? Oh! if you could but enter into His heart—and it, too, has been laid open by a cruel wound—you would find that your name also is enrolled there, and among those of His sinful creatures, for whose redemption so much was cheerfully endured.

He yet bears graven upon His hands those wounds which were inflicted there to ensure our salvation. Upon the accomplishment of this great object alone His thoughts were fixed, amidst the desertion of His friends, the apostacy of His disciples, the tears of His mother. Upon the purchase of this blessing alone His soul dwelt amidst the calumnies of His accusers, the triumph of His enemies, and the smart of His wounds; and fearful lest even the most base, the most brutal, the most sacrilegious of men should be excluded from His anxious desires, He exhausts His last breath in a prayer to His Father, that the very authors of His death should partake of the redemption which it purchased. Oh! truly, my brethren, God does not wish any of His creatures to perish, but that they should all be preserved and gathered into life.

But if He is so anxious for the salvation of all men, must not His wish be necessarily attended with success?

My brethren, I will answer this question by an example from Holy Writ. When the Israelites left Egypt, they were led forth by the Almighty to be conducted into the land flowing with milk and honey, which He had promised to their fathers. To use His own expression: "As the eagle teaching her young to fly, and hovering over them, He spread His wings and took them, and carried them on His shoulders: the Lord alone was their leader." (Deut. xxxii. 11, 12.) "All were under the cloud, and all passed through the sea." When they were hungry, He gave them bread from heaven; when they thirsted, He changed the rock into streams of water. "They all eat the same spiritual food, and they all drank the same spiritual drink." Did not God then desire, and desire with earnestness, the accomplishment of His design? And yet, my brethren, "with the most of them, God was not well pleased, for they were overthrown in the wilderness." (1 Cor. x.) Six hundred thousand men marched out of Egypt; only two of these entered the promised land!

This example is applied by the Apostle to the painful subject upon which I am speaking. "Now all these things," says he, "happened to them in figure, and they are written for our correction, upon whom the ends of the world are come. Wherefore, let him that thinketh himself to stand, take heed lest he fall."

Had the doctrine that few will be saved out of all that hope for salvation, been less clearly expressed in God's word, it might have been considered an ingenious device of pious men to terrify the wicked into repentance, and preserve the good from transgressing. But wherever we look at the history of God's providence, we find but too clearly that the number of those who can hope with reason for this eternal blessing, are but a small remnant; to use the figure of Isaias, like the few grapes which are left upon the vine by the gatherers, like the few ears which may be gleaned from the field after the harvest. Abraham alone is called forth from the land of idolators to be rescued from perdition; only seven thousand men, who had not bent the knee to Baal, form the remains of God's religious kingdom in Israel. Tobias alone of the twelve tribes goes up to Jerusalem to worship God; Daniel alone at the court of Babylon observes the stated hours of prayer, when its practice becomes dangerous ; the three young men alone refuse, of all the satraps, to fall before the golden statue of the king. In the gospel, the same disproportion of numbers is foretold of the true followers of Christ. They were reminded that in the days of Elias there were many widows in Israel, but that only the one of Sarepta was saved from famine ; that in the days of Eliseus there were many lepers, but none were cleansed except Naaman the Syrian. They were told that the way of salvation was difficult, and followed by few ; they were assured, in fine, that many are called, but few are chosen! When you consider by whom these awful words were uttered ; that it was by Him who had come down to preach the gospel of peace and reconciliation ; by Him who was blamed for His condescension to sinners and publicans; by Him who bled and died for the redemption of man ;—oh! however painful it may be, we must conclude, that amongst the thousands whom we see around us, flattering themselves with the prospect of salvation, many—too many—will be deluded and disappointed !

And if we contrast the conditions of salvation required by the gospel with the course of life pursued by the generality of mankind, surely we shall not hesitate to acknowledge the justice of the sentence. For if they hope to attain this greatest of blessings, it must only be because they can assure themselves that they are complying with those conditions which have it provided as their reward. Now, as it is certainly revealed that nothing defiled can enter the kingdom of life, so it can only be upon assurance that they will be found undefiled that they can ground their confidence. Does a superficial view of the conduct of Christians in general justify the conclusion that more than a small and chosen portion can entertain it with justice? Is a life of innocence, esteemed by David so rare, that he thinks no one able to stand the judgment of God; declared so extraordinary by Solomon, that he deems it the height of presumption to claim immunity from guilt; pronounced by Job so difficult, that man must be almost equal to the angels to be able to boast of it: is a life of innocence, then, so common in our days, that we can consider the generality of mankind able to found their right to salvation upon its plea? Can any one flatter himself that he has passed through all the dangers of the world without a stain adhering to his baptismal robe; that he has stood all the temptations of his corrupted nature without having once yielded to their suggestions; that among all the words which he has uttered, not one has recoiled, like an unfaithful arrow, upon himself, and wounded his soul; that of all the thoughts which have glided through his mind, not one has been tainted with corruption, and shed a blight upon his innocence and hopes? Oh! must not that man be presumptuous who can flatter himself of all this? Would you reckon him among those that may justly put in a claim to salvation? And must not the number of men who expect salvation on such grounds be exceedingly small?

Well, then, it is not upon a plea of untarnished innocence of life that the great body of Christians can hope for salvation: "For we all have sinned, and do need the glory of God." What hope remains but that we found our claims upon a life of repentance? We trust that we have expiated our offences by penance, and that as often as we relapse during the remainder of our lives, we shall do the same. But when I examine the word of God, and the practice of His servants, I look around in vain for something to correspond, in the lives of those who trust to this plea. I there find the sinner exhorted to turn to the Lord in fasting, in weeping, and in mourning; and reminded, even after his sin has been propitiated, not to rely too securely upon its forgiveness. I see David, after one crime watering his couch with his tears, and begging of God ever more and more to wash him from his iniquities, and cleanse him from his sins; protesting that they were always before his eyes, and that he ever held himself ready for the stripes which His justice might inflict. I see the publican, proposed as a model of repentance, standing without the temple, pronouncing himself unworthy to raise his eyes to heaven; Zacheus, a converted sinner, distributing his whole property among the poor and those he had injured. I see Peter, rushing out from the hall of the high priests to weep for his denial, reckless of the scoffs of those who had so easily terrified him into his offence, and fearless of the danger to his very life, as a follower of Christ. I see Magdalen, contemning the sneers of the Pharisees, and setting at nought the usual decencies of society, and disfiguring her beauty, and spending her substance, and humbling her person, when it was necessary to expiate her guilt, and obtain forgiveness at the feet of Jesus. I see the penitents in the early ages of Christianity, undergoing years of public penance for one offence; prostrate at the doors of the church, soliciting the prayers of the meanest among the faithful; covering their limbs with sackcloth, and sprinkling their heads with ashes; yet, after this, afraid to be received into the community of the Church, for fear that their guilt might be yet unforgiven. I see, in fine, in later ages, many who, for a single transgression, have secluded themselves from the world, emaciated themselves with austerities, passed whole years in prayer and tears; and then, after all, departed from life with fear and apprehension. This is a life of repentance, as portrayed by the word of God and the practice of His saints; and is this so common as to afford a grounded hope that *many* will be saved in consequence of leading it?

Say that this was more than is required; that these penitents did far more than was necessary to regain their innocence. Yet the words which I have quoted are the words of God; the first examples which I have given are approved in Scripture; the practices of the Church were prescribed by the apostles. We must, therefore, suppose either that God requires less now than He used to do in former times, to secure the salvation of a penitent sinner, or that there is little to hope for those who trust to the ordinary repentance of our days. But, be it as you say; if that were too much, something at least has to be performed. Some difference must be expected between the lives of those who have never offended God, and those who have offences to expiate. Their prayers should be doubled, their fasts more rigorous, their circumspection more marked, their deportment more humble. But could we, when looking around us upon the world, for one moment suspect, from any of these signs, that we are living in the midst of men who, conscious of having once forfeited their claim to salvation by sin, are leading a life on which they intend to establish a new title, as a life of true penitents? To this conclusion, then, we are necessarily forced: that the number of those who lead a life of innocence is very small; that the number of those who lead a life of penance is hardly greater. How frightfully small, then, must be the number of the elect, who can only be composed of these two classes?

Another consideration is no less striking and appalling. The gospel describes but two paths which are trodden by men, of very different characters and of very opposite tendencies. "Wide is the gate, and broad is the way that leadeth to destruction, and many there are who enter by it. How narrow is the gate, and strait is the way which leadeth to life, and few there are who find it." (Matt. vii. 13, 14.) It informs us that the way is rugged, painful, and disagreeable; that those who walk in it deny their own wills, take up their crosses, and track the bloody footsteps of a crucified Saviour; that they weep while the world rejoices; that persecutions, and revilings, and calumnies are their portion, as they were of their Master. They are described as men given to prayer, and accustomed to mortify the deeds of the flesh; as men who find no satisfaction in the fleeting pleasures of this world, but, sighing for a better inheritance in a life to come, anxiously wish to be delivered from the body of this death. The law which they follow prescribes that they be meek and forgiving, just and charitable, humble and obedient, temperate and chaste, vigilant and circumspect. All these, my brethren, are definite and marked characteristics, and they determine those who tread the narrow path of salvation. Where, then, are these? Where are the elect of God? Instead of them, we behold the common mass of mankind moving on in one broad undistinguished crowd; all following the same laws, and all seeking the same pleasures. What road, then, do they tread? towards which gate do they advance? I see no thorns upon their path, no ruggedness to hurt their tread. Are they, then, the followers of a mortified and persecuted Leader? I see no tear in their eye, no affliction on their countenance. Are they the disciples of a suffering and crucified Master? I see no apprehension in their looks, no timidity in their steps. Are they the worshippers of a just and terrible God? Oh! my brethren, if the gospel be not a fable, if the words of the Son of God be not vain and empty, who are these but the many that crowd and push one another forward, on the broad and spacious way of perdition?

If, then, they form the bulk of mankind, and have not the characteristics of those who toil up the steep and rugged path of Christian perfection, how awful, how terrifying the conclusion which we must draw, upon the number of those who enter the gate of life!

But why examine this question as if we were sitting in judgment upon the lot of others, while we ourselves are so closely interested in the decision? The number of the elect is but small: all hope to be included within it; but were that the case, it would be great beyond calculation. Many, therefore, are to be excluded: who of us will be among these? The answer is easily made. There is no middle path; we walk already either with the crowd in the wide road, or with the chosen few in the narrow way.

Do you find that your principles form an exception to those of others? Do you perceive that your conduct contrasts strongly with general custom, not merely by the singularity of some actions, but by its undeviating regularity? Have your friends and acquaintances marked you out as peculiar in your strict notions of morality, and your high sense of Christian perfection? Do you find that what gives the world joy, causes you pain; and that while all around you cast themselves upon the earth to take their fill of the pleasures which cross their way, you, like the few chosen soldiers of Gideon, only taste them, as a pilgrim and a passenger, to obtain refreshment and support? In fine, do you, like Elias, feel that you stand alone in the circle where you move, in opposition to all, and scarcely able to meet a chosen few who share your feelings and opinions? If all this be not the case, I leave you to decide to which class you belong. Beware the path in which you tread: if it be that of the multitude, it is the path of perdition.

One delusion only, my brethren, can remain. Does not the immense number thus included in the dreadful doom, secure them against punishment? Does not the frightful scale on which vengeance is to be taken, preclude the possibility of its completion? Can we suppose that the

Almighty will condemn such a vast multitude of His favourite creatures to eternal suffering? Alas! my brethren, did He hesitate to strike the rebellious in the wilderness by the sword of the Levites, or to exterminate them by the bite of the serpents, because tens of thousands were to be included in the punishment? Did He hold suspended the waters of the Red Sea over Pharao and his army, because the flower of a great kingdom were there, and not rather relax His hand, and bury in the abyss the monarch and his host? Did He close the floodgates of heaven, when He calculated the millions who would be swept from existence by the flood, and not rather put in the balance against them all, the little family of the just in the ark? No, my brethren, the whole world He has told us is preserved but for His elect; the wicked are of no value in His sight. He counts not their number; He only weighs their crimes. They are but the defilement of creation. He represents Himself in Scripture as taking hold of the ends of the earth, and shaking them from its face like the dust of a garment. (Job, xxxviii. 13.)

Well, my brethren, may you ask with the disciples, "Who then will be saved?" (Matt. xix. 24.) He will be saved, my brethren, who, knowing that salvation is only a gift of God, and includes final perseverance, the greatest of all His gifts, earnestly asks with the young man in the gospel, with a disposition to fulfil whatever is enjoined him: "Good Master, what shall I do that I may have life everlasting?" (ib. 16.) He shall be saved, who, remembering that, according to St. Peter, even "the just man shall scarce be saved," (1 Pet. iv. 18) never feels too secure, but endeavours to work out his salvation with fear and trembling, and strives to render his calling and election sure. In fine, he shall be saved, who, detaching himself from the principles of the common mass, endeavours to ascend the mountain of the Lord with the clean of hands and the pure of heart. *He* shall receive a blessing from the Lord, and mercy from God his Saviour. When he shall see the wicked perish, he shall not be moved; when he sees the separation between the good and the bad at the last day, he shall not be terrified. The narrow path which he has followed in life, will have led him to the spacious pastures of eternal enjoyment; and he will hear with raptures the words addressed to the small number of the elect: " Fear not, My little flock, because it has pleased My Father to give you the kingdom."

SERMON XII.

On the Hatefulness of Sin.

PSALM x. 6.

"He that loveth iniquity, hateth his own soul."

It were well for us, my brethren, if sin could be made to appear in its proper figure before our eyes. Could we strip it of its many disguises, of its deceitful colourings, and in its own deformity parade it through our public places, or could we introduce the faithful who hear us into its hideous secrets, and reveal to them its enormities such as they are presented to the view of God and His holy angels, I believe the pulpits from which we address you might be cast aside, as no longer useful, and the tribunals of penance closed up, as no longer necessary, and the warning voice of Christ's Church to sinners be silenced, as unseasonable and unjust. So hateful would sin appear, and so loathsome in the eyes of man, that none would be found to commit it. And for this purpose I would not desire that we should be taken, as Ezechiel was in vision, to some opening in the wall, where we should see "every form of creeping things, and of living creatures, the abominations and all the idols" of men's passions, and old and young worshipping them and serving them; (Ezec. x. 10) in other words, that we should surprise the libertine in the midst of his excesses, or listen to the discourse of the profane, when unconscious of being overheard, or pry, in their unguarded moments, into the machinations of the corrupt. Neither would it, methinks, be necessary to sound the depths of iniquity which lie in the souls of such determined and lost transgressors, so to comprehend the mystery of evil in its uttermost depravity, unchecked by conscience or moral feeling, unmitigated by any lingering of virtuous regret, abandoned, in fine, by God, to the mercy of every passion, and the defilement of every vice. No, my brethren, the sight of such crime and more consummate iniquity would not be requisite to excite our horror and disgust. It would be quite sufficient if each of us could contemplate his own soul, such as it is when defiled by sin. Yes, even such ordinary, petty transgressors of the commandments of God, as we who have sinned indeed often, but yet so that men have not known nor accounted it—even we, did the light of God hold up a mirror to our eyes, while under the imputation of guilt, and show us ourselves, such as He beholds and considers us, would shrink in terror from the sight, and, in the energetic language of my text, would hate our own souls.

But perhaps these words, if well considered, will be found to bear a two-fold sense ; each worthy of most serious meditation, and pregnant with saving instruction. For, first, they may be taken in this sense, that he who loveth iniquity, that is, sin, is thereby guilty of grievous injury to his soul ; and, consequently, proves himself to hate it. The lover and doer of iniquity is thus declared the enemy and hater of his own precious soul. Or they may not improperly be understood as I applied them just now, to declare, that he who loveth sin and iniquity, must come to feel a loathing and hatred of his very self. We will try, with God's blessing, to meditate on those two different views of the same matter. For the two will bring us to one conclusion, of the enormity and hatefulness of sin.

If you knew a person who boasted greatly of his friendship for another, and even overwhelmed him with expressions of his affection; yet you knew and saw that he was, in every possible way, spoiling him of his substance, and reducing him to a state of miserable poverty; if you knew that, by every act, he was estranging from him his sincerest friends, and preparing to leave him, at his greatest need, without their support or assistance; that, in fine, he was many ways aiming at nothing short of his total destruction, and was bringing him within the reach of a most ignominious end;—I ask you, would you consider that man anything less than the bitterest enemy; the most cruel, yet the most refined, hater of his pretended friend? Worse than the gall of dragons and the poison of aspics, you would pronounce the profession of such a treacherous monster. But now, if so it be, that whoever commits sin actually does all this to his own invaluable soul, what more proof can we require of his cruel hatred towards it, which more than all the world else he ought to love?

But, my brethren, will not many listen with incredulity, when I say that the sinner, by his transgression, always robs and despoils himself, and thereby suffers loss? The avaricious and unjust in his dealings heaps up his hoards, and has the homage of the world at his feet. "The gold of Arabia seems given to him, and his glory seems exalted above Lebanon." The man of pleasure, who "sitteth in ambush with the rich in private places that he may kill," that is, seduce, "the innocent," (Ps. ix. 8) is he not "praised in the desire of his soul, and blessed" (3) by the world, as attaining possession of all his wishes? Does not the proud man obtain consideration, and the artful man credit, and the flatterer patronage, and the detractor favour, and the scoffer at holy things willing listeners? Is there any other that so little prospers as the righteous, who is "derided in his simplicity?"

I answer you not that all these gains will one day be shown to have been real and most grievous losses. I will allow them to be fairly thrown into the balance against the injuries inflicted upon the poor soul when plundered by sin. When you read of Adam's transgression, are you not tempted to indignation? He possesses a paradise of delights, with the command of all its delicious produce, with one exception; he possesses an exemption from every pain and infirmity; he possesses the gift of immortality; his happiness is unclouded by the fear of death. All these he, in one moment, renounces: for what? For the momentary gratification of a foolish desire; for the one forbidden fruit which looks fair to the eye; and for the uncertain prospect of greater happiness, held out to him by the tempter. Fool, you exclaim, that he was! to throw away present, sure, and splendid advantages, for such a mean and such an uncertain exchange! And yet, in all that I have enumerated, he lost nothing comparable to what we daily, by sin, tear from our soul's possession, and fling for ever away.

For all these were but earthly and temporal blessings, while we reject spiritual and heavenly gifts.

Oh! that I had words, my brethren, to describe or bring down to your comprehension, the treasures of grace and the inheritance of glory which we renounce by sin. A soul just regenerated by baptism, upon which its Creator, looking down with complacency, sees His image and likeness stamped fresh, and as yet unsoiled; in which the Son beholds the fruits of His redemption full and ripe, without the smallest blight or taint; in which the Holy Spirit dwells in the plenitude of grace and divine favour; is a thing almost too precious for this world of iniquity to be allowed to hold. It deserves a sanctuary apart, in which to be enshrined from the approach of the profane, and from the very look of the wicked. It should be served, as in truth it is, not by an earthly priesthood, but by the ministry of angels. For it is an ark of divine covenant, far more beautiful to His eyes, far more valuable in His estimation, than the one which Moses made of setim-wood and gold. That soul is the bride of the Lamb, decked out with a magnificence of precious gifts, becoming her rank. She is the beloved, the darling child of the Most High, and, as such, entitled to an inheritance in His kingdom, rich beyond calculation, vast beyond measure, enduring beyond all computation of time. God having repaired in it, as far as possible, the mischiefs of original transgression, is willing, and intends, to bestow upon it, every good thing it can require to make it happy. As its period of probation here below advances, it receives fresh instalments of its rich inheritance, in the knowledge of God, in His love, in the use of His sacraments, so that nothing remains that He can do for it, till the time shall come to accomplish its happiness, by taking it into His eternal rest.

Now all these privileges, blessings, and rights, present and future, the lover of iniquity deliberately casts away. I say deliberately. Not that he calculates in the heat of his passion, but still it is with full previous consciousness of their worth, and of his interest in them. He is as Esau, who, when fatigued and hungry, in exchange for a mess of pottage, renounced his birthright with the glorious inheritance of promises made to his fathers. He is like the prodigal, who gives up the advantages and joys of his father's house, for the chance of pleasure, in the riots of a distant land. Each was borne away by the impulse of passion, but each lost, notwithstanding, the blessings which he before enjoyed.

When Adam transgressed, it was at least against the chance of our improved condition, that he threw his stakes. He entertained hopes of a sublimer happiness, by being as a god, knowing good and evil. There was a bold presumption in the cast, but there was no consciousness that he was flinging himself into the arms of misery. He knew not well what death might be; he had not seen it. He was not aware that there was another earth beyond the bounds of Eden, which produced thorns and briars, into which he could be banished. But we, when we offend God, and resign His gifts, understand to the full the terms of our bargain. We know too well what that death is which becomes our due; we know well what the place will be to which we shall be consigned, when driven from this miserable substitute for our lost Paradise.

See, then, this wretched soul, a few moments ago so comely, clothed in righteousness, laden with spiritual gifts, endowed with most abundant graces, in dignity little less than the angels, and crowned with glory and honour, able to hold up its head before God, and be caressed by Him as a child, entitled to look up to the heavens in all their splendour and say, "Ye are mine,"—see it, by one spontaneous act, disfigured and defaced, as though it had been plunged from that moment into an ocean of destructive evil, and drawn thence, base and poor, naked, trembling and hiding itself at the voice of God, degraded to a lower condition than that of things devoid of reason, without power of defence, without a plea of mercy, without a title of grace, stripped of the very name of God's child, divorced for ever from His love, to wander like Cain from before His face, without a home or an inheritance! But yet, not without some inheritance.

He has exchanged, he has not barely renounced, what he enjoyed. He has acquired new possessions, new titles, new rights. He is now "a child of wrath," instead of being, as before, a child of grace. If before, he had the abundant good things of his father's house, he has now the husks of swine in his chosen master's bondage. If he had a place prepared from him in heaven, a throne of light and glory, "Topheth is now prepared for him, prepared by the king, deep and wide. The nourishment thereof is fire and much wood: the breath of the Lord, as a torrent of brimstone, kindling it." (Isa. xxx. 33.) And now let me ask you, did the robbers who met the wayfarer between Jerusalem and Jericho, robbed him of all his goods, stripped him of his fair apparel, and disfigured and disabled him with wounds, leaving him half dead, did they act towards him with a hatred less deadly than we have shown to our souls, every time we have so plundered, and reduced them to utter wretchedness by sin? Could any other being give proofs of bitterer hatred to them, than we ourselves do thus display?

A most glorious prerogative of the innocent and pure soul, is the friendship and favour of God. It is the highest point of ambition to which we can aspire here below. The title we have already seen belonging to the sinless soul, as the child of God, necessarily brings with it the right to a familiar intercourse with Him, and a high place in His favour. It entitles us to His protection, under the care of His special providence, in all that relates to our salvation, and, with due subordination, in the interests of our worldly welfare. It confers the right of being favourably heard of Him, whensoever we present Him our petitions in prayer. "The prayer of the just man is the key of heaven." (St. Aug.) He has special portion in that solemn promise, that whatever is asked in the name of Christ, shall be granted unto us. Beyond these there is a degree of familiarity too inward and too sacred to be apprehended, save by those who have experienced it,—a communion of affection between the soul and God, in holy meditation, in the retirement of religious solitude, and particularly in the partaking of the blessed Sacrament. In the days of our innocence, and in an inferior degree, perhaps, in those of our repentance, we have felt what it was to consider God our friend. He seemed to speak to us almost audibly: we felt that He heard us in our very interior, when we poured forth warm protestations of love and unalterable fidelity. We rose from prayer refreshed, cheerful, and confident. We needed to repress our ardour for combat with our enemies and His, so sure were we of victory under His protection. If we turned in devout colloquies to our blessed Saviour, it was "as one friend speaketh to another;" with a familiarity of address and a sensible affection, which sprung from the consciousness of possessing His favour. We seemed to have Him present when we dwelt upon the most touching incidents of His life; those especially in which most He manifested His love for man: and then, "were not our hearts burning within us," when we heard His words to us, and "knew Him in the breaking of bread"? (Luke xxiv. 35.) How unbounded did His love then seem to us, and how precious beyond all the treasures of the earth! and how sincere and how fervent was our return!

Ah! thus it was with us until we sinned, and in an instant how all was changed! The heavens became to us as brass, hardened against our prayer, and impenetrable to our desires. The throne of God seemed enveloped in darkness; and thunder-clouds of anger, that murmured threats of vengeance, rolled between us and His holy place. The face of our once dear Saviour was changed upon us, and was not as yesterday and the day before. If we had courage to look upon Him, there was anger on His brow; He seemed to reproach us for our perfidy; He looked more like our judge than our dearest friend. Our devotion was fled; our hearts were barren and parched; thoughts of love would not return; the happy hours of intercourse with God were changed into times of heaviness and loathing, the sacraments into objects of dread; and we were left in temptation without confidence, in danger without support, in the performance of good actions without pleasure and fruit. Where before we felt a security of a heavenly guardianship over us, our way became dark and lonely; where before we experienced a remunerating hope that our actions were noted down for our future recompense, conscience told us that no good angel any longer took that care of us. Our soul was changed into desolation and a spiritual wilderness. Happy we, if, profiting by the visitation of this inward sorrow, we lost no time in seeking again the Friend that we had lost! Happy if, like Peter, the reproachful look of our good Master, whom we had just renounced, aroused us to a sense of our guilt, to tears of repentance, and to a lasting reconciliation with Him!

But thrice wretched if, like Judas, not content with having given up the friendship of our God, and most loving Redeemer, we remained in our guilt, and impenitently rushed upon the last and crowning act of hatred which sin displays, the infliction of murder upon our own souls!

"The sting of sin is death;" a sting which, scorpion-like, we drive into ourselves. For, as the favour of God is the life of the soul, we extinguish the one when we abandon the other. But death came not into the world alone; it came accompanied by a train of infirmities and diseases, which are its harbingers, not only to announce its approach, but to prepare its way. And so does the death of the soul, which sin inflicts, bring with it a host of evils, that dispose all things for the last and complete dissolution of the second death, the eternal loss of heaven.

As our bodies, even when full of health and vigour, have lurking in their very constitutions the germs of disease, ready to break out at every fitting opportunity, and take, according to this, a varied form ; so is the soul the seat of every evil propensity, hidden, indeed, so long, as the living power of grace keeps them in subjection. But if, even when controlled by its superior strength, they are as chained enemies that rebel and ever strive to acquire mastery and dominion, what must they be when sin has expelled from the soul the grace and power of God? Their irons are now broken, and eager to make up for the time they have been kept in bondage—finding, too, the soul an unprotected prey at their mercy—they run riot within it, spreading everywhere waste and devastation. Every irregular desire is lord of the moment, till chased by some wickeder and baser usurper. The soul, which before used to govern, is now the slave, under the command of these thousand tyrants. And if this state, of abandonment to the passions, be suffered to strengthen into habitual vice, every faculty, every power of man becomes tainted with its respective evil. The heart, once pure and simple, changes to corrupt and designing, full of evil desires, and of devices to gratify them ; the imagination is abandoned to every train of foolish or wicked thoughts which happen to enter it ; the reason becomes perverted, to the disregard of the awfullest truths, and the belief of the vainest delusions ; the will gradually loses its desires of good, till it actively joins in the pursuit of what is bad ; and only one faculty in the entire man, memory, remains faithful to the trust of its great Giver, and faithfully, too faithfully, treasures up the recollections of the past. Thus does the poor victim, first plundered of all its rich possessions and glorious inheritances, stripped of God's favour and friendship, with the deadly knife that has inflicted a mortal blow standing in its heart, stagger on a few more paces in its blind career, and then falls heavily, to rise no more. Yes, that sin, so brief in its duration, so unsatisfactory in its expected results, was yet a stroke of death, begun here indeed, but to be completed by a hand of juster power. For the word of God has assured us, that after this first, the sinner shall suffer a second and an eternal death.

In what a strange and most unnatural state must the soul be, while placed between these two events, dead in truth before God, but waiting another and a final destination! It would be a frightful and a hideous spectacle, were one who had been laid in his shroud to return to the functions of life, yet so that he should ever bear about him the traces of his dissolution: to see his glazed, unmoving eye, that never sparkles with tidings of joy, nor moistens at the deepest distress, and features devoid of passion or expression, that relax not into a smile of pleasure; to touch the hand ever damp and icy, and find the heart motionless and cold; and yet, to behold this living death partake in the business and pastimes of men, and speak their flattering speeches, and talk of its feelings—oh! how it would poison every joy in which it mingled, and how men would shrink and shroud themselves from the hateful apparition! Not less odious, unnatural, and disgusting, to those beings that can behold the spiritual part of man, must that soul appear, which is truly dead to God as the corpse in the grave is to man, yet animates a human frame, and drives it through the functions of its worldly life, and discharges the other offices of a rational being. A soul without an impulse of grace, without a throb of love for God, without a noble emotion, without an aspiration to heaven, without a virtuous desire, yet holding place among living men, is an animated corpse, a hideous spectre haunting the abodes of men.

If, then, God may ask you, what more He could have done for your soul, to prove how much He hath loved it, may He not likewise ask, what more *you* could have done, if you had wished to display your hatred? Could you have more spitefully despoiled it, or more infamously degraded it, or more treacherously discredited it, or more barbarously destroyed it? And after you have, with your own hand, thus piteously reduced it and disfigured it, do you think that when you look upon it you will ever again love it?

When sin has been so far and so long indulged, that he who doeth it may justly be called a lover of iniquity; when he has, for the time at least, put aside all idea of abandoning his vices, and returning to a course of severe virtue, he must make up his mind to encounter a perpetual storm of reproach within himself, or to acquire an artificial and deceitful peace. But, before he can arrive at this latter state, if it be possible to him, he must needs pass through a series of painful sufferings, inflicted by the lashings of remorse. It is seldom that the consummation of iniquity arrives so early as to extinguish the power of conscience before it has attained its growth. In general, it is not till years of dissipation, or other transgressions, have hardened the heart, that this state of dreadful calm can be procured.

What a useful, but dreadful, illustration of this, the words of the impious Jezabel give! Perhaps no woman was ever more shameless or more successful in a career of crime than she; none had shown herself less encumbered by the fear of God or of man. Yet, wishing to throw the bitterest taunt and curse upon her enemy, though at that moment dressed out and painted, so to prove that the vanity of the world was still in full possession of her unrepenting heart, she addressed Jehu in these words, which she never could have uttered had her own experience contradicted them: "Can there be peace for Zambri, who hath slain his master?" (4 Kings, ix. 31.)

But, my brethren, it might be worth while to consider, of the thousands who betray no symptoms of remorse, or conscientious misgivings, how many really enjoy even a temporary peace, or can refrain from contemplating their own soul with feelings of abhorrence? Could the walls of this or any other church speak, they would probably answer, "None." The ministry of penance, so often discharged in them, presents too many instances of men who have spent years in every species of excess, who to the world appeared cheerful, happy, and unvisited by compunction, yet have come at last to reconcile themselves with God, unable, as they tell you, longer to bear the burden of their own hearts. They will assure you that they have essayed every art to stifle the voice of conscience, but in vain. They have avoided all that could recall them to their duty—the hearing and reading of God's word, attendance on His worship, the company of the virtuous. They have associated with none but libertines like themselves; they have escaped from every moment of serious thought; they have plunged into one excess to drown all remorse of the preceding. But it was to no purpose. There was a sting, a barbed arrow in their hearts, which defied all their efforts to extract it. They loathed themselves, they hated their very souls, till, in a moment of generous resolution, springing from their very despair, they arose to return to God, whom they had lost.

That there may be a few, very few, who have at length smothered all moral sense, cannot be denied; but far more fearful than that of others is their fate. It is only when the last seal of reprobation has been set upon them, that they reach this fatal darkness. When it has come, a terrible retribution is often at hand. The physician hails it not as a salutary symptom, when the patient feels the pain, which his inflammatory disorder caused him, suddenly cease. It is a fatal gangrene that has assuaged and succeeded it. The heart of the wicked is compared in Scripture to a raging sea. Now, the seaman dreads much more than the continued storm, the fearful lull that suddenly interrupts it, when the sea boils up in silence, and the wind that was in the heavens is hushed. He knows that a furious outbreak of the tempest will instantly succeed, and threaten, in earnest, the destruction of his bark. They are compared to mountain torrents that pass swiftly through the valleys. When you have followed one such in its course, and have seen it ever fretting and boiling in tumult and noise, then have observed, all at once, its uproar cease, and its waters, though gliding with equal rapidity, yet flowing sullen, dark, and deep, did you not understand that a few steps further would show you it shooting over some ledge of rocks, to be dashed to foaming fragments in the abyss below? This state, then, of calm is but a more awful judgment, the proof that the store of mercies, of which the calls of conscience are generally the last, has been at length dried up.

But observe, I pray you, the strong expression employed by the Apostle to describe the way by which this callousness of the heart is attained. They are no lenitives, no opiates that procure it; he describes it as a searing of the conscience with a hot iron, (2 Tim. iv. 2) a deadening of its sensibility by a painful operation. Much will they have suffered who attain this awful state. For, in all the word of God holds good: "There is no peace for the wicked, saith the Lord."

The peculiar office of conscience is to draw attention towards ourselves, and make examination how we stand with the duties of which it admonishes us. So long as we can face this inward monitor with readiness, or at least without grievous reluctance, so long shall the examination to which it leads us be a source of comfort, though not unmingled with reproach. But when it drags us unwilling before its tribunal, and forces its exposures on our reluctant minds, it must surely lead to a sickening view of spiritual ills and sores, that will not bear the light.

What, in fact, will such a sinner discover to make him love his wretched soul? So long as he looks around him, he sees proofs of the esteem and good report which he bears among men. But within there is no deceit; he is conscious that if men could see the corruption that stares him in the face, they must despise and hate him. Can he who does see and know it then, forbear to despise and hate himself? He remembers the time when the sight or thought of iniquity was hateful to him: would he not have then hated it as he now sees it in himself? And is he not yet one and the same individual? He feels that however lost to principle himself, the sight of crimes in others, similar to his own, fills him with disgust. In very justice must he not turn that disgust upon himself? It may be thought, perhaps, that pride will be sufficient to quench these feelings. But pride craves daintier fare than the corruptions of the sinner's heart. It looks abroad for something without itself wherewith to be flattered. It finds its nourishment in that gratification which the world's applause can give it. But if a choice could be given to the proud reprobate, of one object upon earth, which he might utterly and for ever forget, believe me, my brethren, his very pride would make that choice fall upon himself.

When driven home upon his own heart, by the very weariness of his evil life, when unfitted through disappointment or indisposition, or any other cause, for the excitement of sin, and brought into unwilling contact with his own thoughts, what a desolation, what an unlovely wilderness does he find! Enough, perhaps, of former cultivation, to show the hopes of early care disappointed; enough of ruin, to show the labour of years spent upon building up his mind by virtuous education, overthrown; enough of generous emotion, to curse his present state; all the rest a blank, uncheering waste, like the cities which the Lord overthrew, once fair as the land of Egypt to them that came down from Emath, but now a scorched and blackened plain, and fetid pools. Such is his soul : shall he not be forced to hate it ?

The night will come, with its silence and gloom, when the voice of the timbrel and the giddiness of the dance have passed away. The burning head will roll in sleepless anxiety upon the pillow, the ever-invisible monitor will sit beside him, and in spite of every effort to repel, will recount the misdeeds of the day, its victims, its mispent time, its wasted opportunities, its worthless conclusion ; and he must fain listen, and consider them, and pronounce condemnation upon them. They are the deeds of his own soul, and shall he refuse to hate it?

The hour of prayer will come, when from even worldly motives he must stand before the face of God. A touching visitation seems to reach him. He remembers himself to have once known and loved Him, and he desires again to find Him. He sees, from the recollection and devotion of all around him, that they have found Him in His temple; but though he knows Him to be there, he cannot feel His presence. He seeks Him where before he used to find Him—in his own interior. But though it be that God of whom David said, that whoso descended into hell should find Him there, yet in his soul he finds Him not. And shall he forbear to hate that soul?

In fine, the days of sickness and sorrow shall come, uniting in themselves the offices of every other season of remorse, the solitude of retirement, the silence of night, the warnings of religious visitations. The separate charges which these have made, they will sum up in one comprehensive indictment, and force him to hate and abhor his own soul, till he curse the hour which called it into existence. The end is now come; he feels there can be no delay: there is no more room for him in God's works. They, by His ordinance, in a concert of richest harmony, give Him praise and honour, from the angel that sings hosannas day and night, to the insect that chirrups in the grass; his soul, unblessing and unblest, is as a dissonance that harshly jars in the universal accord. It is time it should be silenced.

All Nature obeys its Creator's command, moving in the paths He hath appointed, and keeping fair order in all He hath decreed; from the sun that each day commences his course like a giant, to the hyssop that creepeth on the wall: this soul wanders from every track enjoined it, and thwarts and deranges the constituted plan. It is time it be removed. All the works of God's hands are good and fair in His eyes, without blemish in their respective degrees: this soul is a dark blot, a stain upon them, a hideous deformity, a marring of God's works. It is time it should be effaced. Thus must his conscious guilt oblige him to feel, and to see himself such as he is, abhorred by God, and hated by the only one on earth who inwardly knows him—himself. And when thus self-convicted, as a reproach, a burthen, an ill-placed deformity in creation, what remains for him but to expect, in silent despair, when the Almighty, wearied with the sight, even as he is himself, shall crush him beneath His foot, as he would himself a noisome insect that crawls upon his floor?

Hateful, then, beyond all earthly deformities, is this

monster of sin. I have not spoken to you of its essential evil, of its treason and outrage to the Divine Majesty, nor of its treatment of the Son of God, nor of its ingratitude, nor of its madness, nor of the punishment to which it is foredoomed. I have confined myself within a narrow portion of the subject, that of describing its havoc within the soul, and the devastation which it produces in all that is good within. If in so doing I shall seem to have aught exaggerated, what a picture, I may ask you, would have been drawn, had all these other frightful accessories been brought into the composition? But no, my brethren, it is impossible to exaggerate or overdraw the ugliness and hatefulness of this baneful evil. God, who has made the heart for love, might have justly made it incapable of hatred, had He not permitted sin to defile the world. It is the only lawful object of our detestation here below. It is a monster, the only one in creation: how wretched to foster it in one's very heart! If, unhappily, you still retain it there, in God's name banish it for ever. And remember that if he hateth his own soul who loveth iniquity, he who hateth this shall be found truly to have loved his soul unto life eternal.

SERMON XIII.

On Death.

Gen. iii. 19.

"Dust thou art, and unto dust shalt thou return."

And what is there, you will perhaps say to me, in those here present, that can recall to your mind these bitter words, or suggest them as a theme for fitting instruction? Are we not mostly young, are we not healthy, are we not cheerful and gay? Have we not laid out long plans for future enjoyments, saying, " to-day or to-morrow we will go into such a city, and there we will tarry a year, and will traffick, and make our gain;" (Jas. iv. 13) or take our pastime, and after so many years will return again? Are not we the generation which hath made a covenant with death, that he disturb not our pleasures, with his mocking images, nor discompose our speculations with his superstitious terrors? Have we not velvet palls to cast over our biers, that the unseemliness of death may be transformed into pomp; have we not banished the "holy field" of our last repose from the midst of our dwellings, and changed it into a garden of pleasaunce in our suburbs, whither we may resort for recreation or exercise, and know nothing of the nearness of the grave, except from the richer vegetation which it has caused, or the classical monuments it has inspired to delight us? Come we not of that cunning race which hath invented a thousand new arts to prolong life, contrived ten thousand artifices to exclude dangers to our health, and perfected the science which restores it, till we have bound the angel of death in a short chain, and can unclench his gripe from his victim's very throat? And is it to us, so full of life, and spirits, and hope, and promise, that you come with such frightful warnings, and such unseasonable instruction, to tell us that *we* are dust, and must return to dust? Yes, my brethren, even unto you. For to the old and decrepit, the feeble and the sickly, the voice of Nature sufficiently preaches this lesson, reminding them of their mortality: it is to the youthful, the strong, the thoughtless, the secure, that religion sends us to proclaim that they too are dust, and to dust must soon return.

In these few words, preserved like a broken tablet among the fragments of the world's earliest history, how many solemn lessons are recorded! How feelingly are therein expressed the fall of human nature from its first holiness and dignity, the anger of God against sin, and His irrevocable punishment thereof, and the unrepaired damages it inflicted upon the constitution, and, as it were, the essence of His noblest work! How are the banishment from a paradise, and the inheritance of thorns and briars, the loss of the tree of life, and the acquisition of the grave, the forfeiture of a heaven, and the destination to a hell, comprised in this short memorial of the baseness of our origin, and, humanly speaking, the hopelessness of our end—dust in life, dust in death! And with these two simple words, I will content myself this day, and will trace the working of this twofold denunciation;

and we shall find that death is written upon every stage, upon every action, upon every hope of our lives, as plainly, as assuredly as it will one day be read upon our tombs.

Truly a mine of rich and precious meditations is the grave! and the churchyard is a field wherein is hidden a pearl of great price, for those that apply themselves to its discovery! Take but a handful of its mould, and consider whereof it may be composed. It was once, peradventure, a heart that throbbed or writhed, as yours may do, with the best or most evil passions, the centre of much love, and joy, and hope; and withal of much grief and hate, and disappointment; something as warm, as bounding, as lively, as uncontrolable, as is now beating within *your* bosoms. Into that dust too have been resolved, eyes which once sparkled like yours with expression, with intelligence, with life; tongues that cajoled the multitude, or charmed the circle of domestic listeners; features which the ancient chisel would have transformed into marble, that their impress might be unperishing; athletic frames and well-built limbs which seemed to defy the power of destruction. And see what they have all become, since all Nature has been at work upon them! The worms of the earth have curiously dissected them, the strange alchemy of their own disharmonious elements has transmuted their very substance, the winter's damp and summer's heat have macerated and dissolved them, the rains of heaven have filtered through them : till crushed, and crumbled, and mouldered, they have been turned up as dust, to be fanned abroad by the four winds of heaven. And from this change may we not augur another more feelingly involving ourselves? Will not future generations moralize over our scattered remains, even as we now do over those of our forefathers? Will not they say, those graceful forms which in those days inspired such admiration, and appeared to all who saw them worthy of immortality, what were they, after all, but dust? Those supple and powerful limbs which bore the youth of that age through all the bright and interesting scenes of their time, what did they prove in the end to be, but dust? Yes, my brethren, such shall we too be shown to be no less than the generations that have preceded us, slime of the earth, that which ye tread upon with scorn, that which ye shake as defilement from your skirts —dust—dust!

We fly, I know, habitually from these reflections; but in spite of ourselves they will not be shaken off. This ground-work is, indeed, within ourselves, the savour or seasoning of death, which this body of ours hath in it from its formation in the womb, accompanies it through life, and must, in its various evidences and increasing manifestations, too often remind us of the frail and worthless materials whereof we are composed. What else are our almost daily indispositions—our hourly ailings—our perpetual uneasiness in one part or other of our system, but germs and out-buddings of that noxious creeping parasite, death; which entwines itself the stronger round us in proportion to our very growth, and will one day suck out the last sap of life from within us?

In fact, strange as it may seem, the principle of death penetrates so completely the operations of life — the complicated machinery by which these are conducted, tends so essentially to fret itself in pieces, that we can hardly conceive the body's constitution before the fall, nor how it ever existed otherwise than as destined to dissolution. In other words, the principle of vitality is the principle of death; and sufficient cause of our final end, is involved in the simple fact of our having lived. The flood of life, which bounds so briskly through our frame, diminishes at every beat the moments of our existence, and exercises a wearing influence, however imperceptible, upon the channels through which it flows. That shaping power which it possesses of gradually forming and consolidating the bony structure in the infant and youth, which power alone can give consistency and strength to the body, perseveres with obstinacy in its action, after it has ceased to be useful; stiffens and hardens the joints, ossifies the softer textures, and becomes the cause of aged decrepitude, the weakener of the frame, the preparer of its dissolution. That genial heat, which gives to youth its most beautiful glow, and imparts energy and warmth to all its enterprizes, is a fire that cracks and corrodes the walls of its furnace, and disposes it to its final overthrow.

While the operations of spirit know no limit, but are capable of perfectibility without measure, and always go on in the line of their peculiar destination, not contradicting themselves, nor involving their own annihilation, it is precisely the contrary with the body's vital functions. The over-exertion of any organ produces its decay— the palate palls, the eyes are dimmed, the stomach fails, the lungs waste away, the very brain will sear and pine, by the excess of action in those functions whereunto they have been ordained. Their sum is evidently their own overthrow; their strongest effort a fatal blow to their own existence. Justly, then, did the Apostle call this our earthly tabernacle the " body of death ;" inasmuch as it is made up and held together by deadly principles, engaged in constant conflict, which of them shall in the end achieve the destruction of this brittle frame.

And if death is thus "not far from any of us, but in it we may be said to live and move and have our being," neither can we far remove it from our nobler part; for, however unconsciously, the thought, or fear, thereof forms the great moving power of our social and moral existence. A little reflection will convince you that preservation of health, or the prolongation of life, or, plainer still, the delaying of death, is the object which suggests and regulates more than half the changes and movements of your life. If I ask you, what has induced you to leave your native country and domestic hearths, and has brought you to this distant spot; many, perhaps most, of you will answer me, that the delicate health of some member of your family counselled the removal to a more genial climate, or that over-exertion rendered such a recreation necessary, or that the interesting scenes around you sympathize best with your natural temperament. And in all this, what have you done but calculated the chances of adding some years, perhaps only some months, to your own or another's life? It has been the king of terrors that has driven you from your homes, and spurred you forward over seas and mountains, through toils and discomforts, in quest of a longer promise, if not of a longer enjoyment, of life's blessing. And it is this same fear which holds the balance in all your arrangements and deliberations here. The consideration of health shortens or lengthens your proportions of exercise and study, repose and dissipation, to such a degree, that you will reproach yourselves more strongly for having transgressed the rules of prudence than of conscience, in any gratification. And what, too, constitutes the object of half the social arts, but the beguiling of time, and the forgetting that its course is swift; the casting away from memory the proportion of life that is already exhausted; the repairing, by a thousand artifices, the ravages of age; the disguising of the changes undergone in our nearer approaches to the grave? And what so much sharpens the ingenuity of thousands, and gives employment to the industry of millions, as the gratitude wherewith every invention, or production, is received that can remove a suffering or provide a comfort, that can lessen a danger or can add a chance to the frail mortality of our existence? What is the greatest resource of imposture, what makes it such a thriving profession, but the unceasing and trembling anxiety about life, which will make the most sensible men become dupes to the cunning, when they promise them life and health? And thus may we say that industry and commerce, science and art, with their various motives and encouragements, in the end receive their impulse from the love of life, and the anxiety for its prolongation, which are rooted in the affections of all mankind. Hence may we truly conclude, that as our physical, so likewise our moral, being is powerfully under the influence of death; that all which passes in body or mind doth strongly receive its impress and colour from the destructive power; that death is in reality the indefinite, but still necessary, ratio, without which we cannot solve any problem in our twofold existence.

And here, methinks, you might interrupt me with this reproach: You have come to uphold the necessity of always remembering the mortality of our nature; and wherefore, if, as you say, its evidence is always before and within us, so that we may not remove it? Truly, my brethren, it is even so. We are moving and acting all our lives under the influence of this power, but seldom or never is this influence profitable to our souls. And the reason is simple: we look not at these considerations by the light of God. We cannot conceal from ourselves that we are only dust and ashes, but we never act as if we believed ourselves to be so.

This evidence teaches not the strong that all flesh is grass, nor the comely that beauty is as the flower of the field; it checks not their presumption, it chastens not their gait, it lowers not their haughty bearing, it reminds them not that one day under them "shall the moth be strewed, and the worms shall cover them," (Is. xiv. 11) till their warmest admirer would shrink in disgust from their hideous change. It reminds not the rich, as he passes by the poor man, that the same Lord fashioned them both with His hand from the same slime of the earth, and that but a few more years will reduce them both to one condition; it teaches him not to respect him as an equal before God, to love him as a brother before Christ Jesus. It instructeth not the proud of heart, how foolish and groundless is his pride, and how unseemly it is in a thing of clay to raise itself against the potter who shaped it; nor the sensual man, how vile and filthy is the flesh which he serves; nor the violent man, how soon his staff will be broken; nor the ambitious, how quickly they will pass who give him glory, together with him who seeks it at their hands; nor the covetous man, how the time for enjoyment may never come, but his short life be wasted in the pain of gathering and hoarding up. It warneth not the sinner, green and flourishing in his iniquities, that the next passer-by will see him seared and withered; that he is swifter than the running water; that mercy shall soon forget him, and the worms shall be his sweetness, and he shall be remembered no more, but be broken in pieces as an unfruitful tree. (Job, xxiv. 18–20.) And if the thought of our mortal condition produce not these reflections, if it render us not before others meek and charitable, before ourselves lowly and self-despised, before God humble and resigned, of what more use is it than any gloomy speculation of philosophy, or the impression of a melancholy dream?

But there is another stronger motive besides this of self-improvement, for God's having thus written upon and within us, these records of our frailty, leading us to the serious work of preparation. We cannot avoid thinking of death, but it is only to learn how we may fly from it, not how we may meet it. I will not speak of that false philosophy which makes the mind indifferent towards the awful transit. I trust it is not common; at any rate it is but one sort of cowardice, and cannot be called a preparation. Yet this surely ought to be the strongest influence which the knowledge of our nature should exercise, to keep us in a constant and humble mood of watchfulness and readiness, knowing that One standeth at the door and knocketh, and we know not when He will have it opened; to fix our eyes steadily upon our lamps, that they be trimmed when the Bridegroom shall come forth, though it be at the middle of the night; to make us stand ever ready, girt about our loins, expecting our Master, though He should come in the second watch, or in third watch; that so we may be called happy. For, therefore, only are we, in God's holy word, reminded that we are dust, that we may never forget that we shall once more return unto dust.

And having discoursed thus largely of the first part of God's commination to man, it now only remains that I briefly touch upon the second. It is a task at once difficult and painful, to analyze those feelings with which the approach of that last dissolution into our original composition will be viewed, by such as during life have neglected the first portion of their sentence, and refused to take it as warning and preparation against the second. For these feelings must be so modified by the peculiar circumstance of each case, by the sudden or leisurely approach of that moment, by the character of its causes, by the bodily pain which precedes it, by the clearness or dulness of the mind, by the sensibility of the conscience, by the apprehension of God's justice and sin's enormity, that it is impossible to trace a picture resembling every individual, or likely to be approved by the experience of any. But it will not be difficult to specify some general characters of that fearful season, which must be common to all, and must produce some impression upon every unprepared sinner.

First, it must come as a day of bitter and multifarious separation: a separation of the affections and the heart from all that has ensnared and fettered them; from friends, from family, from home, and from the world: a separation of the passions from all that has excited and engaged them; of worldliness from riches, of ambition from honours, of pride from station, of lust from pleasure, of sin from profit: a separation of the body from the soul, being riven, torn, wrenched from it like a poisoned garment, which has eaten and insinuated itself into its substance, till the very spirit had become tainted, as it were, with the corruption of the flesh, and now working torture unutterable in the violence of its final tearing off: and last of all, strange as it may seem, a separation of the soul from God. For though the veil of the flesh is about to be rent in twain, and the barrier of its separation broken down, so that he shall seem to be brought nearer to God than ever he was before, yet will his soul feel within itself none of that pure adhesive power of love which can alone join spirit unto spirit, and will, on the other hand, see all those bonds, whereby it has felt itself some way hanging to Him, snapt insunder; such as the carefulness of His providence, the communion with His Church, the encouragement of His ministers, and the unction of His sacraments.

It will come as a day of curious balancing of accounts, and of a righteous judgment of things. A voice will say to him: "Give an account of thy stewardship, for now thou canst be steward no longer." (Luke, xvi.) Then, presently, he will fall to casting up scores; and against him he will see much wealth, or splendid parts, or lofty station; and opposite to those, he will try to set off the good he has effected by relieving the distressed, by enlightening the ignorant, or by encouraging virtue by example; and he will see on one side a weight as of a thousand talents, and on the other, hardly the dust of a balance; and he will wring his hands in anguish, and exclaim, "What shall I do, for my Lord taketh away my stewardship?" Next, he may calculate the unremitting toil and struggles of a long life, to gain some pre-eminence, or glory, or pleasure; he will measure the unwatered deserts, and the crooked paths, and the rude thorny roads in which he has trodden all his days; and he will compare with these the short intervals of gratified desire, more like the traveller's halt, under the tamarisk-tree in the wilderness, than the repose of contentment; and he will say to himself, striking his breast : " Truly I have been but a sorry usurer to my soul, and have but little understood the ways of peace." He may sum up, too, all the scattered moments in which his passions have been satisfied, and try to join them into a connected estimate of pleasure and happiness ; and he will find a fearful payment already made in the whips and scorpions of conscience, and in those really lasting seasons of remorse, which such instants have only interrupted with their paroxysms of frenzy. And, in the end, he may try to measure the rate and proportion between the mercies and the judgments of God in his behalf : and it will seem to him that His mercy, though stored up for him in huge reservoirs, have been dealt out with such unthrifty liberality, that not a drop remains in reserve for him now; while His judgments, though pent up in small vessels, have been distilled therefrom in such sparing drops, that their stock seems yet unabated, and no way remains to establish the balance with the others, save at once to break the phials upon his head, and drown his soul in their unquenched bitterness.

It will appear a day wherein the whole end of life is summed up, and included ; as the only day for which he hath so long lived. For, as in a race, to use the figure of St. Paul, it matters not who set off most gallantly from the starting-post, nor who bore himself most bravely round the course, nor who was most loudly applauded by the multitude; but, when the goal is near, all this is clean forgotten, and each one stretches forth in eagerness that he may snatch the prize—even so will it be now ; all the past years will seem but as a striving after this day, as a hastening forward towards its decisive effort ; and all that has been done and suffered will only be estimated according to the influence it has upon this crisis. Then virtue, simple and unadorned, shall appear something more lovely and winning than empires and their treasures; and every little action that seems marked by moral excellence, will give sweeter consolation than brilliant achievements. And, on the other hand, how paltry and nothing worth will many passages in his life now seem, upon which, until this moment, he has dwelt with unqualified admiration—how unprofitable all those accomplishments, which have not disposed him for this hour !

Now, sensible how the whole of his life was but intended as a preparation for this one day, he will recount, in the bitterness of his soul, the iniquities of his youth, and the unrepentance of his old age. And as it was thought by the ancients, that men on the verge of death did acquire a sudden sharpening of their faculties and perceptions, so that their last words should have been held oracular and worthy of notable observation, so may we truly say that the last glance over a wicked life must be so quick and penetrating, as to bring forth from a thousand corners and lurking holes, offences and shameful sins, long forgotten and almost lost. There will be a comprehensiveness in that look of the sinner, which will take in at once all the measurements of his iniquities; which will strip these completely of their disguises and concealments, and increase them with all the additional circumstance of ingratitude towards God, and scandal of men; of graces despised and duties neglected; of interior villany by others unseen, and of a thousand hidden aggravations; and there they will all stand between him and his destined goal, closing his prospect of a happy issue, and extinguishing the last spark of hope within his soul. And though we attribute much to exaggeration or enthusiasm which we read, of spectres sometimes surrounding the dying sinner's bed, and of evil spirits haunting visibly his latest hour, yet is there that in memory which can open tombs, and bring forth the forms of many awful witnesses against us, and arm them with torches and scornful looks of vengeance; and there is in conscience a domestic demon, which knows and awaits the fitting time to vex and torture the soul, dressing itself out in such hideous mask as best may suit its mission of particular terror.

But it may be thought that such a representation is contradicted by experience: inasmuch as the last hours, or even days, of the most reprobate are generally passed in a heavy senseless torpor, hardly capable of feeling and reflection, and interrupted only by transitory gleams of consciousness. And yet I doubt whether even so the view is more consoling; whether the indefinite sense of pain, the raving incoherences of the last dream, made up as it must be of fragments from a worthless life, and refreshed by short glimpses of bitter realities, are not more frightful and oppressive than the collected look upon the most appalling dangers. For, we can imagine faintly the condition of a man who, having fallen into a deep water, first plunges and struggles fearfully, astonished and amazed at the obstruction about him; how his ears are stunned by the moanful murmur of the deeps; how his eyes stare upwards at the pale horny light that gleams upon him, how his feet beat about impatiently for a standing place, and his hands grasp and squeeze, in vain, the oozy and slippery element; how his chest and throat gasp and strain in agony, and all the flesh of his body creeps and trembles with exhaustion. Then, when his senses are becoming bewildered, and his perceptions confused, and the holy spark of existence just extinguished, he is borne up by the buoyant spring of life once more up to the surface, and whirled round for a moment above the waters; and in that moment he sees the clear blue sky gazing upon the calm mirror around him, and the green hills, and the pleasant fields, and the habitations of men, all standing quiet and at peace, or he hears the little birds singing in the trees, and the fisherman in his skiff; and all the love of life returns with its images, and seems to tie his soul to the meanest bulrush upon the bank. Then does he stretch forth his hand for help, and utter a faint scream of agony, and takes one long draught of air as he feels himself dragged downwards again, and plunged and tossed more wildly in the pathless deep; and the waters seem now more bitter, and his abandonment more complete, and his life more hopeless, from the renewed images thereof, which he has borne with him to this his final struggle. Even so may we imagine the sinner in those long intervals of fancied unconsciousness, tumbling in the waves of an ill-defined existence, trying in vain to grasp and seize hold thereon by each of his senses, with all his confused recollections, of hideousness and beauty, of pain and delight, of childhood and old age, of virtue and lewdness, swimming around him in the bewilderment of a nightmare; with all the sorrows of domestic mourning days, and the savage hours of youthful debauch, the altar and the gaming-table, the banquet and the charnel-house, staggering before his amazed sense: then comes one of those momentary gleams of recognition, a fitful upflaring of life's lamp, in which a clear view is once more caught of the world and its attachments, the domestic walls, the weeping friends, the tabernacle of the flesh; and withal the consciousness of past evil, and the dread of future uncertainty, the sense of responsibility, and the terror of doom, flash once more upon the mind, and renew all its remorses; yet without the time or power to receive help or comfort: and so again the sense is hurled back into darker and more fantastic dreaming, into a gloomier lethargy, and a more frightful forestaller of death's final sleep.

But to accomplish all, this day will come to many a sinner as a day of doom. Our blessed Lord hath described, with many circumstances of terror, the coming of the last great judgment; yet may we say, that those signs will then appear some way verified in respect of that man's last hour. " For, in the tribulation of those days, the sun shall be darkened;" (Matt. xxiv. 29) being admitted into his chamber only like unto faint twilight, and even that falling dull and heavy on his vexed eye-balls: "and the moon shall not give her light;" changed as she will be for the sullen glimmering of the watch-lamp: "and the powers of heaven shall be moved," inasmuch as all Nature shall reel and stagger with his sickly brain. To his irritated senses, all things will seem unhinged and disorganized, and the distant sounds of life will come to him with such a grating harshness, as if it were the uproar of an universal confusion, and utter overthrow. But these are only the beginning of sorrows; for to them, he knows, will succeed an instant of sudden and eternal change—a shock, as though of a lightning stroke—a suspension, as it were, of one beat in life's pulse—a rending of the sanctuary veil—a resurrection of the spirit; and he will stand an unembodied culprit before a dreadful bar, in full consciousness, but helpless and alone. And there is something truly overwhelming in this idea of a doomsday all to oneself.

We flatter ourselves that at the day of general assize, we who have crept through the world unobserved, shall be able to shrink and conceal ourselves from notice behind the men on whom all will be curious to gaze, and whose enormous crimes will sink our private guilt into insignificancy. But here the entire scene is ordained for one: the hushing murmur of expectation which is excited when the officers of justice, who have a notable culprit in charge, are first seen; the concentrated gaze upon his wan countenance, when he rises at the bar; the deep silence and undivided attention will be for him alone; and here it is the keen, piercing gaze of spirit upon spirit—of angels, who ministered unto him in life—of saints, who walked with him upon earth, intensely bent upon his doom. There he will have to stand face to face with Him who died for him, and who ransomed him with His blood—the Holy One, who hateth iniquity, and who judgeth in righteousness, to answer for all that he has done while in the body. There he will have to stand with all the evidence of the law clear and incontestable against him; accused by his infernal tempers, convicted by conscience, reprobated by all he ever loved, and accursed by Him who made him. And now that all this scene will be no longer a distant event or a vague futurity, applicable to all men, but something at hand, and even at the gates—now that he gazes upon it with all the earnest assurance of immediate completion, and the interest of a personal concernment; that the course is finished, and he just touches the goal, and even above him are moved the palm branch and the fiery sword, and on each is written—" for ever ;" that the road will seem ended, and before him stand unbarred the two gates of life and of perdition, without power of retreat or escape; that the thick separation he once saw, as ye do now, between him and them, has gradually melted away into a thin cloud—a haze—a film—a nothing; and the fear is now become a certainty, that but a few more flutterings of his pulse, and he shall be borne through the one on seraphs' wings, or dragged through the other by infernal chains,—O God! O God! must he not, in the bitterness of that moment, curse the life during which he had forgotten Thee!

You will peradventure have heard, how, in distant lands, the wretch who, through malice or accident, has spilt another's blood, is pursued even to death by the nearest relation of him that he has slain. And we are told, that it is not difficult to recognize those who daily live in fear of the avenger of blood, whose duty it is, by artifice or strength, to strike down his victim when best he may. There is a restlessness in such a one's eye, a keen, searching look at every turn, a measuring back, from time to time, of the way he has trod, and a redoubling of caution at any dangerous pass. But besides, he always goes forewarned and armed, with his lance in his hand, and his target at his back, and his sword girt upon his loins. Knowing that he may at any moment be called to meet his danger, he is resolved it shall not surprise him, nor take him unprepared. Need I apply this parable to you? Need I repeat that there is an avenger, not of blood, but of sin, tracking and pursuing you without ceasing; and, more than in the other case, *sure* of taking you some time at his advantage, and of accomplishing, in your regard, his stern commission? And if so, will not you, too, be always armed and prepared to encounter him? And how? "Remember thy last end, and thou shalt never sin;" and sin alone it is which can make thy last hour bitter and insupportable. This is the whole art of dying well, resolved into that simple precept with which I commenced: Never forget that thou art dust, and that unto dust thou shalt return. Or to sum up in the words of inspired wisdom : " Remember thy Creator in the days of thy youth, before the time of affliction come, and the years draw nigh, whereof thou shalt say: they like me not: before the sun, and the light and the stars be darkened, ... and the dust return unto its earth, and the spirit return to God that gave it." (Eccles. xii. 1, 7.)

SERMON XIV.

An Unprepared Death.

Luke, xii. 16–20.

"The land of a certain rich man brought forth plenty of fruits. And he thought within himself, saying: . . . . . . Soul, thou hast much goods laid up for many years; take thy rest, eat, drink, make good cheer. But God said to him: Thou fool, this night do they require thy soul of thee; and whose shall those things be which thou hast provided?"

The life of man upon earth is but a pilgrimage and a passage. But while in every other state of progress we look forward with eagerness to its termination, the last close of our existence is only an object of dread and aversion. Forced on, by an irresistible hand which grasps us, towards the boundary of our career, we avert our eyes, or endeavour to beguile them with the fading pleasures that cross our path, that they may not contemplate the fatal goal from which our most violent struggles cannot detain us. When this expedient fails, and when the memorials of our mortality cannot be removed, we still use every art to strip death of its terrors, and view it in its mildest form. It was a law established by the ancient Egyptians, that in all their entertainments and banquets, a seat should be reserved for the image of death. But their degenerate posterity soon became wearied of this stern, unyielding monitor. They concealed its shrivelled limbs with drapery, they cast a veil over its ghastly features, and they wove a chaplet round its fleshless brows. Such is *our* practice no less. The rich clothe the tomb with marble, the poor scatter the grave with flowers. The trophy of death thus becomes only an object of curiosity or admiration to the living, and we willingly forget the chill and gloom of its interior, the corruption which rankles and the dust which moulders within its cell. "O death," justly exclaims the wise man, "how bitter is the remembrance of thee to a man that hath peace in his possessions, to a man that is at rest and prosperous in all things." (Ecclus. xli. 12.) But if we are careful to practise these acts of self-deceit, the word of God has been no less careful to provide against it by unsparingly reminding us of our certain fate, and painting it in its proper colours. It tells us that this is the common end of all the sons of Adam, the punishment of their common transgressions, from which no rank, no power, no virtue can redeem us. "One man dieth strong and hale, rich and happy. But another dieth in bitterness of soul without any riches; and yet they shall sleep together in the dust, and the worms shall cover them." (Job, xxi. 23, seq.) It tells us that we are nourishing and caressing our bodies only in order to mature them for a decay at which all senses revolt, "for man is corruption, and the son of man a worm;" (Ib. xxv. 6) that we are instructing and refining our minds, only to prepare a nobler victim for the universal destroyer.

But, my brethren, there is a more important instruction than these in the inspired pages. They teach us to consider the dissolution of this our being as the moment, on whose decision waits an everlasting compensation of good or of evil. It is the gate which leads from a state of probation to one of retribution; it is the day when a final balance is to be struck between our duty and our practice, and a sentence pronounced accordingly, from which there is no appeal. Anxious for a happy result, the Spirit of God raises His voice to exhort us to hold ourselves ever in readiness, that so we may be found watching at its approach. For if any of us, thinking his time is yet far distant, shall continue to occupy himself only in the pursuit of sinful pleasures, "the lord of that servant shall come in a day that he looketh not for him, and at an hour that he knoweth not; and he shall separate him, and appoint his portion with the hypocrites: there shall be weeping and gnashing of teeth." (Matt. xxiv. 50, 51.) To guard against the misfortune of such a surprise, is the great duty of our life: and I will, therefore, propose to your serious consideration two important points: first, to allow ourselves to be surprised by death is the most unpardonable blindness, because we are every moment warned of its approach; secondly, to be found unprepared by death is the most inexcusable madness, because instructed of the dreadful evils which this will bring.

The all-wise Author of our being has been graciously pleased to endow us with a love and tenacity of life, which is necessary to interest us in its preservation. Besides this natural attachment, the world and our passions continually cast their toils over us, and fasten us down on every side to the earth, with a thousand complicated ties. We know perfectly well that this connexion is but temporary and passing; we know that the day must finally come, when a rude hand will tear us from all around us, and number our names with those that are long since forgotten. But this knowledge and conviction are only cold and general impressions; and when at last our term is come, we fancy that it must be premature, because we had not expected it: we complain that we are surprised, because we had been wilfully blind to the approaches of our enemy. Had we looked abroad upon the crowd around us, had we paid attention to the changes which occur in ourselves, had we listened to the voice of religion, we should not have been thus deceived.

You see no reason to calculate that your hour can yet be come. But correct your calculations by those of the victims who daily fall around you. Does not death, the tyrant, year after year, make his unceasing round through the world, sweeping down whole ranks of its inhabitants, and decimating without mercy the rank, the genius, the worth of society? Have you yet discovered that his aim is taken by rule, or that his strokes descend by measure? Have you perceived that there is a certain rotation in which he calls for his victims, and that, till a specific number have been preferred, your turn cannot possibly arrive? Or can you say, " We have entered into a league with death, and we have made a covenant with the grave: when the overflowing scourge shall pass through, it shall not come upon us"? (Is. xxviii. 15.) While "thousands fall at your side, and ten thousand at your right hand," have *you* alone anointed your door-posts with the blood of some mysterious sacrifice, which will charm the angel of death from your dwelling? You, perhaps, have an advantage in your youth and constitution. God grant that it may prove so; but how many, whose spirits were as buoyant, whose vigour was as fresh, whose health was as blooming as yours but a twelvemonth ago, are already numbered with the dead?

Every age, every condition, must contribute its proportion to the annual lists of death, and its victims are already marked, for the ensuing year, from the gay, the healthy, and the young. On what ground, then, can any one amongst us assure himself that he is a solitary exemption, or that he does not stand in the same liability to choice, to which all in a similar position are subject? If the example of the thousands who have been, and who daily are, summoned unexpectedly from the world, is not a sufficient lesson of the necessity of holding ourselves always in readiness for our turn, let the conduct of those who survive afford us instruction. From them we shall soon learn that it must be an infatuation which blinds us, when we reflect not on our approaching end. For does not the aged and decrepit make his plans for the next year, and for many that will succeed it, without once calculating on the innumerable chances, that he will never reach the completion of one? Does not the invalid lay out projects that require years, which he will never see, for their fulfilment, and do you not smile, and pity him when you hear them? Do you not freely judge that every one around you far over-calculates the age which he will reach, or the duration of health which he will enjoy? Do you not then feel and acknowledge that this is a case in which all men are deceived, and in which no one is capable of judging, while his individual interest is concerned? The same is your case.

If you shall ever reach old age, the same fascination will continue to blind you, the same love of life will continue to pass in your mind for an assurance of its continuance; and you will be as unprepared for death, and as surprised at its arrival, as you now would be in the full glow of youth and health. But happy, indeed, must you be, if you have to look so far abroad for experience upon this point. Happy and fortunate must be your portion, if you have passed through life without more domestic proofs of its uncertainty; if you yet see yourself surrounded by all those in whose company you entered life, and with whom you made your first calculations of its probable duration; if the friends of your youth are yet the counsellors of your maturer age. Have you not seen them cut off, one by one, by diseases against which they seemed best secured, or by accidents which had never once entered into your reckoning? And, oh! happier still, if hitherto you have beheld the angel of death, as David saw him on the threshing-floor of Areuna, only unsheathing his sword in the house of your neighbour or your friend. Has, then, the tyrant spared the sanctuary of still more endearing connexions? Has he never broken in upon your most sacred affections, and carried off in triumph before your eyes the object that you valued most—a son upon whom you placed your hopes for the perpetuation of your line, the daughter whose opening charms had most engaged your heart? The course of nature seemed to promise that these should have closed your eyes, and mourned after your bier.

But it is the delight of death to invert this order, to snatch his hostages for our future obedience to his summons from all that we most value, and to give us a lesson where it may best pierce our souls, that no age, that no situation, that no value which we may be to others, can avert the blow suspended over us, when our day is come.

Every hour that we live we are approaching, or drawn, nearer to that fatal term. Our occupations, our amusements, our frame-work, expose us daily to accidents that may hasten it. We daily hear and read of others perishing in circumstances in which there could be nothing dangerous, and in which we have been a thousand times placed; some while travelling in the pursuit of their innocent occupations, by casualties which no prudence could avoid; some in the bosom of their homes, by occurrences which no foresight could have predicted. We instantly remember that we have repeatedly stood in the same situation; sometimes we too have had our narrow escapes. But this recollection only gives ground for a pleasant security, never for a reflection, how frail and brittle a blessing is our life. The delicate formation of our organs, the complicated operations which life requires within us, the conflicting principles which struggle for victory in every throb of our pulse, make its enjoyment still more precious. Almost from our infancy the seeds of our future dissolution begin visibly to unfold. Disease, generated from our own substance, developed with our growth, strengthened upon our nourishment, broods within us, a lurking enemy, slowly but unceasingly filing away the stamina of life, till our constitution is undermined, and we sink unresisting victims of its power. Almost every year we receive some intimation of this constant action. Some complaint every now and then attacks us, occasionally, perhaps, sufficiently strong to excite the alarms or the despair of our friends, at others merely reminding us of our weakness and mortality; while we feel that the slightest additional irritation, perhaps a current of air, had it accidentally played upon us, might have aggravated our disorder, and even rendered it fatal. But these warnings, too, pass over us unheeded and without profit. The weakness and danger of relapse, which they leave behind them, are not considered as any proof that death has gained upon us, and that a few attacks thus repeated may suffice to complete our fall. "Waters," says holy Job, "wear away stones, and with washing, the ground by little and little is washed away: so in like manner Thou shalt destroy man. Thou hast strengthened him for a little while, that he may pass away for ever: Thou shalt change his face, and shalt send him away." (xiv. 19, 20.) While life is yet in its vigour, these warnings are repeated at certain intervals; as it declines, and our danger becomes more imminent, they are more frequently renewed, and at length become completely habitual. But they are hardly the less disregarded on this account. Year after year imprints deeper wrinkles upon our brow: old age gradually impairs our senses, and blunts the power of enjoyment; continual use paralyses the limbs; but, in spite of all, the old man, covered already by the badges of death, totters towards his grave with as little care or reflection, as if he confidently expected some miraculous renovation in his shattered frame.

Oh! blind, indeed, my brethren, must we be, thus to

delude ourselves, and to close our eyes to these evidences, which daily meet us, of our ever-approaching dissolution. You pass not your threshold, but a funeral procession crosses you; you enter not a church, but the monuments of the dead environ you; you tread not the soil, but it is enriched by the ashes of the deceased; wherever you stand, you press the grave of departed empires. Within, a principle of destruction is creeping through your veins; at every step you take, your enemy has gained upon you. The dominion of death is on every side and within you, and yet you feel not that you are in its reach. All around you speaks of death; and it stalks beside you as constant, but, alas! as unheeded an attendant as your shadow. After all this, was it necessary that religion should interfere to remind us of our mortality?

Was it necessary that a prophet should remind man that all flesh is grass, and all his glory as the flower of the field? Was it necessary that the Son of God should so often tell us, that His last visitation will arrive when we least expect it; and that He will come upon us like a thief in the night? Was it necessary that year after year a solemn day should be observed, to remind the children of clay that they are mortals, and that they should be summoned to the foot of God's altar, and be there ordered to remember that they are as weak, that they are as crumbling, that they are as easily dispersed from the face of the earth, as the kindred ashes with which this lesson is written on their foreheads?

If, with all these admonitions, it must be the height of infatuation not to live in the constant apprehension of death, by what name shall we call this blindness, when we reflect upon the dreadful evils attendant on an unprovided death? By an unprovided death, I mean not only that tremendous judgment of God, when, for the public terror of the wicked, some signal sinner is struck down in the fulness of his iniquity; not merely when the impious sensualist, like Baltassar, receives his doom in the midst of his excesses; not merely when the irreligious scoffer is struck, like Herod, by the angel of God, while profaning and bringing blasphemy on the name of his Creator. These are the thunderbolts laid up in the "storehouse of God's wrath" for rare and terrible lessons; and yet His justice daily surprises unprepared and unthinking Christians. It surprises the man who, passing his days in the ordinary rounds of dissipation, scarcely ever affords himself time to think that he has a salvation to secure, or a God to propitiate. He hears, indeed, whenever public decency obliges him to observe the outward forms of religion, that there is some object of greater importance to man than the gratification of passion, the accumulation of wealth, or the study of ease. But the truths of God make no practical impression on his soul, and he is accustomed to dismiss from his mind every serious thought and every religious counsel, as the Roman governor removed the terrifying preaching of the Apostle—"For this time go thy way; but when I have a convenient time I will send for thee." (Acts, xxiv. 25.) He does, indeed, flatter himself that as his last hour is yet far distant, so it will be long before he need listen to these importunate advisers; he allows time to steal on without ever thinking that the fatal term has approached nearer than when he first calculated. He has been for a long time unaccustomed to the remorses which his first crimes produced; the memory of his early offences has died away; and, undisturbed by a thought upon himself or his final destiny, his unruffled course glides on, like the stream which expands and smoothens its waters the more, the moment before it shoots them over some frightful precipice. At length the number of his crimes is filled up, the time of his probation has run out, and he finds himself in that fatal condition which he knew must come, but which he never expected.

The forerunners of death have seized him, and secured its prey. The anxiety of those around him that he should dispose of his affairs, the doubtful and faint encouragement of his attendants; above all, the decay of strength, and the gradual exhaustion of life, convince him that the threatened hour has at length arrived, that one scene only more remains to be acted, and that then his doom is sealed. During life and health his thoughts had many occupations; they could easily fly from himself. But, oh! to what a narrow space is the world now reduced for him. Accustomed before to wander over the fair face of heaven, though without ever blessing Him who reigns there; to draw delight from the beauties of creation, without ever thanking their bountiful Maker and Preserver; in fine, to seek relief or pleasure in the charms or dissipation of society,—his view is now confined to range within the unvaried limits of one small apartment, of which he is the centre, and where all that he beholds makes his thoughts recoil upon himself and his hopeless state.

Whatever of the external world reaches his confinement, can serve only to aggravate his condition. Instead of the crowds in which he used to mingle, and where he diffused cheerfulness and gaiety, he now sees only the few friends who are allowed to approach him, and is obliged to beg from them a few insincere words of consolation. Instead of the riot of amusements in which he used to be involved, the distant murmurs of the world just reach him to remind him that all without is going on as well and as happily as if he were still in the throng; that his rivals are pushing forward during his absence, and his enemies rejoicing at his situation. Now does he begin to see and feel the nothingness of the idol which he had worshipped. He had thought that to him who possessed its favours, nothing could ever be wanting: he had obtained them, yet he finds himself abandoned and forlorn in the day of his distress. He had imagined that riches could place him above the danger of ineffectual desires: he is surrounded by them, and yet cannot purchase one hour of feverish repose. He had fancied that reputation and applause would support him in the greatest difficulties: he has enjoyed them beyond his hopes, but the flatterer's breath cannot infuse one moment's vigour into his failing frame.

At the same time, he may see ten thousand schemes thwarted which he had nearly matured, a thousand undertakings interrupted which he had almost completed. But, alas! "he hath built his house as a moth, and as a keeper he hath made a booth. Poverty, like water, shall take hold of him, a tempest shall oppress him in the night: a burning wind shall take him up, as a whirlwind it shall snatch him from his place." (Job, xxvii. 18–21.)

Yes, happy would it be for the sinner if, when surprised by death, the worthlessness of his past life were his only torment. But a new power within his soul, whose energies he has hitherto repressed, now asserts its rights, and seizes upon his attention. Religion had long been banished from his thoughts; but in the day of distress she is sure to make her appearance, and he who has not cultivated her friendship, must then be content to meet her as a foe. He hears a voice that once more whispers in his ears the simple and touching queries with which his early teachers first instilled into him the truths of religion. Who made him, and for what object was he sent into the world? Oh! what a long train of painful, torturing recollections does this simple inquiry excite in the mind of the dying sinner! He now recollects how carefully the principles and duties of Christianity were impressed upon his mind, and how he endeavoured to practise them. He remembers how sweet and easy they then appeared to him, how resolved he was to order his life according to their rule. He remembers how soothing and cheering was the thought that he had a Father in heaven whom he could daily invoke; how consoling to reflect that He would reward him for his smallest acts of virtue. He remembers the slight transgressions of his early days, and how feelingly he then used to weep for them. But, alas! as he proceeds, how the picture gradually darkens! He now recollects distinctly the progress of his first and fatal seduction from this happy path, into the wild wanderings of his worldly life; how his first transgressions were wrung from him with difficulty, and were accompanied with remorse; how he gradually lost all sense to their commission, till crime at length became his occupation, and the very food without which he could not subsist. At first sight, these appear involved in impenetrable obscurity; it seems like one dark mass of evil which casts a gloom over his thoughts; but by degrees the cloud opens in his sight, one by one he begins to trace, through all its complications, the guilt of each succeeding offence. In vain does he try to avert his eyes from the disgusting and alarming array; the crowd closes round him on every side; sins force themselves upon his notice, each single and distinct, and deeply imprinted with every trace of time and circumstance which can render its character more marked, and its features more odious. A host of tormentors appear to surround him; all whom he has wronged during a long course of unscrupulous dealings and unguarded conversations, all whom he has seduced by his pernicious maxims and loose expressions, all whom he has misled by the open and unblushing wickedness of his life; their broken forms flit before him in his delirious dreams; during his long, sleepless nights, their ghastly figures watch around his pillow, and his moments of consciousness only aggravate his sufferings, by making him feel that they are real and merited.

It is when the sinner is in this condition, my brethren, that the charitable assiduity of friends, or of the ministers of religion, endeavour to train his mind to reflect on the truths of salvation; and this is the completion of his wretchedness, that the most consoling doctrines of Christianity are become for him the most piercing torments. They tell him that God is infinitely good; that His bounty and mercy are inexhaustible. Alas! he knows and feels this more strongly than their words can express, but the thought only serves to enhance his despair. He knows how long God has borne with his repeated transgressions, and heaped His blessings upon him, without exciting any feeling of repentance ; how often He has called, and he refused to hear; how often He stretched His hand, and he regarded not. And he knows the threat which the Almighty has pronounced, as the consequence of such conduct : " I also will laugh at your destruction, and will mock when that which you feared shall come upon you." (Prov. i. 26.) They remind him that He willeth not the death of a sinner, but that at whatsoever hour he shall be converted, He will receive him to mercy. But he feels that for him that day is past; the fountain of tears is dried up within him ; and he remembers the awful denunciation of the Holy Spirit : " Delay not to be converted to the Lord, and defer it not from day to day ; for His wrath shall come on a sudden, and in the time of vengeance He will destroy thee." (Ecclus. v. 8, 9.) Perhaps, indeed, to satisfy the importunity of his friends, or to comply with what he knows to be the custom, he may, at this critical moment, go through the forms prescribed by religion, and receive those sacraments at which he has so often scoffed, and which he has so long abandoned. He may attempt to unfold the hidden guilt which loads his conscience to the minister of God. But, oh! who will insure him that, after so many years of guilt, uninterrupted and unchecked by one moment of repentance, his mental powers enfeebled by disease, his soul racked to despair by the sense of his situation,—who will insure him that he has sincerely and fully exposed the whole of his iniquity? After a life of attachment to all that is odious to God, without one affection of the mind having ever been turned to Him, who will dare to hope, that, in the moment when his crimes are at their full, he is able to break through all their engagements, and transfer at once his heart and his affections, from all that had hitherto engrossed them, to an object which had never for a moment occupied his thoughts? What an extraordinary grace must, indeed, be required for the sinner who has despised the commands of God, when enjoined in sweetness and meekness, now on a sudden to esteem and embrace them, when enforced by the pangs of a mortal illness; for him who has neglected God, when He heaped blessings upon his head, now at once to love Him, when He has let loose upon him the storms of His vengeance!

Oh! no, my dear brethren, God is not to be mocked, nor His vengeance eluded. One more crime only is now wanted to set the seal of final reprobation upon his guilty soul: that, like Judas, he should receive the pledge of our salvation into a traitorous bosom. No sooner is this perpetrated, than he is delivered up without mercy to his enemies: the toils of death encompass him, and the terrors of hell environ him. His soul no longer casts back its unavailing regrets upon the unexpiated guilt of his past life; all his faculties are absorbed by the dreadful prospect of the future which begins to open on his view. The veil which had hitherto concealed this appalling sight, gradually withdraws, and he beholds the awful preparations for his speedy trial. Already he sees the Judge seated and awaiting, with calm indignation, the moment, when his last gasp shall separate his impure soul from its hateful body. Already he sees his accusers preparing their account, and adding to it the last blasphemies which his despair forces from his pale and quivering lips. Already he sees the place of his torments, "prepared deep and wide, which the breath of the Lord, as a torrent of brimstone, kindleth," (Is. xxx. 33) and the welcoming shrieks of his early companions are ringing in his ear. The friends and relations who crowd around his bed to implore the mercy of God upon his last moments, appear to him like so many hideous spectres, that press upon him and suffocate him in order to accelerate his doom; and the beautiful prayer which the Church has appointed to usher the soul into a life of bliss, pierces his ears as a call for vengeance, and as the sentence of reprobation.

"Go forth, Christian soul," it seems to say, in the name of God the Father Almighty, who created thee when He made thee to His own image and likeness, and appointed thee little less than the angels. Restore thyself to His hands, degraded below the brute creation, His image defaced, His likeness obliterated from thee. Go forth, Christian soul, in the name of the Lord who suffered for thee. Go, claim the mercies purchased by the blood on which thou hast trampled, the glory reserved for those who follow His example. Go forth, Christian soul, in the name of the Holy Ghost, who was poured out upon thee when thou wert washed in the waters of baptism; present to Him, now torn and defiled, the white garment in which He then clothed thee, with an injunction that thou shouldst bear it unspotted to the tribunal of Christ. Go forth, Christian soul, and as thou issuest from the body, may the splendid choir of the angels meet thee, to mourn over thy fall; may the army of saints environ thee, to reproach thine ingratitude;

may the mild and sweet form of Jesus Christ come before thee, but only to pronounce thy condemnation. The final moment of reprieve is at length expired; and before the last glow has chilled upon his countenance, while the hand which closes his eyes yet presses upon his brow, his soul has already been judged, condemned, and chained down to its place of eternal punishment!

Oh! my brethren, it is a dreadful thing to fall into the hands of the living God! For this is the lot that awaits us, if we are unprepared for our last end, and suffer it to surprise us. We know not the day, nor the hour, but experience shows us that it is generally earlier than we anticipate; and prudence, therefore, requires that we should be always in readiness. If we are so soon, and on so short a warning, to be summoned forth to leave all that the earth can give us, why should we rivet our affections to it, and so increase the pain of our final separation? When you have laid up a provision for the future, when you arrange plans for the years that are yet to come, let the salutary reflection ever cross your mind, that long before the expiration of that time is come, they may require your soul at your hands; and whose will those things then be which you have provided?

Yes, my brethren, judge of the future by the past. Whose are already the pleasures of your infancy, when everything around you breathed joy and satisfaction, which you never doubted would be durable? Whose are now the liveliness and spirits of your early youth, which made you promise yourselves that life would be one tissue of unvaried happiness? Whose are the first zest and relish of novelty in your pleasures, which you flattered yourself would remain unimpaired at every repetition? "All these things are passed away, like a shadow and like a post that always runneth on; and as a ship that passeth through the waves, whereof, when it is gone by, the trace cannot be found, nor the path of its keel in the waters." (Wisd. v. 9, 10.) The past, when you review it, is only covered, like the plains of autumn, with the withered remains of former charms. Oh! why, then, will you trust to the deceitful promise of the future, and to the opening pleasures which it seems to exhibit? Your touch is fatal to their freshness and bloom; and the moment you have plucked them, you will have cast them behind you, to add to the desolation and bleakness of the past! If youth and health seem to give security, trust not to the delusion: death too frequently prefers such victims. But if age has begun its work of destruction upon you; if your step has become more heavy, or your eye more dim than it used to be; if your whitening locks or your wrinkling brow admonish you that the first step towards the final dissolution has commenced—oh! then, ye sons of men, how long will you be slow of heart, and in love with vanity? Ask not counsel of the world, or your passions and prejudices, how long your life may yet last, but listen to the gospel and its warnings. Send not, like Ochozias to Accaron, (4 Kings, i. 2) to consult its idol whether you shall live, while there is a God in Israel who has ordered you to put your house in order, for you shall certainly die.

Behold! your Judge stands at the gate and knocks; hear His voice, and despise not His admonition, that when He at length summons you, He may find you watching: then will He make you sit down with Him, and, passing, will minister unto you, in the everlasting banquet of His joy.

SERMON XV.

On the Last Judgment.

Luke, xxi. 27.

"Then shall they see the Son of man coming in a cloud in great power and majesty."

It seems, my brethren, as if the attention of our blessed Redeemer was so habitually turned towards the melancholy end which awaits all earthly grandeur, and all human enjoyment, that objects which excited in others feelings of confidence in their sincerity or duration, only recalled to His mind their worthlessness, their instability, and their certain termination. It was thus that on His triumphal entry into Jerusalem, when all around Him seemed to indicate the commencement of His reign, in acceptance of His authority by His people, and when " the multitude of His disciples began with joy to praise God with a loud voice," (Luke, xix. 37) then did Jesus, drawing near the city, weep, (41) for *He* only thought of the speedy days of desolation, when the very walls which He approached would resound, not as now with the hosannas of His triumph, but with the fierce battle-cry of an unsparing foe; and when the very road whereon He moved would be covered, not with the palm branches and garments that overspread it now, but with the shattered weapons or the lifeless corpses of the unthinking little ones who strewed them upon His path. It was a similar train of ideas which led Him to deliver the awful lesson from which my text is chosen. "As He was going out of the temple," His disciples directed His attention to the massive stones which supported the edifice, and whereon, together with it, they considered the perpetuity of their religion to be solidly based. "Master, behold what manner of stones, and what buildings are here." (Mark, xiii. 1.) Once more the same fatal period rises before His thoughts, and once more He foretells the terrors and tribulation of the avenging day, when, of all these goodly and splendid buildings, there should not be left a stone upon a stone. But on this occasion, His prophetic mind bears Him forward to a kindred but more fearful epoch ; He glances on from desolation to desolation, from ruin to ruin, until He rivets the attention of His disciples to that day of wrath and final destruction, when not merely the enormous masses which they so much admired, but when the very "mountains" from which they had been hewed, "shall melt as wax before the face of the Lord," (Ps. xcvi. 5) " because He cometh to judge the earth." (xcv. 13.)

This, my brethren, is indeed the great goal to which all created beings hasten on. For this sun, which once withdrew its light in sorrow over the sins of man, though they were being atoned by the sufferings of his Redeemer, will now totally extinguish it; when the same crimes, filled up to their measure, are to be avenged with rigour by his wrathful Judge. Then shall the stars, which once before "fought, remaining in their order, against Sisara," (Jud. v. 20) " fall down as the leaf falleth from the vine and from the fig-tree" upon the guilty earth, (Is. xxxiv. 4) and bear its ruin and conflagration through their lawless course. Then shall the waters which once, by an universal deluge, washed from the earth the iniquities of the human race, once more produce "distress of nations, by reason of the confusion of the roaring of the sea and of the waves." (Luke, xxi. 24.) In fine, then shall the whole of Nature be convulsed in its last fatal stage; the earth shall tremble to its centre, and then remain still and lifeless, till God ariseth in judgment; (Ps. lxxv. 9) the powers of heaven shall be moved, and then shall they see the Son of man coming in His majesty. "The books shall be opened," and the judgment will sit. (Apoc. xx. 12.)

This, my brethren, is the great action for which the preceding troubles will but only have prepared the scene. And this is the point which should engross our entire attention: for little will it matter to us, who will long before have slept, that these fearful woes should be poured out upon creation; little can it import us to reflect that the last destructive earthquake will scatter our ashes from their splendid urn, or only mingle them more intimately with the kindred earth of a mere humble grave; so long as we are assured that, whether from the winds of heaven, or from the dust of the earth, every particle will be demanded back, in order that we may stand in the flesh before the tribunal of Christ, together with all the tribes of the earth, that so each of us may be judged according to his works.

And it is just, my brethren, that we should so stand; it is fitting that the sinner should render an account of his doings in the flesh, in the presence of man, and before the face of his God, for against both has he offended. He has sinned in the world to the ruin or injury of his fellow-creatures, and it is just that they should be there to receive his reparation; he has sinned to the outraging of God's glory, and it is just that by Him it should be avenged. It is to these two circumstances of the last judgment I desire to engage your attention.

The wicked man, through life, is a source of ruin or injury to thousands besides himself. The bold and daring in iniquity, he gathers in his train by the force of example; the timid and wavering in virtue, he allures to fall by the arts of his seduction. To each of these, the great day, when he is exposed, in all his infamy, to the gaze of the whole world, affords ample and public satisfaction.

From the beginning, vice has exalted itself into the high places, and success seems ever to have attended its followers, in proportion to their daring. We see that it is the most unbending pride which has ever secured the humblest submission; that it is the most reckless ambition which has infallibly seized the highest prize; that the most unfeeling oppression, or the most sordid covetousness, has generally amassed the greatest wealth; that the most shameless imposture has frequently seduced the largest proportion of followers, and that the most unsparing and indiscriminate calumny, regularly insures the liveliest attention. There are men whose spirits, bold and forward, prompt them to aim at these apparent advantages, heedless of the guilty ways by which they must be attained, and who, originally drawn forward themselves by the example of those who preceded them, in their turns become leaders in the path of iniquity, and give additional volume and strength to the torrent, which at first simply involved them in its course. Such are the men of renown—the giants of vice in their generation ; such are the thousands who, even now, blushingly run a career of irreligion, or who openly follow the bent of their passions, without showing that they are even sensible of restraint from conscience or the gospel. Surrounded here by wealth, by honour, and by reputation, they diffuse the evil through an enlarging circle: they have it in their power to overawe resistance, or to purchase connivance ; and instead of being hated and abhorred for their iniquity, they are admired and imitated for the advantages it has procured them.

But, ah ! how has the vision changed ! The passage of the tomb will have stripped all of whatever is not strictly their due : possessions and dignities, glory and esteem; of all, save their works. And its purifying action will go further still. At present, the partiality of Nature, or the modelling hand of early care—often even artificial embellishments—can bestow elegance of form or comeliness of feature, without reference to the corruption and uncleanness which lurk within the breast. But the whited sepulchre will have long crumbled into dust. Long before that period, the moth will have rioted at pleasure upon the lineaments which this day bloom in youth and health, and the feeble worm will have unknitted the limbs of the vigorous and the strong. According to the expressive image of Isaias, for many days shall we all have slumbered on the foul pallet of corruption, and decay will have cast its loathsome covering over our repose. (xiv. 11.) The bodies which we shall resume from the elements of our previous existence, will receive their form and their qualities, no less than their animation from the soul which returns to dwell within them; and as disease and deformity, no less than death, came into the world by sin, so, like death, they are the wages of sin, and the destined and eternal portion of those who have incurred the second death. Such are the changes which the sleep of the grave will cause in the sinner.

For, inverting exactly the order of that transformation which is daily exhibited in Nature, he will first have lived for a short time a painted, gay, and thoughtless insect, fluttering, without repose, from pleasure to pleasure, adding grace and animation to the scene in which he moved; then have been involved, for another brief period, in the dark stillness of the tomb; to emerge what guilty man really is before his Maker, a bare, a helpless, and a loathsome worm. In this condition is he dragged forth from the crowd of culprits, to be exhibited in the face of the whole world, one, indeed, of millions no less guilty, but, for the present, absorbing and concentrating the attention of all, as completely as if they were assembled to gaze on him alone. Behold him, then, separated from the rest of mankind as a leper, and one struck by God; his features distorted with the convulsions of frenzy and despair; his crippled and palsied limbs reeling beneath the iniquities which weigh upon his very frame; his whole exterior ulcered by the foul blot which is the emblem of sin; and his bones, into whose very marrow the Scripture describes the crimes of his youth to have penetrated, bearing in them, though resuscitated, the cankering rottenness of the grave. Thus he is exhibited to the crowd of his former admirers, who, dazzled by the splendour of his course, once used to court and revere him; to the multitude of his treacherous friends, who encouraged him in his iniquities, that themselves might receive corresponding support; to the army of more servile followers, who made his guilt the model of their own, and were proud to emulate, in their meaner sphere, the bold and unchecked flight of his impiety.

But no longer are they his admirers, his friends, or followers. They shrink in horror from his side, and wonder how they could ever have applauded or esteemed so miserable and so odious a wretch. But his abandonment is not yet complete: all his treasures and advantages have escaped as " water from his hand;" and of the wealth which he once owned, he now possesses not even, with Job, one broken potsherd, wherewith to soothe the smart of his noisome flesh. He must see all those things, for which he so often perilled his soul, not merely departed from, but turned faithlessly against, him; his wealth, and the things of price, wherein he gloried, his chartered possessions, and his titled dignities, thrown in an indiscriminate heap into the scales of the sanctuary, together with the iniquities which bought them; and he must hear his former admirers and friends greeting him in the insulting words of the prophet: " Thou also art wounded as well as we; thou art become like unto us. Thy pride is come down unto hell; thy carcass is fallen down." (Is. xiv. 10, 11.)

Oh! how abundantly does the wicked, merely by being exposed to the whole world, as he has been, changed by sin from what he was here below—oh! how abundantly does he atone before those whom his brilliant and successful course of iniquity had hurried forward in his train.

But it is not always that vice can assume a bold and daring front ; often, not to say generally, it is too odious to obtain public applause ; and it is by more covert arts that it must seek gratification or reward. Indeed, even the most unblushing sinner would tremble to have a thousand deeds of his guilt dragged into the light. Again and again he is obliged to act the hypocrite, and put on the mask of virtue, or, at least, of decorum, that he may succeed in his plans of villany. He must assume the character of a man of honour, if he wish to secure the intended victims of his passions; he must pretend to a rigid integrity and probity, to procure participators or dupes for his schemes of injustice ; he must appear true to moral principle, if he wish to direct by his advice, and to influence by his authority, those whom he needs ; or to ruin, by his imputations, those whom he fears in the advancement of his views. At every step he silently draws a new prey into his toils ; he loosens in some the principles which had bound them to virtue, so artfully and so gradually that they are scarcely aware, through life, of having been *his* victims ; he can place the temptation so suddenly and vividly before others, that it becomes resistless and appears excusable ; and many discover only at the close of life, that though once they had been upright, simple, and inclined to virtue, they have spent a life of sin, in consequence of the perversion or influence of others whom themselves and the world would hardly have deemed the authors of such guilt. And these, also, my brethren, must be publicly avenged; the deceit which the wretch has practised must be exposed. For this purpose it is necessary that not only his outward condition be held up to abhorrence, but that the secret and interior baseness and worthlessness of his soul be exposed to public execration. He must be his own accuser, and that with the most painful rigour. There is no degree of humiliation which we can conceive more trying and more repugnant to our feelings, than the manifestation to others of our hidden guilt. But there are circumstances attending this last and dreadful revelation, which render it without parallel, in any public confession which can be made here below.

First, were we compelled to expose our secret crimes before the world, the confession can be but *partial*. It can hardly embrace all the offences of our life; or if we have submitted to such an humiliation, thousands of transgressions will have vanished from our memories, and those that remain will not be viewed, and cannot be described, in the vivid and glowing form that they bore at their commission. Indeed, we can hardly conceive the circumstance which could compel us to betray the minute and secret workings of our heart. But here, the manifestation must be *entire*. A superior power is in the soul of the culprit, tearing and rooting out from its most hidden recesses the guilt which had there lurked so long; an irresistible spell is upon his tongue, compelling him to recount them, with a clearness and minuteness of detail which his sincerest efforts, in life, would not have enabled him to give to any single transgression. Nothing can be omitted, nothing extenuated, nothing disguised. From the first passionate wilfulness of early youth, to the cold irreligion of decrepit age, from the petty and mean designs or roving schemes of more thoughtless hours, to the dark perpetration of most artificial crimes, all must be recounted, detailed, depicted, precisely as, at their commission, they were beheld by God.

Secondly, any confession here below must be necessarily circumscribed in place. Compared to the limits of the globe, they can be but few who are present to receive it. Suppose all the publicity be given to it that is in the power of man, it will seldom reach a foreign country; nay, in our own, it can excite no lively interest beyond those who are acquainted with the actors or the scene; and of even their interest the culprit cannot be a witness. Far otherwise will it be on the last day of trial. Not the men of our own kindred or of our own tongue only, not even those of our own colour and feature alone, but every individual, of every climate and of every nation under the sun, every mortal who will have dwelt upon the earth, from its creation to its dissolution, will be present; all equally able and equally eager to catch every syllable of the frightful history, each for the moment become, in one's regard, a prying searcher into the reins and heart, able to comprehend and feel to its fullest extent the blackness of his guilt.

In fine, a confession upon earth has necessarily some advantages resulting to him that makes it. Occasionally its humility softens the indignation of those who would punish; generally, even with the murderer on the scaffold, it secures him a degree of sympathy and secret compassion;

always, it unburthens the mind, and brings relief to the conscience. Not so the self-accusation of the sinner at the tribunal of God. From his Judge he can expect at every step, not a mitigation, but an addition to his sentence. From all around him, instead of compassion, he elicits nothing but scorn and execration, loathing and malediction; and every eye of the millions that gaze keenly upon him, is as a two-edged sword, penetrating to the division of his heart and soul. And in himself, alas! instead of ease or relief, at every new recital, the rack on which his conscience is placed receives an additional pressure, from the increased force of the passions which torment it. Of *shame*, such as the most delicate feelings on earth cannot conceive. For the excitement of passion, which once disguised his excesses, has long been extinguished in the tomb; the intoxication of pleasure, in which he drowned remorse, has totally evaporated, and he can see no circumstance which could excuse, or even palliate, the crimes which he is obliged to lay open to the world. Of *rage*, to behold himself the reproach, the scorn, the abhorrence of all mankind, impotent to utter even a defiance or threat against his insultors, unable even to interrupt the narrative by which he draws such painful scrutiny upon himself. In fine, of *despair*, from the full consciousness that for each particular he has deserved, if possible, a distinct, yet eternal, hell; and that additional torments *will* be laid on, in proportion to the guilt which he is forced to reveal; torments not merely measured from past experience, but calculated upon the additional sufferings of the body to which he has been re-united, and upon the prospect of his prison door being now, at length, sealed down for ever, without even the anticipation of a change, if not of relief, with which he had hitherto looked forward to the day of trial.

Oh! how will those who have been the victims of his seduction, and the less guilty participators of his crimes, exult to see their betrayer thus held up to public shame! "Behold," they will exclaim—"behold the man, with all his loathsomeness, and all his abominations, whom, alas! we thought so fair and wise."

My brethren, if the terrors of this day went no further than I have described; if we suppose the Judge to vanish from the scene with the power and majesty which environs Him, and the legions of His heavenly host who minister unto Him; if we imagine the sinner doomed to nothing but this dreadful exposure, both outward and inward, to the attention and the execration of all mankind, surely you will own it to contain a measure of sorrow and of wrath, which the diadem of earth could not compensate. It is, indeed, but a moment of time for each—but a drop compared to the ocean of eternity, to which it is united; but it is a drop of gall, whose bitterness will amply wash from the mind the remembrance of years of pleasure, and pall it to eternity for the slightest sensibility to good. It *is* but a moment, yet in the destitution of that moment, how fully is an empire of unjust wealth outbalanced; in its ignominy, how abundantly is a guilty renown through the whole universe requited; in its desolation, how is an entire life of lawless enjoyment a thousand times overpaid! But hitherto we have seen the sinner only confronted with his fellow-man; it is time that "God arise, and His enemies be scattered." If so much has been suffered to atone before guilty man, what will be endured when the Almighty comes forward to claim the reparation due to His outraged honour.

"Give glory to the Lord God of Israel," was the summons by which Achan was called forth to confess his guilt in the presence of the whole people, before being cast into the flames which were to punish his transgression; (Jos. vii. 19) and "give glory to God" will be no less the adjuration, whereby the sinner will be commanded to manifest his iniquity before the assembled world, previous to being thrown into the eternal fire that has been kindled for his punishment. Through life he had contemned and neglected the law of God, given him for his salvation, and he has thereby changed it into a law of death, by which he must now submit to be justly condemned; he has rejected the proffered mercies purchased by his Redeemer, and he has thereby converted Him into an angry judge, from whom he must receive his final doom.

The evil which the sinner commits by the injury inflicted upon his neighbours, is but a comparatively trifling accession to the direct violation of God's law; and it is to avenge this, that he is principally summoned before the bar of divine justice. From his earliest years, this law was proposed to him for acceptance, coupled with promises of the most perfect happiness, if he received, and with threats of the most signal vengeance, if he refused its yoke. At the same time, he was assured that "this yoke would be sweet and its burthen light," whereas, if he pursued the crooked paths of sin, he would soon find his way hedged up with thorns, and finally conducting him into perdition. In spite of this caution, he chose the latter course; and consequently set the law and its provisions at defiance. He neglected to comply with its regulations, and observe the outward practices which it enjoined; or only partook of them so as rather to insult by his misconduct, than to benefit by his attendance. He thus separated himself from the people of God, and joined the opposite standard of his enemy; he upheld the maxims of the world, and he scoffed, at least in practice, at the commandments of the gospel. And yet his transgression seemed to have passed unheeded. In youth, he was seen successful and happy; in old age, he appeared tranquil and composed: his course was evidently prosperous, and his end was reported to have been in peace. The just who beheld him thus, were tempted to waver and be scandalized in their way, upon seeing this open and still unpunished violation of the Almighty's commands. In their presence, then, He is pledged to vindicate the efficacy of His menaces, as well as the wisdom of His decrees; and therefore does He come with the thousands of His saints to call to judgment before Him the wretch who has dared to set His power and authority at naught. In his own person he must be forced to prove and proclaim that this law was reasonable and just; how, at every period of his life, he felt its evidence come home to his heart, however he might harden it against its influence; how, at every change of course, the more he deviated from its maxims, the more bewildered and uncertain his steps became; how, at every transgression of its precepts, until conscience had been lulled within him, he was sensible of a violence done to the natural and purer dictates even of his own dispositions. But his tribute of reparation to the law of God must be fuller still. From the experience of his own life, he must acknowledge it to be not only conformable to justice, but necessary to happiness. The pain and agitation caused by his early crimes; the uneasy though concealed forebodings of his latter days; the cold apathy and joyless indifference of his middle course, when vice had lost its charms, though virtue had not regained her influence; the perpetual apprehensions, contentions, and anxieties which the acquisition of every new, yet worthless, pleasure cost him; the distaste, uneasiness, and discontent which its gratification left in its place; the secret envy towards those who had chosen a different path, felt even when actually holding them up to censure or derision; the repeated gnawings of the internal worm which nothing could ever perfectly subdue; in fine, the raging despair, or the chill hopelessness of his death-bed scene, when his crimes, starting up in a thousand hateful shapes before him, made him suffer, by anticipation, the tortures he now endures, or when, abandoned by God, he lay in a torpid insensibility, uncheered by a gleam of consolation or of confidence, so as to make him feel with ten-fold rigour the first full rush of torment which poured upon his departed soul; these feelings and these scenes, now at length revealed and described with a sense of bitter but useless regret, will surely justify to the full the truth, the justice, the beauty of the divine law. It will satisfy those who suffered so much on earth to discharge its precepts, that, putting aside their heavenly reward, they had really chosen happiness even here below; and the secluded devotions of the virgin, the hair-shirt of the anchoret, and the sword of the martyr, will appear as a lighter price to have been paid for heaven, than the reprobate has laid out only to purchase eternal woe.

Having borne testimony to the truth of the divine law, the most painful act yet remains—to acknowledge the justice of the sentence it inflicts. Having separated himself through life from the assembly of God's people, he must now own himself justly excluded by it for ever from their blessed society; he must bid an eternal farewell to that heavenly court to which he feels that he was himself originally destined, as no longer worthy even to stand in its presence. Within its circle are included many who once loved him sincerely, and were beloved in return; perhaps the mother who bore him, the darling infant on whom he doated with a father's fondest affection. But, alas! they know him not; and while not a glance of compassion on *their* part soothes the eternal separation, envy and rage of the blackest dye agitate his soul, as he considers the loss which he has incurred, and condemns his own folly as its only cause. He attached himself during life to the enemies of God, and he must justify the divine law, which had warned him that he would be the partaker of their torments. He sees the hideous legions of his infernal allies standing below, and stretching forth their hands to seize and enchain their prey; he hears their insulting scoffs, their jeering invitation to hasten to the new and eternal abode which they have fitted for his body, there to revel with the friends whom he has chosen; and he feels obliged to plead for their right, and to maintain the justice of their claim. He insists that he is their lawful portion, their purchased victim, sold over by himself for pleasures long since vanished, and for prospects which were never realised; and, flinging himself at length before the footstool of his Judge, he invokes upon his own head the sentence which the divine law has so justly awarded, and entreats that he may be suffered to depart, accursed, into the fire which has been prepared for the devil and his angels!

But no, my brethren, there is a sign in heaven which yet seems to plead for an arrest of judgment. The standard of the Son of man is borne by the angels above his tribunal, the instrument of mercy, reconciliation, and peace. It is the altar to which the most despairing criminal may cling in safety; it is as the bow set by the Almighty in the clouds, upon which, when the iniquities of the whole earth seem to demand a deluge of wrath, "He will look, and will certainly have mercy." (Gen. ix. 16.) Surely it is not from beneath its shadow that sentence of eternal damnation will be passed against a redeemed soul, by Him who expired thereon to ransom and to save it!

But, alas! my brethren, the sinner has despised the mercies which it purchased for him while they were within his reach; and this is the consummation of his misery, that what should have been his hope and his protection, is converted into the strongest plea for his condemnation. Strange it is, that, from the beginning, the great benefit of redemption, and the incalculable graces and advantages it procured us, should have been so little valued and so easily contemned. According to St. Paul, the sinner of every age, like the Jews, loads the Son of God with indignities, with injustice, and with blows; but with this difference, that while His earthly persecutors knew not the Lord of glory, or they would not have crucified Him, the Christian professes to believe that it is He; they maltreated His flesh while in a state of sufferance, but he outrages His glory, raised to the right hand of God; the first offended to the accomplishment of the work of redemption, while the latter transgresses to the impeding of its efficacy. But to both He makes the same appeal.

For even while in the hands of His ruthless enemies, the mark for the spite and indignities of the rabble, the object of the blasphemies and taunts of the high priest, meek and enduring as He was, He reminded those who were insulting Him of this hour when full retribution must be made, and when the outrages they were committing against the Saviour of the world would be atoned to Him as its Judge. "Nevertheless, I say to you, *hereafter* you shall see the Son of man sitting on the right hand of the power of God, and coming on the clouds of heaven." (Matt. xxvi. 64.) Then shall be fulfilled to the letter those ominous words, "that they shall look upon Him whom they have pierced." (Zac. xii. 10.) But far stronger is this challenge when made to the Christian sinner.

For, besides the mercy of redemption, received in common with the Jews, the cross which stands before him is a lively and touching record of all that Jesus Christ has done for him individually, from the first time that it was signed upon his breast and forehead in baptism, through all the long series of graces and blessings which were purchased by its expiation; to the last moment when, perhaps, his closing lips pressed its sacred emblem. It will remind him that with the first he received a white garment, which he was commanded to bear unsullied by vice, and unrent by error, before the tribunal of Christ; that through the various dispensations of grace, whereof he partook, he was gradually invested with new privileges in the Christian profession, or received fresh aids to discharge their obligations; that, at the close of all, the minister of God bid him go forth joyfully from the body, to meet the mild and cheerful aspect of his dear Redeemer! Now, then, in the presence of this symbol and source of grace, he must account to Him for the use he has made of all these helps, and the mode in which he has discharged his solemn engagements. Convicted at once, by his own confession, of having rendered them all void, nothing remains but that he surrender at its foot the dignities with which he was therein vested; that he should give back the token of reconciliation which his Father placed upon his hand, as he returned from the more early of his prodigal wanderings; that he should strip himself of the wedding garment with which he was clothed at the nuptials of the Lamb, at His holy table; that he should resign for ever the glorious title of a child of God, and renounce all claims to partake of his inheritance. Thus, retaining nothing more of his elevated condition than may serve to increase his punishment, the tarnished robe of baptism, which as a vest of fire must burn around him for eternity, the character of a soldier of Christ, which, stamped by the holy chrism on his brow, is converted into the branded mark of a deserter from his standard, thus despoiled and degraded, he must await a still heavier doom, because he has been more signally blest.

Already self-condemned to separation from the saints of God, already self-condemned to the eternal company of fiends in unspeakable torments,—oh! what shall that doom be? One, my brethren, which He will inflict upon himself, but to escape which he would cheerfully endure all the other pains of hell—eternal banishment from the face of his Redeemer and his God. He now feels towards Him a longing desire of possession, which all heaven besides could not even partially satisfy. His attributes appear in their most lovely form before his imagination: the mild and encouraging sweetness of His aspect here below, His unvarying kindness to him through life, the moving scenes of His agony, His sufferings, and His death, endured for the love of him; all are vividly painted before the eyes of his soul, and bear it forward with resistless vigour to enjoy and possess Him. But these very feelings recoil with ten-fold pressure upon the unhappy wretch: the more lovely his Saviour appears to him, the more deeply and fearfully unworthy he feels even to look upon Him, the more dreadfully and insupportably His wrath and indignation seems to flash forth against him. "Then," says St. John, (Apoc. vi. 16) "shall he call upon the mountains and to the rocks to fall upon him, and hide him;" not from the unsparing fury of "the leopard,"—as the Almighty promised he would be to His enemies on the way of Assyria; (Osee, xiii. 7) not from the irresistible strength of the Lion of Juda, who is to arise and beat down every foe—but "from the face of the Lamb,"—of the meek Lamb, that bled and was "slain for his salvation." In this manner, flying of himself from His sight into the deepest recesses of his prison, he shuts himself out from the blessed vision of God, after which he will thirst in vain, for all eternity; and "the smoke of his torments shall ascend before God for ever and ever."

Thus will God finally avenge His glory in the condemnation of the sinner, for his contempt of His law and the rejection of salvation. My brethren, remember that we shall all be there; that each of us in his turn will stand forth to receive his sentence. But you have it in your power to prevent a condemnation by anticipating the trial. For, " if we would judge ourselves," says St. Paul, " we should not be judged." (1 Cor. xi. 31.) The code by which we shall be tried is already in our possession—the gospel of Christ; the accuser who will give witness against us is within our own bosoms. The indictment is being gradually drawn up, as we multiply our transgressions.

But our merciful Judge leaves it during life in our own hands; and it is not until we have ratified its validity by an impenitent death, that the record becomes unchangeable, and its doom irrevocable. He has established a court here below, where his minister, invested with powers from Him, may receive in secrecy the manifestation which must otherwise be displayed before all the world, and pronounce a sentence of absolution which will be registered in heaven. Oh! one penitential tear will cancel the whole act of accusation by the forgiveness it will obtain. Lose, then, no time; if involved in guilt seek its forgiveness; preserve yourselves for the rest of your lives from whatever may defile the soul; and then, on that dreadful day, you will lift up your heads, knowing that your salvation is at hand, and that your eternal crown is going to receive its last brilliancy and perfection.

SERMON XVI.

On the Character of Faith.

1 Cor. xiii. 12.

" We see now through a glass in a dark manner, but then face to face Now I know in part; but then I shall know even as I am known."

WHEN God led Israel out of Egypt, He guided them by a pillar, which changed its appearance in a most remarkable manner, so as to represent the opposite extremes of light and darkness. During the night it was a column of flame, and during the day it was a volume of cloud. And when the Egyptians had come up with God's people on the shore of the Red Sea, this miraculous guide placed itself between the two hosts, so as on the one side to appear bright and cheering, and on the other dark and perplexing. Hence, while those, whose freedom God was working, derived from it comfortable assurance and efficacious assistance, those who, through their obstinacy, were strangers to His mercy, saw in it nothing but obscurity, uncertainty, and fear.

Under this emblem, my brethren, I think we may consider as represented to us, that faith of which the Apostle speaks in the conclusion of this day's epistle. It is the guide which God has, in His goodness, given us to lead us through the weary wilderness of this earth, into the promised land of our inheritance. At times, and under certain aspects, it presents itself to us as a bright and cheering light, showing us a clear and easy path wherein to walk. Again, when viewed under another form, it shall seem to us full of mysterious darkness, wherein are enwrapped doctrines of unsearchable obscurity, principles of impenetrable depth. And, moreover, the resemblance may be even discovered in this, that while divine faith, to those whom it guides, is a source of most blessed assurance, hope, and joy, to those who are estranged from it, it appears but as a cloud, a mist, full of error, uncertainty, and gloom. This two-fold character of faith is intimated by St. Paul, in the words of my text. For, he tells us, that by it we see, indeed, and know, but then adds, that it is only darkly, and in a borrowed light, as though reflected in a mirror; so that our knowledge is only partial and imperfect, especially when compared with that which one day we hope to acquire in the full light of God in heaven. With these two opposite characteristics of faith, its light and its darkness, I wish to engage your thoughts this day, if so, haply, the entire counsel of God, in His revelation to man, may be better manifested unto us.

When we speak of the first appearance of the Christian religion upon earth, we are wont to compare it to a bright ray breaking upon a night of deep and universal darkness. We consider the world as immersed in awful ignorance and corruption, without God, without morality, without any certain principles to guide man in virtue, without any definite end towards which to direct his steps, without any stable assurance of a final retribution. When upon this abyss, this chaos of thoughts, surmises, and perplexities, the light of true religion first dawned, it must have appeared as charming and as joyful as that of our visible firmament, when the first creative command for its existence was spoken.

But, in this view, we do an injustice to the glory of God's truth. Never, on the contrary, had the world been in a state of greater intellectual refinement, than at that period. Every art that could humanise or ennoble man, had reached its perfection; every branch of literature that tends to the exercise of the best faculties, had been cultivated with success. School after school had discussed the abstruser sciences, and sought a solution of the mysteries of man's existence, and his relation with the world and with other beings. The opinions of philosophy had, on many points, come nearer the truth than in remoter ages; the ethical code of some schools had proposed a higher and purer standard of morals, than had been imagined in the pagan world at an earlier period; and even on the subject of the Godhead, heathenism might be said to have thrown off many grosser ideas, and aimed at reaching principles of a more intellectual character. The peculiar feature of the time, with regard to these improvements, was their general diffusion; for, no longer confined to a small territory, and within that to the conflicting followers of small sects, who were looked on as separated from the mass of society, philosophy, as it was called, had become the solace of the statesman, the meditation of the poet, the topic of social conversation, a branch of every polished education—in short, the pursuit of every rank, age, and sex.

Compared, then, to what the world had been several centuries before, it must be owned that it had made a progress great as that from night to day; and the powers of human genius had developed themselves to a degree that left little hope of their being able, by the most energetic strain, to reach a higher eminence. And, in fact, experience proved, that the next step in the social progress, was one of downward direction towards decay. Now, if we can imagine this sun of ours, in the very pride of its meridian, and even tropical, splendour, while men were shading their eyes from its dazzling beams, surprized by such an outburst of glorious light, as that all should seem to themselves, from the contrast, to have, in one moment, passed from the gloom of midnight to the brightness of noon, we should form some notion of the transition which took place in man's intellectual knowledge, when, upon the variety and richness of his rational acquirements, the ray of heavenly revelation falls. For thus is the effect, in some sort, described in God's word, when we are told, that "the light of the sun shall be seven-fold as the light of seven days, in the day when the Lord shall bind up the wound of His people." (Is. xxx. 26.) But in two respects, particularly, does this comparison seem to hold, in the simplicity, and the universality, of this light.

For, when men desire by artificial means to supply a brilliant light, either in the earthly or in the spiritual order, they must needs have recourse to many most complicated, and yet most imperfect, means. If you wished thoroughly to light up but the interior of one large edifice, you would require a multiplicity of lamps and tapers; and yet, after all, there would be nooks and recesses which their rays will not reach, and many parts would seem but the darker from the contrast with the brightness of the rest. But let the sun, though one and alone, rise, not only upon it, but upon all the world, and let it find but a few small openings through which to send some of its messengers of light; and presently every part is steeped in an even and well-diffused radiance, which gives to every object its natural hue, and winds into every angle and deeper cleft, till no part has escaped its searching influence. Even so was it with the intellectual world. Many separate researches were considered necessary for the illustration of one single problem among the thousands that involved the nature of God; the most various theories were devised to explain any one of the moral phenomena which surround our present existence, and its connexion with the past and the future; conjectures and capricious fancies were brought to give some light to the unfathomable mysteries of good and evil, as existing in the world and in man's interior. And, after all, far greater was that portion of the moral edifice which remained in total darkness than what enjoyed this glimmering light, and many were the objects, even amidst the latter, which seemed incapable of receiving, or reflecting, even the brightest of its beams.

Now, when revelation came to remove these difficulties, it proposed no deep, nor learned, nor complicated maxims. It brought with it no long chain of axioms, theorems, and corollaries; it told not those who wished to be truly wise, first to decide whether the Grove or the Portico, the luxurious couch or the hard ground, would best suit their meditations, then to settle whether a system of progressive induction or a method of constructed argumentation was more favourable to the investigation of truth; and after that to proceed by many difficult steps to the formation of great and novel systems of religion, morals, and belief. No, it came as the light, simple, complete, and universal. It dealt at once with the past and the future, as decidedly as with the present; with eternity, as with time; with the creation of all things, as with their final end; with man in the greatness of his destiny, as in the littleness of his origin; with his spiritual being, as with his earthly. Man, as a free agent, reconciled to the right and true knowledge of God; man, as a miserable dependant upon a superior power, yet responsible for his actions; man, in short, evil in heart, yet bound to be virtuous; a slave to passions, yet called to perfection; an outcast from paradise, yet heir of heaven; presented no insoluble contradictions to the simplicity of its great principles. God, the perfect and the infinite, the inscrutable and the inconceivable, the stumbling-block of every religious system till then, was in it the centre, from which all its light proceeded, in the simplicity, yet completeness, of the idea it presented of His nature. Before the splendour of the new system, all the many feeble lights of human knowledge, which before looked so bright, waxed pale; and in the fitful contrast they presented, decided which was of earth and which of heaven.

We cannot be astonished if, to minds well disposed, Christianity, thus presented, seemed at once to carry sufficient evidence of its divine original. For, if different persons had been seen successively to try the notes of a complicated instrument, and had on every attempt only produced harsh discords, or at best but imperfect and feeble harmonies, then, at last, one came, who, running his hands lightly over its strings, at every touch awakened a new, perfect, and thrilling accord, we should say that he had a right to call himself the master of that instrument, and to command attention when he explained its properties. And so, after the experiments of ages had been tried upon the constitution of things, yet naught but jarring theories produced, the Divine Founder of Christianity came, and by the simplest declarations of His saving faith, brought all Nature so into harmony, from its Creator's attributes to the destinies of its meanest objects, as that all must confess Him to have possessed knowledge and control in all its complicated movements.

Such was the light of faith in reference to the objects of previous speculation: what shall we say of its perfectly new manifestations? It is not necessary for me even cursorily to enumerate those great dogmas, which the deepest meditations of the sublimest genius, though prolonged through centuries, would not have been able to imagine, nor those institutions for our benefit, which it would not have entered the heart of man to devise, even when his self-love had pushed him to the most extravagant desires. For it would seem as if God, determined to show how high His thoughts are above our thoughts, had been pleased not only to satisfy the longing of humanity after knowledge of the highest order, but to go even further, and open to it stores of whose very existence it had been ignorant till then.

But the words of St. Paul seem principally applicable,

not so much to faith, as manifested to the world, as to its acting on the individual. He speaks of that light and knowledge which he himself possessed, and not, indeed, as a highly privileged apostle of truth, but as one member of Christ's Church. For he contrasts the imperfection of present vision and knowledge, with the perfection of that which is to come. If faith was given to the world to supersede the uncertain guidance of human speculation, and to substitute unvarying principles for vague conjectures, we must be able to trace its action, for the same purposes, into the souls of men, and to discover in them a similar substitution. Hence, St. Paul speaks of it as knowledge, however imperfect that knowledge may be, and not opinion, and as of vision, however faint, not of inquiry. Yet, had God so ordered faith that it should be the mould of each one's reasoning, subject to all the changes which his intellectual growth might undergo, to all the vacillations that his ordinary sentiments may suffer, to the chances that every species of human knowledge has to encounter, of being discovered false, or despised as useless, by the variable mind; surely He would have elevated man but a short step above the unsteadiness of his previous course, and would have done but little towards removing him, from the sphere of opinion to that of knowledge. But, consider faith as a fixed and unalterable standard of religious assurances; as a system of belief invariable from the beginning of its manifestation to the end of time; subject to no alteration from the influence of temporal events, or the character of nations or individuals: bring the mind of each man under its absolute control, making it the guided and not the guide, the instructed and not the teacher; make, in other words, religion the law, and us, all and severally, its subjects; and you have harmony in the scheme of providence, the same great end attained, in the substitution of security for instability and uncertainty, whether in the ideas of men in general, or in their individual minds. And no doubt but the means whereby such an object is attained, will possess, in one, as in the other, order, the same characteristics of simplicity and universality. It will be by no complication of reasoning and study, by no great variety of methods, by no multiplicity of independent investigations, but by some one simple and obvious principle, which shall be found to contain in itself the entire system of truth, and the completest assurance against error. It will be a principle which at once frees you from all reliance upon fallible and partial methods, and affords you a guarantee for the certainty of your convictions. It will be a principle that takes in the whole of revealed truths, not leaving one part to be reached after another, but, by its comprehensive nature, putting the mind at once in possession of all.

I am far from intending or desiring to place this matter before you in a polemical point of view. I content myself with deducing a few simple analogies, leaving the consequences to be developed by your own minds. God, for instance, thought it right to put an end to the many and contradicting opinions entertained concerning His nature, by a revelation of Himself. As the result of this revelation, some maintain the sublime mystery of the Trinity, others impugn it as little better than Polytheism. Can God have given a scheme of revelation which can lead to either of these opinions, according to the peculiarities of men's minds? To overthrow the power of evil, and reconcile man to God, He sent a Saviour into the world. Most Christians hold the solemn belief that He was true God, and that His blood wrought real atonement for sin. Many others, professing to believe in the same manifestation of truth, maintain Him to have been a simple man, and to have purchased no salvation for us by death. Can God have given a standard of faith which may justify either one belief or the other, according as each one may apply it? To secure an unfailing source of grace to weak man, Jesus Christ, on the eve of His passion, instituted a solemn rite, commemorative of His passion. A large body of Christians, taking His words in their most obvious acceptation, believe, in consequence, in a sacrament wherein His flesh and blood are really present; others reject such a belief as a blasphemy, and the practices to which it necessarily leads as superstitious and idolatrous. Can we imagine the grounds of belief for this institution to be of such a nature as to support either opinion, according to our different plans of viewing it? Again, some affirm, that to heal the wounds of sin, which had corrupted all mankind, He appointed other sacraments, as baptism and penance, whereby it is forgiven; and others assert that no such provision was ever made.

Now, every one of these instances belongs to doctrines and appointments, which, if taught or made, were for the express purpose of correcting the ignorance and corruptions of the world, before revelation came. If the belief in them be true, their denial must go a great way, though in different degrees, towards leaving men in the condition they were previously in. Can we, then, imagine the foundation of faith, the principle of revelation, such as leaves it to individual man to decide, whether or no he shall affirm or deny any or all these and many other points, or whether he shall to-day think differently upon them from what he yesterday did? And yet is it not evident that so many as believe in them, merely because they are satisfied that they have found them plainly declared in God's written word, do believe them upon the very same ground as the almost equal number who deny them, because they tell you that conscientiously they find them rejected by that same written word? And can this possibly be? Can this be the faith that knows and sees, in contradistinction to the opinions of men, when they groped about conjecturally for truth? Can this be the only substitute given for the ignorance of man, respecting these great objects of his former fruitless research?

If, therefore, we discover our scheme of faith, such as to leave all that follow it in uncertainty, and to lead some of them into error—for of contradictory opinions one must be wrong—our minds naturally turn to seek some other system wherein this perplexity is escaped, and all the difficulties of its rival obviated. And here the simplicity and the universality of the Catholic rule naturally presents itself to our minds; for by it we see how all that embrace it are brought to the belief of exactly the same doctrines, in exactly the same form, and to precisely the same extent. They who hold it may be said truly to *know* what they profess; their belief, like Him on whose guarantee it rests, is the same yesterday and to-day; and while the convictions of others are as a garment which is changed, and which too often wears away and perishes, it, like the God that gave it, ever remaineth, and its record is unto generation and generation. They who cherish it have the assurance of peace, for they know that they can change no more. And as they that go down to the sea in ships care but little how their bark rolls upon the billows, or how its spars and cordage wave to and fro, but take care so to secure the compass which has to guide them, as that no shock or reeling shall disturb it from its even and level position in the heart of their vessel; so will such a one but little heed the variations of opinions and principles which daily occur in the social world, nor the jolts and disturbances which they must cause him, so long as this, his card that guides him, remains steady and unchangeable in the midst of his soul. They who have at one time tasted the miseries of an unsettled faith, or of a religion based upon human grounds; who have been, as little children, tossed to and fro by every wind of doctrine, and have been brought by God's mercy to the knowledge and acceptance of a solid belief as only attainable in the Catholic Church; they well know what I speak.

I have dilated somewhat more than I intended upon the first characteristic of faith, its light. To treat of the mysterious darkness which the Apostle mentions, it should seem necessary to contrast the imperfection of our knowledge here below, with that fulness of it that will break upon us in the light of God, when, face to face, we shall contemplate His glory, and in it view the entire of His counsels. But I feel that to make such a contrast requires a calmer mood of contemplation than the general tenor of this discourse will allow—a completer abstraction from painful thoughts than religious differences here below, so lately considered, will allow the mind to reach: I will, therefore, rather explain the darkness which accompanies faith by reference to the imperfections of our present condition, than by contrast with that for which we hope.

God would have seemed to wound when He meant to heal, had He enlightened our ignorance at the expense of our humility. He had been offended in the very first instance, by the ambition of man to be like to God, with his eyes open to the knowledge of good and evil. This overweaning desire of unwholesome and unfitting knowledge, led to man's fall; and ignorance, one of its principal consequences, was the offspring of pride. In repairing the mischiefs of this fall, and once more revealing to man eternal truths, God took care that no room should be left for the exercise of our pride: but so communicated them, that in themselves we should find the confusion, and the remedy, of this baneful inclination. Hence, even in those points wherein He cleared up the dark errors of a corrupt religion, this knowledge which He imparted was a mystery so deep, that, in believing it, the mind must no less own its incapacity to fathom or to comprehend it.

Thus, the idea of God, in the natural condition of man, was one of perplexity and doubt, from the conflicting and degrading notions entertained of Him; from the corruption in His worship, and from the incapability of man ever properly to rise from the forms of heathenish idolatry to a pure, or even a clear, idea of His spiritual nature. All this error and darkness was dissipated at once, by the revelation of God as a pure spirit, one, eternal, and infinite. But the grandeur of this simple idea was, at the same time, overpowering. It removed man to a distance from God, whereof he had entertained no previous thought, at the same time that it taught him to see His power, and wisdom, and providential care in every part of creation, and every incident of his own life. It thus at once placed him in contact with Him, though infinitely removed from Him; it set the grandeur of God's attributes beyond the sphere of his contemplation, while he was ever moving and living within the sphere of their action; it made the very tabernacle of brightness, wherein God seemed enveloped, an impenetrable veil to his dazzled sight; and when he thus knew God reflected completely, yet darkly, in the glass of faith, his frame could not but fall prostrate before Him; he covered his face, as the prophet in the cavern of Horeb, and adored Him throughout the depths of his spirit. The busy inquisitiveness of his mind was bound up by the cords of salutary fear, and the brightness of truth seemed to flash from a brandished flame, that forbade access to a nearer view. It was holy ground, and the shoes needed to be loosed from the feet of all that approached.

Every other doctrine of Christianity, the sweetest manifestations of love, equally with the most terrible revelations of justice, are involved in mystery that defies our penetration, and forbids too close a search. Is there less darkness in the wonders of redemption than in the awful prospect of resurrection and judgment? Who shall fathom the depths of a love that devised the scheme of our salvation, and that accomplished it? Who shall understand but most remotely the motives that suggested that marvellous accord between justice and mercy, that compact between unyielding rigour and infinite power of propitiation, which, on the one side, demanded a God-victim, and on the other, gave it? Whose eyes can gaze upon the cross, if tears will let them, without being overpowered by the magnitude of the mysteries which it displays, the sufferings of Him it bears, and their mystical effects upon heaven and earth, on man and God? And if so, should not the heart and soul of every one who embraces Christianity, be despoiled of every proud inclination to pry into what God has taught, beyond the terms of His teaching, so as to be without a power to doubt the resources, without a desire to search into the ways, of His omnipotence? Nay, I will go further, and ask, should he not be surprized, and begin to hesitate, when he hears its doctrines so proposed to him as to seem brought down to the level of his understanding, and fear that it cannot be what God has taught, the moment it has lost all mysterious sublimity, and presents no more than a higher order of human wisdom? At least, in the nobler and more spiritual institutions of Christian practice, should he not be prepared for something more akin to the infinite grandeur of all God's revelation? When, for instance, he reads the inauguration of the eucharistic feast, knowing it to be the last and solemnest of his Saviour's actions while master of Himself; knowing it to have been meant for a permanent ordinance as a fountain of grace to the end of time; knowing it intended for an enduring memorial of love to all that loved Him; knowing it to be the last legacy which He bequeathed to His friends; knowing it, in fine, to be the great and principal instrument for applying to our souls the infinite benefits of His death and passion: shall a Christian feel anxious to discover in it nothing mysterious and sublime beyond the possible devices of man, nothing save a commemorative rite, devoid of efficacy and all saving power? Shall he think it necessary to depart from the clear and most obvious meaning of his Redeemer's words, because they would otherwise lead him to acknowledge a mystery of love, which his reason cannot comprehend? No; in the name of God and of his redemption, let him bow as low into the depths of his humble gratitude, as he knows the height of God's wisdom to be above his conception. Let him throw away the fathom-line, with which he was tempted to sound the abyss, and commit himself, with fearless confidence, to its bosom. For know, that if God hath loved to triumph over the resistance of the world and its interests, to the acceptance of His holy faith, there is another triumph dearer to Him still, over the heart of man. In both, the wisdom, and the pride, and the strength of man, must be broken down and confounded, and led as captive to His conquering wisdom. To the eye of flesh, the one seemed most glorious, while the other can hardly be observed. But, believe me, small as the conquest seems, and narrow as its field; to Jesus, that passionate lover of souls, it is a source of sincerest joy. His victory over the tyrants that opposed the triumphant progress of His faith, and over the public resistance of great and national errors, was a triumph of vengeance, a treading under foot of a people in the wine-press of His wrath, and reddening of His garments with their blood.

His victory over the heart of man, the subduing of his pride and weakness, is a triumph of love, wherein He wins those whom He subjects, and leads them, not as captives, but as friends, not in chains, but with palm-branches, to the glory of His Father.

Let us, then, approach with gladness, but in due humility, to the light of God; let us in it seek guidance and protection during this our wearisome pilgrimage; and let it be our fervent prayer, that if any there be among us to whom as yet the dark and cloudy side of His pillar be turned, they may speedily be brought into the congregation of the faithful, wherein they may enjoy the comforts of its light, faintly, indeed, now, but in its fulness hereafter. Amen.

SERMON XVII.

On Religious Unity.

MATT. xiii. 24.

"The kingdom of heaven is likened to a man that sowed good seed in his field."

AMONG the painful offices of our Saviour's ministry, that must not be overlooked which consisted in His being too often obliged, Himself to foretell the failure of so much that He undertook for mankind. Knowing as He did the greatness of His own work, and also the humiliations, sorrows, and pains, that it cost Him; understanding the immensity of the benefits which He was procuring, or rather bestowing, upon us, it must have been grievous to Him, indeed, to foresee how much of all these things would be utterly rendered void, by our ungrateful neglect, or obstinate contradiction. We may easily believe, that with some such feelings He pronounced the parable of this day's gospel. He represents Himself as a husbandman who sowed his field, that is the world, with a good seed, able to produce an abundant return. But while His servants slept, the enemy, taking advantage of their want of vigilance, sowed tares, that is evil principles, among the wheat, and thus disfigured and, in part, spoiled the labours of His hands. It is, indeed, true, coming to the application, that the heavenly Husbandman could have secured His work against any such ruinous surprise. He might have surrounded His field with a fence of hewn stone, such as no power of earth or hell could possibly break down; He might have bound the enemy in a short chain, so that he should not roam abroad to spy his opportunity of mischief; or He might have rendered His servants so wakeful and diligent, as to leave no moment for those wicked attempts.

Who shall say that He could not have done this, and more? But it hath pleased Him as yet, that is, until the harvest, at the end of the world, to leave a freer range to the powers of evil, that so His elect may be tried and approved, and the reprobate convicted and justly doomed. On these grounds we can understand what our divine Redeemer, on another occasion, says: " It needs must be that scandals come ;" (Matt. xviii. 7) those scandals which, in the application of this parable, He tells us His angels will gather out of the world at the last day. And St. Paul, in a similar sentence, explains these words, when he says: "There must be heresies, that they also who are approved may be made manifest among you." (1 Cor. xi. 19.) This necessity, therefore, of evil principles and false doctrine, arises from the state of imperfection in which we now live upon this earth, and which makes a trial requisite of those who truly love Christ, by the observance of His law. And thus it would seem that this two-fold evil may be understood by the bad seed, which the enemy of God and man hath sown over that part of the world, on which our Saviour had cast the good seed of His word. The first consists of the baneful maxims of a false morality, the second, of erroneous principles of religious belief.

But as there would be too much matter for one discourse, were it to treat of both these points, I will confine myself to the inculcation of the second. And to handle it with greater clearness, I will, first, endeavour to convince you, by a few obvious considerations, how much our Saviour took to heart that there should be but one seed scattered over the world, producing everywhere the same fruit; in other words, how dear to His heart is the maintenance of religious unity: and then I will propose to you some motives for aspiring and striving after the restoration of this blessing, where it hath been spoiled or impaired amongst us.

The figure of a husbandman is evidently a favourite one in the word of God, when speaking of the pains taken by His providence for the welfare of mankind in general, and of His more chosen people in particular. It, in fact, describes more accurately than any other could do, the exact relation between the will of man, in his present state, and the power of God, which directs and assists him. When He speaks of having created us, He compares Himself to the potter who fashions the clay at his will, and makes it a vessel of whatever form he may have designed. For such a one's work is entirely in his own hands; the success of his labour depends completely upon his skill; and it comes forth from his fingers perfect as he intended it, unable to thwart his design, or to disappoint his expectations. And so, in like manner, God, when He created us, asked for no co-operation from us. We know not how it was with us till we had been formed by Him, perfect in body and soul, fitting vessels for His mercy and grace. But very different does the other image represent Him to us, in explaining His providential action upon us, after this first favour has been conferred. The husbandman toils more than the potter, to insure himself success. He ploughs up the hard soil again and again, he cleanses it of all that can hurt his future crop, then he casts upon it a choice and well-prepared seed, which he covers over, and protects from the birds of the air. He sits not at home, as the other, to his work, nor finishes it in one brief hour. But in the sweat of his brow he toils abroad, under the fiercest sun in summer, amidst the drenching rains of winter; he labours through weeks and months unceasingly, and gives little or no rest to the apple of his eye. And when he hath done all this, when he hath exercised all his science, and exhausted all his ingenuity, and busied himself all the year, can he make sure of his success? No; but he waiteth patiently, to see what the earth will repay him for all his labour. It may be an abundant return; but the ungrateful soil may disappoint all his hopes, render vain all his exertions, and bring down his curse upon itself.

When this image is applied, as it so often is in Scripture, to things spiritual, when God is the husbandman, and man the earth, it affords matter for awful considerations. But my subject requires at present only one or two. What an earnestness it supposes in the desire of the husbandman that his labours should succeed! We may, indeed, truly say, that God puts forth no material strength, and toils not in the ordinary government of the moral world, especially in the souls of men; but even then the very imagery used implies a variety of means employed, a richness of application of His power, and a serious wish of a proportionable success. But when we speak of that cultivation which the Son of God bestowed upon this world, in sowing the seed of His doctrine, literally and not figuratively, must we say that He toiled and wearied Himself far beyond what the most active husbandman on earth can ever do. For, had it been His intention or plan that belief should vary from country to country, or that private conviction should be the basis of faith, He need not have laboured as He did, to break down every opposition which society or the passions presented to unity of religion.

In fact, my brethren, if we examine the great tendencies of Christianity, we shall find them all towards unity in its most perfect form ; and if we study the action which from the beginning it exercised upon the world, we shall discover it directed to overthrow every distinction that could prevent the entire fusion of men's souls into one great intellectual and moral community. And first our Saviour commenced this work of demolition amidst His own people. Unity of belief in all essentials, nearly prevailed throughout the Jews in His time. At any rate, the various sects which existed seem not to have excluded each other from the pale of salvation ; and St. Paul speaks of the one to which he had belonged as the surest among them. But to none of them did our Saviour show mercy. He reproved the exuberant pretensions of the Pharisees as much as the scanty belief of the Sadducees ; He respected not the claims of popular favour, nor of long respect, nor of the zeal for the cause of God, nor of stricter observance of His law ; He made no compromise with one for the overthrow of the other, but turned the weapons of His close reasoning, and hurled the thunders of His indignant eloquence, first upon one, and then upon the other, till both were confounded, and glad to join their forces to resist and to destroy Him.

But when Jesus had thus proved His opposition to all sectarian spirit in the customs of His own people, He had effected but little towards preparing the ground for planting this unity of religious faith ; for had He succeeded in effacing all the shades of difference which passed between Jew and Jew, He would thereby have only strengthened the national abhorrence for all religious commerce with the stranger. I need not recall to your well-instructed minds the carnal ambition of this stiff-necked race, to become, under the guidance and rule of the Messias, the lords of the world, and the avengers of their wrongs upon all other nations. You know how, even after the Holy Ghost had descended upon the apostles, they could not, till after a special revelation, be induced to think that the Gentiles could be called to religious communion with the privileged Jews. This was not, therefore, a merely popular prejudice, but a sentiment founded upon serious religious scruples. It was not because the Hebrew people had so long been the prey of every powerful neighbour, and had been spoiled, degraded, and subdued by every conqueror that passed his armies over Western Asia, but rather because they were the inheritors and depositories of God's covenant and promises to the patriarchs, to Moses and the prophets, and because the others, by their rejection of the true God, and the defilements of idolatry, were deemed unworthy to partake therein, that the apostles shrank from the very idea of giving holy things to the uncircumcised heathen. At the same time, there was a sentiment of scorn against the Jews prevalent among the other nations of the earth; they were personally despised, and their religion was an object of derision.

Now, this mutual alienation, not to say hatred, Jesus, through His almost reluctant apostles, set about removing. He gave to the most eloquent and most energetic of them the title of Apostle of the Gentiles; He bade him preach that, before God, there was no longer any distinction between the two classes, for all were equal in His sight. One only saving doctrine was announced to all, giving to the adopted children of the covenant all the rights of the children of the house; declaring the fruit of the wild olive equal in soundness to that of the wholesome stock on to which it had been engrafted. By the power of God, the wall of separation was broken down, and both parties were soon astonished and delighted to find themselves joined in brotherhood, worshipping in common, believing and hoping alike, and cemented together in a common body to Christ their head. Still was not the work of preparation complete. At first sight it may appear that the union of such a large portion of the habitable globe under the dominion of Rome, was greatly favourable to the attainment of religious unity, as it certainly was to the preaching of a common faith; and so it would have been but for two serious obstacles. The first was in the prevalence of strong national prejudices between the different provinces of the empire, equal almost to that between Jew and Gentile; for we find St. Paul equally anxious to denounce all distinction between Greek and barbarian, as between Gentile and Jew. But, moreover, the limits of Christianity were not to be merely commensurate with those of Roman power; to the north, and south, and east, the propagators of the new doctrines had a field for conquest from which the Roman eagles had plucked no laurels; nor would the fierce nations against whom the spreading flood-tide of their invasion had broken, as the billows on a rugged shore, be easily tempted to receive a religion whose emissaries crossed over their guarded frontiers. Would the Britain, whom the Roman legions had hunted untamed into the western fastnesses of his island, love the creed which bade him acknowledge for his religious chief the pontiff of that very city whence issued the decrees for his extermination? Would the Parthian, whose quiver could never leave his shoulder, in his restless hovering upon his desert boundaries, to keep back threatened aggression, abandon his post to receive instructions from subjects of a detested foe? Yet was this strong barrier of social feelings overcome by Christianity, that one faith might reign over all. The envoys of Pope Eleutherius may pass unharmed into the heart of the British camp, and receive from its king a spiritual fealty, which he scorns to pay to the world's emperor. The Christians of Persia come, in times of Roman persecution, to comfort their brethren across the boundary, and even lay down their lives in the same witnessing, because they profess the same faith.

But these destructions of great international enmities, would not have sufficed for attaining the great object in view, without the uprooting of darling prejudices, implanted in the very heart of all the civilized world. Such, for instance, was the immense distance between the lord and his slave. The latter, whether possessed by the prescription of generations, or by the right of purchase, or as the captive of the bow and spear, was degraded, by public opinion and practice, into an order for which no hardship seemed too severe, no humiliation too deep. To have at once condemned the outward distinction between the two classes, would have been contrary to the spirit of Christianity, and would have drawn down upon its preachers the punishment of disturbers of social order, and the public peace. They trusted to the working of their principles, and to the mildening influence of Christian love. But they fell little short of this. They boldly proclaimed that the soul of the bondsman was as precious in the sight of God as that of his master. This, to men who looked upon their slaves as almost a distinct race of mankind, who thought little, in a moment of moody caprice, of punishing them for a slight offence with death! They made the very name of servant, or slave—for the two were equivalent—most honourable, by assuming it to themselves, as the servants of Christ. They received all such, without distinction of persons, into the Church; they exhorted masters to treat them with affection, "not as servants, but as most dear brethren, both in the flesh and in the Lord." (Philem. 16.) And why this revolution in the social world, except to procure, through it, a basis for the establishment of perfect unity in religious belief and religious sentiment? To pass over many, another powerful levelling of distinctions, likely to operate injuriously upon this intended unity, consisted in the throwing open to the humblest individual the highest dignities of the Christian priesthood, the abolition of all caste and family prerogative in its exercise: so that the most noble, the most learned, and the most powerful, might have to sit and learn at the feet of one far his inferior in every earthly advantage.

Thus, and in many other ways, did our divine Redeemer break the ground, if I may so speak, of the entire world, and prepare it to receive one only good and perfect seed, that so everywhere the same fruit of faith and holiness might spring up. Surely, in all this preparation, there was a magnificent display of power, that well may convince us of the importance of its object. It involved no less than the re-organization of society, both in the relations between all great component parts, and in those between individuals. It required nothing less than a sacrifice of prejudices, deeply seated in the heart of entire nations; a surrendering of prescriptive rights, tenaciously grasped by individuals; a lowering of the highest, and a raising of the lowest, in the social scale, till all were equalized before God by the sure link of a common religion. But there remained still one greater proof for the Son of God to give, of the earnestness and anxiety wherewith He desired to secure this unity of belief; and this He gave through the unity of redemption. Every other prerogative connected with the foundation of His religion, He shared most liberally with His apostles; but this alone He jealously preserved. He laboured for three short years in His heavenly ministry; He gave them the glory of toiling, during their long lives, in the same cause. He confined His teaching to the land of Judea; He sent them as His emissaries to the furthest bounds of earth, and gave them the honour of being the apostles of the world. He performed, indeed, miracles stupendous and most mighty; but to them He gave the power to do even greater works than He had done. He withheld nothing from them of authority or power, with which His Father had invested Him on sending Him into the world, save the right of dying for man's redemption. Towards Himself, they were allowed to testify the greatest of possible love, by laying down their lives for His sake; but for man, He alone was to have the privilege of such affection. For them all, He had wreaths of laurel, unfading coronets, prepared; but the royal crown of thorns, He would have to be but one. One only redemption was to save all, that so all might be one! Some have erred by maintaining that this unity may be considered secured by the common belief in this our common redemption, but His blessed Apostle has carefully guarded us against this error. For, in the most energetic language, he protests against those who believe Christ to have died for all men, forming sects, or professing to follow different names. Hear how he writes to the Corinthians: " For it hath been signified unto me, my brethren, of you, by them that are of the house of Chloe, that there are contentions among you. Now this I say, that every one of you saith: I indeed am of Paul, and I am of Apollo, and I of Cephas, and I of Christ. Is Christ divided? Was Paul then crucified for you?" (1 Cor. i. 11–13.) What doth this signify, if not that we virtually deny the unity of Christ's death for the redemption of all, when we allow ourselves to follow a division, and multiplicity of religious opinions, grounded on the teaching of different men? What doth it imply but that the doctrine which Christ taught can be but one, even as His redemption was one, so that they who prize the one should value and seek to attain the other? And could a higher value have been possibly set upon this unity of belief, than by thus making it co-ordinate with so solemn, so vital, so fundamental a dogma?

We have seen, then, our Husbandman go forth to sow His seed; we have seen the pains which He took to prepare the soil. That the grain which He scattered was chosen and perfect, who can doubt? Most certainly, when it first sprung forth, it was green and beautiful; but it was not long before the tares, which the enemy had silently planted, sprung up, and impaired its primitive beauty. I do not intend to lead you through the wearisome history of error, nor to detail the arts whereby it has, from the beginning, been propagated and upheld; neither will I bear you back to older times, but seek rather to fix your thoughts upon the present days, and ask you to reflect upon our own condition. It is impossible, my brethren, for us to speak of religion as presenting an aspect the very reverse of unity, or rather divided into a countless multitude of discordant sects, without our thoughts wandering to our dear country, as the theatre of the most varied religious dissension that the world has ever displayed. Did I name it as the land of enterprise, of wealth, and of generous emotions, I could not characterize it more distinctly than I should, by calling it the land of religious dissension. To other nations we are a moral problem; for they cannot conceive how, with the acknowledged good sense which distinguishes the nation, so great a diversity of sentiment can possibly exist, without even the attempt being made to bring such jarring pretensions to some final settlement. This will surely never be the case, until the majority are convinced of the importance, not to say necessity, of religious unity.

Variety of opinions in any object involving the search of truth, may be an earnest of an anxiety to find it, but must no less imply great imperfection in the method. Did we see men who dedicated themselves to some of the nobler branches of science, unceasingly busied with deep speculation and active research, discussing, debating, answering, and reconsidering, then each coming to a different conclusion from his neighbour, though professing to start from common principles; moreover, did we find leading men among them avowing that this year they thought differently upon some points than they did the last; think you not, that such science would soon fall into disrepute, or that all men would, at least, conclude, that the methods pursued must still be in a state of infantine imperfection? Let me, then, be allowed to come to this mildest of conclusions respecting the individuals, or the religious societies, which present a similar aspect at home. But let me push the comparison somewhat further. Suppose, for a moment, that these men of science, when not together, openly said that it mattered not for the interests of true science that their reasonings and researches should ever bring them to uniformity of sentiment, for it was quite just that each one should have his own views upon the subject; should we not reach a severer conclusion, that these men had but a very mean regard for truth, and rated their science exceedingly low? And is religion, the eternal truth, the knowledge of God, such as He has been pleased to manifest Himself, to be placed below all mere human pursuits, and the arrival at some great universal conviction to be considered an object of no account?

But contenting ourselves, for the present, with the first conclusion, where, let us ask, is the imperfection of method which prevents all men arriving at according conclusions in their search after truth? It consists primarily in overlooking the great characters whereby it is distinguished; in seeking it by parts, instead of considering it as an indivisible and perfect whole. The moment the unity of the truth is acknowledged, that is to say, the principle that of many conflicting opinions only one can be correct, it will be easily discovered to possess an unifying power. For, if all who possess of those many opinions the true one, *must* necessarily agree, while the holders of the rest may differ, and likewise change, so did we observe that many professed to have one belief perfectly accorded in every particular, and never altered their convictions, while all others broke away from one another on every side, and were each easily led to pass from one to another opinion; we should conclude, on a strong ground of probability, that they who agreed were right, rather than those who, so individually and relatively, varied. At the least, it would lead any reasonable man to give the earliest and most impartial consideration to the claims of that body which possessed that unifying power, which is so obvious a consequence of the unity of truth.

Further, our dissensions are kept alive by men seeking individual truths, rather than the principle of truth. The former may be found, mixed with errors, in the most corrupt or the most absurd religions; where the latter exists, error can have no place. A generous and feeling, as well as upright and determined, mind is necessary for its discovery. It requires the entire system of religion to be considered on a comprehensive scale, the quenching of many prejudices upon individual points, the suppressing of partial curiosity, to investigate practices, and search out abuses, rather than follow out principles to their root and foundation. It demands the accurate comparison of first postulates in different systems, referably to sound reason, the divine attributes, and the word of God. And, beyond all, it requires the willing determination to embrace any principle, when discovered, with all its consequences, however individually they may seem, to contradict our previous convictions, or thwart our desires. Let the study of jarring claims be assayed and judged in their first elements and fundamental principles alone, and the cause will soon be decided.

But these investigations would be most surely successful, if the nobler feelings of the heart were allowed to play the part they deserve in it, and not kept chained down, as too generally they are, as though intruders, whenever truth is in question. For truth is but the reflection of the eternal mind of God, and partakes of His beauty. As such, the heart and soul have as deep an interest in its discovery, and may be as fitting organs to discover it, as the understanding itself. But to this, at least, they must lead all, whatever their religious profession, to value religious unity, and deeply to admire it, and so earnestly to desire its accomplishment.

The idea that religious truth is not merely the creature of man's thoughts, an image passing through his mind, and having its reality only in his conviction, but that it is a portion of the everlasting knowledge of God, and has consequently an objective entity, is the only worthy view we can entertain of revelation. Only thus is it worthy of this name; for only thus is it a lifting up of the veil of the sanctuary, and a real, though indistinct, view of its mysteries. It ceases to be the object of mere speculation; it is a solid portion of heaven's treasure, weighed out in nicest scales before committed to him, from which he must not clip the smallest fragment, as he may not add thereto the least dross, because his own. It is not as a meteor, which now may shine, then vanish, which rises in one age, and waxes and wanes in brilliancy, according to circumstances, and disappears after a time, to be called forth by some spiritual magician at a later period; but it is as the sun, that sets not and fades not, even though men, for a time, in some parts of the world, lose sight of his brightness. And who will not love the truth, when thus considered, as the light of every age, of every place, of every mind, and of every soul?

For, this is another beautiful property, arising from universal unity of belief, that it levels the interior distinctions between all men, as the institutions of Christianity do the outward. No sooner is truth considered a divine manifestation, having an existence independent of our apprehension of it, than it subdues the will, and captivates the understanding, of the most soaring genius, as of the simplest peasant. The intellect of man may break its natural ties, and stray beyond the boundaries of permitted conjecture; it may roam into regions of wild and dangerous theory, and lose all remembrance of its lowlier duties; but, if well trained, the voice of religion, however gentle, has power to call it down from its wheeling flight, and make it submit to be hoodwinked and fettered in becoming humility. If we sometimes wish that we could weep, or smile, or forget, as when we were children, we, at least, have the consolation to think, that we may believe as we then believed. For, in truth, we shall the better believe, so much as our faith shall more resemble what it then was.

Such will religious truth appear to him who considers it as an universal truth, incompatible with the admission of other systems, save as objects of pity and regret. And now, my brethren, I exhort and entreat you in the bowels of the Lord Jesus, and by the price you set upon His redemption, that ye all and severally resolve, above all things, to exert yourselves, wherever Providence gives you influence, for the removal of this reproach from amongst us, and the bringing of men's minds to the uniform and unvarying possession of religious belief. "Be instant in season and out of season; reprove, entreat, rebuke in all patience and doctrine;" (2 Tim. iv. 2) urge on all sides the importance of this great investigation, and of settling such important claims. Oh! do not say that such an object is beyond hope, and that religious party has run too high, for all to be again brought back to unity of religion. Tempt not the jealous God, by surmising that His arm is shortened, or that there is a sore He cannot cure. That which once has been, may be again, through the might of His hand. Think, then, rather of the days of old, when we were an united people, linked in brotherhood with every other nation, and closely knitted together among ourselves in the profession of a common faith; when, instead of several mean and puny conventicles springing up suddenly in every town, those majestic monuments of ancient unity, our matchless minsters, rose majestically from the earth. Imagine what a spectacle it would be, to see those vast aisles once more filled with men that worshipped with one heart, and hear those harmonious vaults ring to the notes of thousands praising with one voice. But when, not from one alone of those sumptuous temples, "the eyes of England,"—to borrow an expression from an ancient writer,*—but from many all over the face of the land, at the same hour of day and of night, the peals of simultaneous homage and thanksgiving rose swelling up to heaven, what a choral strain they must have borne to the ears of celestial spirits, woven together, as they ascended, into a rich and soothing harmony! And as upon a building, exposed to the storms of heaven, men place at intervals metallic points, which silently steal away its thunderbolt from the cloud, so did the towering pinnacles of these holy edifices, placed almost at sight over the country, stand between it and the wrath of heaven, and charm away the scourges which sin might provoke.

Oh! had our forefathers judged as our generation, or

---

* Ocelli Italiæ. Plin.

thought it possible that a few years would have torn the nation into morsels, each creeping to its peculiar worship in some hidden nook, they would have plucked down their own noble work, rather than see it shamed by the desertion of their descendants, and the desolation of their sanctuaries. Have not three centuries of experience proved, that when the unity of faith was once violated, the grandeur of religion, and its power over the soul to command great sacrifices, disappeared from amongst us?

But let us not brood over the past and its judgments; let us rather turn to the future and its hopes. So long as we remain a people of conflicting creeds, it is impossible that the vital functions of our social being can be properly discharged. For, believe me, a nation, being a body fitted together for magnificent purposes, hath well need of great and healthy organs for its life. It shall have its hands in the strong grasp wherewith it holds together its large possessions, and gathers up its riches; it shall have its arms in the strength wherewith it beats and holds off an assailant; its mouth, in the wisdom of its laws, and the justice of its decisions; its sense and intelligence, in the prudence of its policy. But its heart must be its religion. Through this it must love both God and man: and woe to that nation wherein this necessary action is long suspended. If, then, our heart be divided, shall we not perish? not, perhaps, in the material grandeur of this world, but in moral greatness, in nobleness of character, in loftiness of mind. Already has religious acrimony engendered civil hate; nor will human policy, or the statesman's art, find the plant to sweeten this Mara, this bitter fountain, at which all now drink, save that which the Son of man came to raise, when He cast His seed forth upon the earth. Let us be again, as the first Christians were, firmly united in one faith; and we shall soon be as they, possessed of one heart.

Who will refuse his co-operation for the attainment of so noble, so beautiful, a purpose? Who will decline, in his own sphere, however humble, to arouse attention to this great lesson of our gospel, that amidst the various plants that overgrow our country, one only can have sprung from the seed which Jesus cast? And, O blessed Saviour, if ever it be lawful for us to depart from Thy injunctions, let it be in this: that we may exert ourselves, not as the imprudent servants would have done, by violence and strong hand, but by gentle arts and persevering diligence, to pluck up the tares which have sprung up in this crop, that when the harvest shall come, Thou mayest find nothing but wheat to be gathered into Thine eternal granary.

SERMON XVIII.

On Charity.

JOHN, xiii. 34.

"I give you a new commandment, that you love one another, as I have loved you, that you also love one another."

NOTHING, my brethren, can be more affecting, than the details which the Evangelist St. John has left us of our dear Redeemer's conduct on the eve of His passion. He prefaces it by remarking, that "Jesus, knowing that His hour was come that He should pass out of this world to the Father: having loved His own, He loved them even to the end." The greater part of the discourse which follows this emphatic introduction, tends to prove its truth. Our blessed Master recalls to the recollection of His disciples, the love and affection which He had ever shown them, and was yet to manifest; how He had treated them as equals and as friends, when, of right, He was their master; and how He was going to lay down His life, that He might prepare a mansion for them in their Father's house. "Greater love than this no man hath, that a man should lay down his life for his friends. You are My friends." (John, xv. 13.) But soothing and consoling as this manifestation of our Saviour's love towards us may be, it is, at the same time, coupled with a serious obligation. This excess of divine affection is not merely displayed for our comfort, it is cited as the ground and motive of an injunction to love one another; and what is still more important, it is proposed as the model and *rule* of this mutual affection: " This is my commandment, that you love one another, as I have loved you." The commandment of loving one another had been long before given in the Mosaic dispensation; it is the measure of the love, prescribed by our Saviour, that forms the new commandment, here given.

Jewish virtue had not afforded a single instance of friendship so pure, as to have induced one man to sacrifice his life for another; and if it had, the disproportion between Jesus and those for whom He died, would have made His love, in this respect, still quite without a parallel. Nor is this the only peculiarity in the love of our neighbours, taught us in the New Law. The extent of its influence, which is not limited to any particular individuals; the supernatural motive of divine love, on which it has to be exercised; and the eternal rewards proposed for it—all form grand distinguishing features of the precept of charity, delivered by our heavenly Master, and justly claim for Him the praise due to so beautiful and so perfect a system. Yet, beautiful and perfect as it appears, it is, in practice, full of difficulties. For, how am I to love a multitude of persons with whom I have not the slightest acquaintance, or in whom I do not know one single good or amiable quality that can challenge my affection? How am I to love persons against whom I feel a complete antipathy, or from whom I have received anything but kind or even

Christian behaviour? How, in fine, am I to love every fellow-creature, however loathsome, that I meet, and who may, indeed, excite my pity, but cannot rouse any affection? Such, my brethren, are some of the difficulties in observing this divine precept, difficulties which must vanish so soon as the motives are weighed on which we have to love our fellow-creatures, and the manner of practising this love is considered. Let us, then, see the different objects towards whom this love is to be directed, and in what manner our divine Master expects us to exercise it.

This charity towards our neighbours, comprehends every individual of our species. Difference of country, of sentiments, of religion, cannot exclude any one from a right of participating in it. Our Saviour has clearly and pathetically illustrated this in the parable of the good Samaritan; in which, on being asked who is the neighbour meant in the second great precept of love, He taught us that every person was comprised in it, though, according to the common practice of society, he might be supposed to be excluded from it. He teaches us to consider the whole human race as one family, who have all equally God for their common father, whose souls were all equally redeemed by the blood of the Son of God, the first-born of these many brethren, and whose welfare and interests are all of equal value with our own, in the eyes of Him who made all for Himself. He teaches us that we are to love every creature for His sake; and, as a sincere affection towards Him necessarily implies that we should love all that is dear to Him, He requires, as a pledge of our charity towards Him, a love of all those whom He has loved more than His own life. "If any man say, I love God, and hateth his brother, he is a liar. For he that loveth not his brother, whom he seeth, how can he love God, whom he seeth not? And this commandment we have from God, that he who loveth God, loveth also his brother." Such, my brethren, is the general love exacted in the new covenant, from all who wish to be reckoned disciples of Jesus Christ. But how is this love to be exercised? Are we to feel for every individual that warmth of affection which we do for our near relations and friends? Our feelings, I fear, are not sufficiently under our own control, to be directed thus by such pure motives as charity requires; our hearts are not sufficiently enlarged, to diffuse such generous love through so extended a circle. But the love demanded of us by the precept of charity, is more of a practical virtue, which should be manifested in our actions.

In the first place, then, it forbids the doing of any thing which can tend to injure our neighbour in any respect, in property, in body, in reputation, or in peace of mind. It was a principle of conduct fully admitted in pagan morality, that we should do nothing to any individual which we should not wish to be done to ourselves. This principle holds equally in the law of grace, with this addition, that whatever injury is done to our neighbours has become a crime against the God who has sanctioned the rule. Nothing can be more simple and easy than this maxim; and yet, at the same time, to what an astonishing degree is it transgressed. What, for instance, can be a more direct violation of it, than to search out and endeavour to detect the faults of others who have probably done us no injury, and in whose affairs we can have no interest? Making these the subject of conversation, and often of entertainment; pointing them out to individuals who had not observed them, and that, frequently, with considerable exaggeration, are scenes which we daily witness. Nor does uncharitableness stop here: it puts a bad construction upon the best performances; it extracts its poison from a casual and indifferent action, or a thoughtless expression, and construes it into a crime. It is not thus, my brethren, that the word of God depicts the true charitable Christian. "Charity," says the Apostle, "is patient, is kind: charity envieth not, dealeth not perversely, is not puffed up, is not ambitious, seeketh not her own (interests), is not provoked to anger, thinketh no evil . . . . beareth all things, believeth all things, hopeth all things, endureth all things." (1 Cor. xiii. 4, seqq.) Thus, true charity endeavours to see only the good side of our neighbour's conduct, and to throw a veil over his faults, where duty does not oblige us to notice them. It teaches us to make every allowance for his circumstances and temptations. It brings before our eyes our own weaknesses, greater, perhaps, by far than what our keen observation has detected in him, and bids us extend towards him that pity and indulgence which we should wish to be shown to us by others, who are, doubtless, trying no less to discover the flaws in our own character. Thus it was that St. Peter acted, who, though he saw, and must have felt, the black and flagrant injustice done to his divine Master by the Jews, in having so falsely accused and so barbarously crucified Him, still endeavours to palliate their crime by attributing it to ignorance: "And now, brethren, I know that you did it through ignorance, as also your rulers." (Acts, iii. 17.) Thus, our Redeemer Himself, when His apostles abandoned Him to His agony in the garden, notwithstanding their protestations of fidelity, attributes their fault to human frailty, and expresses His conviction that their spirits were indeed ready to assist and pray with Him, if the weakness of their bodies only allowed it.

Not only must we avoid all uncharitable conduct and all uncharitable thoughts towards every neighbour, we must wish and be ever ready to do him all the good in our power. Had our Redeemer contented Himself with the negative part of the precept towards us, our condition would, indeed, have been still wretched. But no charity could be more active than His, which He has proposed to us as a model. Hence, He prescribes that, in our daily prayer, we should not address God for ourselves only, but that we should implore for others the same blessings, the same forgiveness of sins, the same deliverance from evil, which we beg for ourselves. There is not a vice more odious than that of selfishness and envy, nor is there any which more completely brings its own punishment to its victim. He fancies that every blessing bestowed upon another is so much taken from himself; that every good quality in a neighbour is a reflection on him, every good action a condemnation of his own inferiority. To one so disposed, the idea of good done to a neighbour sounds as if it necessarily implied injury done to himself; and if he does not prevent it, he will at least look at it with an evil eye, and be sorry to see it happen.

Now, true charity proceeds on directly opposite principles, and pursues a directly opposite course. For, it recognizes in every neighbour a brother who is to be loved as one's-self, and consequently sees with pleasure everything good which falls to his share. It considers the blessings bestowed upon others as spontaneous gifts from the hand of God, which the Almighty Giver has a right to confer on whom He pleases, and which, coming from His infinite riches, can no way diminish what He may have in store for us. And thus it sees in His conduct nothing which injures us, but it makes us, on the contrary, rejoice that others too should partake of His beneficence. Nor does it stop here.

It considers itself happy in being selected by Him to be the instrument of His goodness, and the channel of His benefits, whenever an opportunity occurs of rendering service to others. No disposition can be more amiable than this. One possessing it, finds his enjoyments multiplied as manifold as he sees good or happy persons around him; and instead of brooding over the faults or misfortunes of others, seeks every opportunity of remedying them, and ever finds a consolation and a recompense in the exercise of this benevolence. What a beautiful picture does holy Job draw of his own happiness, in the exercise of this general attention to the good of his neighbours, his readiness to do them all service and kindness, and his willingness to extend his protection and assistance to all that required it! "The ear," says he, "that heard me blessed me, and the eye that saw me gave witness to me: because I had delivered the poor man that cried out; and the fatherless, that had no helper.

The blessing of him that was ready to perish came upon me, and I comforted the heart of the widow. I was clad with justice: and I clothed myself with my judgment, as with a robe and a diadem. I was an eye to the blind, and a foot to the lame. I was the father of the poor; and the cause which I knew not, I searched out most diligently. I broke the jaws of the wicked man, and out of his teeth I took away the prey. And I said, I shall die in my nest, and as a palm-tree shall multiply my days... My glory shall be always renewed, and my bow in my hands shall be always repaired... If I had a mind to go to them, I sat first, and when I sat as a king, with his army standing about him, yet I was a comforter of them that mourned." (Job, xxix.)

Such was eminently our divine Redeemer, who went round dealing benefits to all who needed them; giving counsel to all who asked it; imparting instruction to all who sought for it; bearing with patience the obstinacy of the crowds, the vexatious and captious curiosity of the rulers, the dulness of His apostles, and sometimes the ingratitude of those whom He had healed; never suffering His warm, active charity to be cooled or damped by any of these discouragements, but persevering to the end in the same benevolence; healing the ear of the wretch who came to apprehend Him; offering reconciliation to the murderer, Judas, when betraying Him with a kiss; consoling the pious women who wept over Him; and meekly forgiving the unfaithful Peter, who denied Him, when dying for his sake.

It is evident, my brethren, that the charity which I have described, excludes the very supposition that we can have any enmities; and yet, it is impossible to go through life without frequently exciting them. Were the mutual forbearance which Christian charity prescribes observed by all, there would be no need of giving directions how we are to conduct ourselves towards enemies, even in the most mitigated sense of the word; but, far from this being the case, there is so much misconstruction, and often so much even of malice, in individuals, that the most correct conduct, the best-intentioned acts, will raise against us persecution or dislike. Nothing, my friends, can be more explicitly prescribed in Scripture, than our conduct under such circumstances.

The law of charity is most positive: we must forgive all who offend against us—we must bear no enmity towards them. "For if you forgive men," says Jesus Christ, "their offences, your heavenly Father will also forgive you your offences; but if you will not forgive men, neither will your Father forgive your sins." (Matt. vi.) He has enforced this principle by the parable of the debtor, who, appealing to the mercy of his lord and creditor, obtained a remission of all he owed; and then refused the same indulgence to a fellow-servant, who owed him a trifling sum. "Then his lord called him, and said to him: Thou wicked servant, I forgave thee all thy debt because thou besoughtest me. Shouldst not thou, then, have had compassion on thy fellow-servant, even as I had compassion on thee? And his lord being angry, delivered him to the tormentors, until he should pay the whole debt. So, also, shall My heavenly Father do to you, if you forgive not every one his brother from your hearts." (Matt. xviii.)

The principle on which we are to use charitable

forgiveness of our offending neighbours, is here plainly declared; it is the remembrance of our own dependence on the justice of God. We daily stand as suppliants before the throne of grace; we confess our numerous treasons and misdemeanours against our Lord; and, notwithstanding their magnitude and numbers, implore His clemency, beg that He will have pity on our frailty, and forgive us our iniquities. But if, at the same moment, a brother, who is our own frail flesh, have offended against us, every motive which prompts us not to forgive him—every reason which our minds suggests to us why we should be inexorable—is no less efficacious an argument in the hands of divine justice for a similar dealing with us. If we argue that our previous kindness towards him, makes his ingratitude and baseness unpardonable, how shall we turn to implore mercy from Him who has loaded us with every blessing, and whom we have, nevertheless, so wantonly offended? If the unfeelingness or violence of his conduct, or the blackness of his enmity, be the plea for our unforgivingness, with what ten-fold strength can it be retorted by the Being whom we have outraged in every manner that is most hateful to Him, and whose most sacred commands we have so repeatedly violated? To insure our remembrance of this rule of forgiveness, our blessed Saviour has inserted it in the prayer which He Himself taught, and which we all daily recite: "Forgive us our trespasses, as we forgive them that trespass against us." Who shall dare to pronounce these words, while hatred or enmity rankles in his breast? When proceeding from a relentless disposition, which knows not how to pardon an injury, instead of ascending as a prayer for forgiveness to the clemency of God, it flies in the form of a dreadful imprecation to the bar of His justice, and addresses it as follows: If I, O Lord, have been guilty of any treasons against Thy infinite goodness, and have abused Thy benefits to offend Thee, cut me off for ever from Thy friendship; for so *I* forgive those who are ungrateful towards me. If I have transgressed Thy commandments, or contemned Thy injunctions, cast me from Thy face, reject me from the number of Thy servants; for so *I* treat those who dare to be negligent to my mandates. If I have profaned Thy holy name, or have not paid it due respect; if I have offended against the sanctity of Thy temple, by irreverence or negligence in its worship; if, in fine, I have, either in deed, word, or thought, slighted Thy honour, hurl Thy bolts upon my head, and blight me in the very bloom and promise of my days; for nothing less than the ruin of my neighbour can atone for the slightest imputation against mine.

Such is the prayer of him who implores forgiveness, without first granting it; and thus it will be heard: "He hath loved a curse, and it shall come to him;" for, "judgment without mercy to him who hath not shown mercy." Indeed, so dangerous is prayer, when not accompanied with mutual forgiveness, that our Saviour prescribed to His disciples: "If thou offerest thy gift at the altar, and there shalt remember that thy brother hath anything against thee, leave there thy gift before the altar, and first go to be reconciled to thy brother, and then come and offer thy gift." (Matt. v. 23.)

But forgiveness is not the only duty prescribed by

Christian charity, towards those who have offended us. The gospel enjoins far more: "I say unto you, love your enemies; do good to them that hate you, and pray for them that persecute and calumniate you: that you may be the children of your Father who is in heaven." (Matt. v.) St. Paul prescribes the same conduct: "Bless them that persecute you: bless, and curse not. Render to no man evil for evil: but if thy enemy be hungry, give him to eat; if he thirst, give him to drink. Be not overcome by evil, but overcome evil with good." (Rom. xii.) The precept, then, of charity, orders us to be ever willing to do good to those who, on their part, may have done us evil; and instead of repaying them in the same manner, to be ever ready to assist them, and particularly to obtain blessing upon them, by our prayers, considering them even as instruments in the hand of God for our trial and perfection. The same command to exercise charity towards an adversary, existed long before in the law of Moses: "If thou meet thy enemy's ox or ass going astray, bring it back to him. If thou see the ass of him that hateth thee lie underneath his burthen, thou shalt not pass by, but shalt lift him up with it." (Exod. xxiii. 4, 5.)

What instances of this charity we have in holy writ! David, persecuted by Saul, almost to death, obliged to take refuge in the mountains and deserts, had his adversary twice in his power, and yet suffered him to escape unhurt. And when he heard of his death, instead of rejoicing and rewarding his supposed murderer, he makes the most pathetic lamentations over him, and repays the false traitor by capital punishment.

The holy Levite, St. Stephen, when bearing the cruel shower of stones, and upon the point of expiring, made his last prayer for his barbarous executioners: "O Lord, impute not this sin to their charge." St. Paul wished to be "an anathema from Christ," for those Jews who had so constantly persecuted him since his conversion. (Rom. ix. 3.) But both these illustrious men were only disciples of that Master, who was the first to pray for His enemies, and to suggest excuses and motives of forgiveness to God for the most inhuman and impious conduct towards Himself: "Father, forgive them, for they know not what they do."

Charity thus extends its sweet influence towards all our neighbours, without excluding from its objects even those who, human feelings would suggest, deserve nothing but enmity at our hands. There is, however, one branch of it peculiarly pleasing to God, and repeatedly recommended in holy Scriptures—charity to the poor and distressed. It is this office of charity which our heavenly Master has taken most particularly under His protection. To do this more efficaciously, He has substituted the poor in His own place; He has assured us that they are His peculiar favourites to such a degree, that whatever we shall do to them, He will consider as done to Himself. Had we it in our power to minister to His distressed humanity here upon earth, we should, doubtless, dedicate, with pleasure, a portion of what we have, to support so good a master and so affectionate a friend. In the person of the poor, this is perfectly within our reach. We can, like Martha and Mary, receive Him into our house; we can, like Zacheus, or the rich Pharisee, admit Him to our table; we can, like the pious women of Galilee, console Him in His sufferings; we can, in fine, like the apostles, have Him always with us, and exercise towards Him every friendly office. The efficacy of this virtue, for moving divine goodness, is described, in Scripture, as almost unbounded: "Prayer is good with fasting and alms, more than to lay up treasures of gold: for alms delivereth from death, and purgeth away sins, and maketh to find mercy and life everlasting." Nabuchodonosor, king of Babylon, loaded with innumerable crimes, and already sentenced to a most severe and exemplary punishment in the decrees of God, is exhorted, by the prophet Daniel, as a last resource, "to redeem his sins with alms, and his iniquities with works of mercy to the poor."

It is impossible for you to invest yourselves with the feelings of those poor creatures who suffer under privations or misfortunes; you can never, in fancy, realise what the distressed father feels, when he solicits your relief, with the remembrance of his famishing little ones, who are expecting his return, and whose support for the day, perhaps, depends upon your commiseration; you can never work yourselves up to imagine correctly the sentiments of degradation and shame with which a person, perhaps, once in prosperous, or at least comfortable, circumstances, holds out his hand for your relief, nor of the wound which you inflict by a repulsive denial.

But if motives of compassion cannot move us to grant relief, let the reflection that this is a sacred duty, pleasing to God, and highly advantageous to ourselves, have the power of eliciting it. Not a cup of cold water, given in obedience to this precept of charity, shall be without its reward. The prayers of the poor never fly into the presence of God, in behalf of their benefactors, without being heard : " He will not despise the prayer of the fatherless ; nor the widow, when she poureth out her complaints." (Ecclus. xxxv.) What a remarkable instance we have of the efficacy of such prayer in the Acts of the Apostles! We there read, that " in Joppe was a certain disciple named Tabitha, which, being interpreted, is called Dorcas. This woman was full of alms-deeds, which she performed. And it came to pass in those days, that she was sick and died." St. Peter was in a neighbouring city, and two men were instantly sent to bring him. " And Peter, rising up, came with them. And when he was arrived they brought him into the upper chamber : and all the widows stood round about him weeping, and showing him the coats and garments which Dorcas had made them." This silent eloquence was more powerful than any words. Peter well knew what it meant, and that no favour was too great to be granted to such petitioners. He knelt down, prayed, and restored her to life. " And when he had called the saints and the widows, he presented her alive." (Acts, ix.) Such was the efficacy of the prayers of the poor in favour of their benefactress; in that age of miracles they procured her return from death : but far more efficacious is their voice, when it implores a heavenly reward. They are directed to a heart far more tender and compassionate than even that of an apostle ; and on that dreadful day, when the sentence of invitation to the mansions of the Father, or of rejection into everlasting fire, will be pronounced according to our discharge, or neglect, of charity to the poor, what advocates can be more powerful, or what patronage more irresistible, than that of the poor themselves, should they surround our Judge as they did Peter, and hold up to His view the alms which we have in our lives afforded them! And if there be any season for being liberal with our deeds of mercy, it must be this, when the Church almost daily calls upon us to hide our alms in the bosom of the poor, and sanctify, by works of mercy, our fast, that it may be such a fast as God has chosen; and more especially, as the commemoration of our Saviour's charity towards us in His passion, is approaching, which cannot be honoured in a manner more pleasing to Him, than by imitating it towards our indigent brethren.

These, then, my brethren, are the duties of Christian charity; and if you want one short, impressive motive to influence you to study and observe them, take that of the Apostle Saint Paul: "Owe no man anything, but to love one another. For he that loveth his neighbour hath fulfilled the law. . . . . For if there be any other commandment, it is comprised in this word, Thou shalt love thy neighbour as thyself. Love, therefore, is the fulfilling of the law." (Rom. xiii.) Hence, in his epistles, he constantly exhorts the faithful to mutual love and forbearance. For this is the badge which his Master had given His disciples, whereby to be distinguished from the rest of men: "By this shall all men know that you are My disciples, if you have love for one another." Hence, in the infant Church, the multitude of believers had but one heart and one soul; those who had property sold it to relieve the distressed: and so effectually were the Christians distinguished by this mutual fraternal love, that the pagan writers notice it as one of the most remarkable characteristics of our religion. It was thus that the Church flourished; it was thus that all the members of Christ really formed one mystical body; it was thus they emulated the unity and charity of the blessed in heaven, and were represented by the Apostle as already joined to the city of the living God, the heavenly Jerusalem. By emulating on earth this really primitive spirit of the first Christians, we shall secure to ourselves, in the most efficacious manner, the acquisition of the same rewards which it procured for them.

SERMON XIX.

On the Love of our Neighbour.

LUKE, x. 29.

"But he willing to justify himself, said to Jesus: And who is my neighbour?"

THE answer to this question appears to us now so natural and so simple, that we feel almost indignant at him who could thus interrogate the Son of God; and yet, when that question was put, there was but one upon earth who was capable of answering it. Had it been placed before the greatest of heathen sages, connected with the precept which had been just recited from the Old Law, he would have known no meaning that he could apply to the word concerning which information is asked, beyond its crude and literal meaning, which would not seem, even to him, to establish the commonest claim to affection. "Who is my neighbour?" he would ask. It may be, perhaps, he who lives in my immediate vicinity. It may mean one with whom I am in some way connected by ties of citizenship. But beyond some such narrow limit as this, he could have had no idea who was meant by "neighbour" in a Christian sense, who was to be loved as we love ourselves. Or, if the question had been put to the interrogator himself, to a man learned in the Jewish law, "Who is your neighbour" whom you are thus to love?

he would have at once recurred to the mysterious lesson of his law, that " Thou shalt love thy friend, and thou shall hate thine enemy;" and he would have drawn a line between those two classes of men, as caprice, or passion, or human interest might have dictated ; though but a small sphere would have enclosed the one, while the great bulk of mankind would have been spread over the vast and unbounded extent, which is beyond that limit.

Then it was no chance, it was a providence, that this question should have been put to Him who alone could answer it, and who has made that answer so familiar, that now the least of Christian children know instinctively how to reply to it. Well may we thank him who was in some way raised up to ask that question, that so we might have its answer ; not merely because it brought forth from the rich treasures of our Saviour's wisdom that most beautiful, that most tender, that most divine of all His parables, that of the good Samaritan, but because it led Him to lay down that Christian principle of charity which has become the very heart of Christian society—which has been the first great principle of all Christian policy, and all Christian civilization, and all Christian enterprise—" Thou shalt love thy neighbour as thyself."

"And who is my neighbour?" With what deep wisdom did our blessed Redeemer answer this question, when He showed to the Jew the Samaritan, in whose character was to be found all that was requisite for a reply to this demand. For while He so severely reproved the enquirer, by giving the example of charity which He desired, in the Samaritan, He taught the Jew that as the Samaritan had included one of his race among *his* neighbours, so he likewise must learn to expand his heart, and to embrace all mankind in that new love, which was to be the great lesson, the great inheritance, of the Christian race. For, my brethren, the Samaritan was not an enemy of the Jew; he was worse than this—he was his rival. He was looked upon with that peculiar feeling of low hatred which is a compound of contempt and of jealousy. The Jew might have been generous, and almost loving, towards the inhabitants of distant regions, whom he scarcely knew, who never came across his own path. He might, and did, no doubt, hate the Roman, who had usurped over him, and over the whole world, that dominion which the Jew claimed for himself and his race. But there was fear and awe mingled in that sentiment; and he felt, too, that under the mighty dominion of Rome he enjoyed security, and peace, and prosperity. But the Samaritan was one who had crept into the very heart of that land which should have been appropriated to him as his own inheritance. He had usurped a worship which the Jew considered as exclusively his own; he was the only one who presumed to offer sacrifices to God in a holy place, and to despise the ordinances of Jerusalem; but, at the same time, observed, even more strictly than the Jew, the spirit of the law. He was enterprising, and he was charitable; he was kind, and remarkable for his social virtues, and cast a reproach on those in the midst of whom he lived, and with whom he shared that spiritual equality which the Jew considered exclusively his own.

Then, when our blessed Saviour thus told the Jew that

the Samaritan was to be included in the number of those whom he was to call his neighbours, He at once threw open the bounds of human love, and made it embrace whatever among men might seem necessarily objects of antipathy to us, or make us most naturally shrink from loving them.

Such, my dear brethren, is the great principle which our blessed Saviour laid down and gave to His Church, and which has been the rule of her conduct from the beginning. And you will allow me, therefore, this morning, to trace for you this principle in the action of the Church, to show you the influence which those words have exercised over the whole of the world, over society, over civilization, and over whatever has sprung from it, wherever the Christian name has been known, or heard. Whatever our blessed Saviour undertook upon earth, whatever He did for man, whatever He bestowed upon him, He wished to imprint with two characteristics, which, to human ingenuity and human power, would have seemed inconsistent one with the other. All was intended by Him to be, at the same time, universal, and yet one. He redeemed the whole of mankind. There was no exception to that great work, which formed the object of His existence upon earth; but all men, of whatever race, of whatever country, and of whatever age, were to be redeemed by one single action, at the same instant. There were to be universality and unity in that act; and faith, which springs from this great mystery, but which was intended to act upon that portion of man's constitution which proverbially is asserted to be the most varied in its action, his mind; that faith which, therefore, it might have seemed impossible to impress with these peculiar characters, was, in like manner, intended to be universal, and yet one. One faith, one doctrine, was declared to all nations—to all the world; and it was the wise and holy intention of divine Providence that all mankind should believe that one faith, should possess the same belief—the learned and the unlearned, the civilized and the savage. Whatever might be the variety of their ideas, of their thoughts, and their wishes, upon every other subject that interested them, they were intended to be placed on exactly the same level, as to that supernatural revelation which was communicated through the incarnate Word. All, whoever they might be, whenever they might be called into existence, were to believe alike; a oneness of faith was to be as sure a characteristic of His teaching as universality. And so, likewise, with regard to His Church: He meant that society of the faithful united to Him to be as completely one, as are the members of the same body a part of the same being. As the separated portions of a kingdom subject to the same rule form one State, so was that kingdom of the Messias, which was to extend to the bounds of the earth, to be one, under one kingship, one headship, one rule, and one law.

Then, in like manner, was it to be with charity: our blessed Saviour, having given this as a great gift, as a new virtue, unknown to the generations that had gone before Him, stamped it, likewise, with the same impress of His own power, and made the precept of loving mankind universal. It had to embrace the whole of our race, yet, at the same time, to be observed by one single act, centred completely in each individual; so that the whole of mankind should reciprocally love one another, because each one loves all ; as the various elements which compose one man are united by self-love within his heart. For all our neighbours must be loved as we love ourselves.

But how was this to be accomplished? For it would appear as if love of God's creatures were diffusive rather than concentrated, as if, in loving others, we had to go forth towards them from within ourselves, instead of gathering them into us. Love, which had not been known upon earth as a virtue, but merely as an instinct, or a passion, was of earthly growth. Each human plant gathered around itself the kindly influence of whatever was immediately in its neighbourhood, and these might entwine their branches together, in close friendship; they might bask in the same sunshine, or enjoy the same congenial soil, and thus have a sympathy, a correlative growth one with another. But rooted to the spot, fixed on that soil, how were they to take part in what was beyond their sphere, their reach, or their consciousness? This was the great problem to be solved—to give to charity or fraternal love the same characteristics which belonged to every other great gift of the New Law: and thus it was done.

The concentration of love was directed from earth to heaven. In the same manner as men, in every part of the world, naturally turn their eyes towards one and the same sun, and admire and glorify it; and as, in return, from that sun are shed over every part of the earth, rays which, coming thence with diffusive power, may be said to form an intermediate means of communication between things most distant upon earth—all gazing on one sun, and that one sun shining on them all: so God gives first the precept to love Him, to love Him with all intensity of love. Then all men thus loving God (oh! that they did so! but such is the design and the wish of His blessed love) —all men loving Him, who alone is the great, the single object of universal love, towards whom all, from every corner of the earth, may turn, and in whom they will find enough to love and to adore; all the affections of mankind are drawn towards Him, and centered in Him.

He manifests to all that love Him, that He, the universal love, loves all that He has made, and man, whom He has redeemed, above all; and so from Him descend over the whole earth those rays of fraternal charity, whereby we perform that great mysterious act of love, unknown before the magnificent revelation of Christianity, but which is one of its most wonderful privileges—the loving of all other beings, all other things, in God, and for His sake. We see reflected in Him that love which He bears to all mankind; and, endeavouring to exhibit a likeness to Him, the natural result and fruit of love for Him will be a striving to the utmost to love all as He loves.

And surely it is not too much to ask that we should love them as ourselves. For He has loved them as He loved Himself, and more: for He has given Himself, and stripped Himself of His glory, robbed Himself of His majesty, abased Himself, and, as St. Paul expresses it, "emptied" Himself, for man; and has even submitted to ignominy, and died to redeem him. Then, instead of having to strive for what is beyond the power of man, to feel distinct love for what he sees not, our love of God makes us love all other beings in His love, who loves them all. Our affections first rise to Him, where all is concentrated, and thence is distributed to all.

Now, what must necessarily be the working of a principle like this—an intense love, that is, of God, and, as a consequence, as intense a love of our neighbours? Why, that throughout the Church, in every age, in every place, all distinctions between men have vanished before her, because before God they are equal; and whatever of distinction or division there was of old, has been broken down; and active charity has sought to pursue its objects everywhere, without reference to any natural, social, or domestic tie.

Look at that venerable man, who bears upon his countenance the clear marks of high and noble birth and refined education—nay, in whose solemn and austere, but, at the same time, benignant, countenance, you may suppose that you behold the venerable features of some sacred Pontiff. See him bending over the rough labour to which his hands have not been accustomed, breaking with feeble and aged hands the soil that is committed to his cultivation. Who is that? It is the venerable Paulinus, one of the noblest of Rome's sons, one of the most learned of her bishops, a man respected and revered by the whole of Italy and Africa. And wherefore do we see him thus changed from his natural condition? Because he has given himself as a slave to the conqueror, to the devestator of his diocese, concealing his dignity; that he may purchase the freedom of his flock, that he may ransom them from slavery.

See, in later times, the meek and cheerful St. Peter

Nolasco, even giving himself up to bonds, that he may free the slave; the slave who, at the time the question was asked, "Who is my neighbour?" would not have been accepted, by the wisest and best of men, as an object of kindness or of love. And wherefore? Because he has, in his love of his God and in his love of his Redeemer, truly read the lesson, that He became man, and that He humbled Himself, and suffered, in order that He might rescue man, the captive of Satan and of sin; and thinks that he cannot better copy Him than by imitating, for man, that very example of charity.

And who is that? A poor and, outwardly, a mean-looking person, who has not in his countenance a trace of great or noble achievements, who, a short time before, had been followed by crowds of children mocking him in the streets, who had been treated by the wise of this world as no better than insane, and had been chained up among those who were suffering from mental disorder. And now see that magnificent hospital which has been raised in Granada. A fire has broken out in it—it is full of patients, without power to move themselves. Every one shrinks from lending them assistance, and he who, unaided and despised, has contrived—God only knows how—to erect this first magnificent building, founded to receive the sick, is to be seen there, running to and fro, fearless of the flames, and carrying them one after the other to a place of safety, so that not the hair of the head of one is scorched. This is the ignoble John of God, as he was before men, but now glorified through the entire Church, because he was an instrument of divine Providence, to manifest, and bring up to that splendour which its development has reached, that charity, which assists the sick, the feeble, and the decrepid. And how has he learned this love, that poor and bookless man? By loving God above all things; by loving Him with that intensity of love, which takes in the whole heart, and soul, and strength of man, and feeling that the love of his God is to be again diffused in the form of charity: upon whom? Upon those that first love us? Upon those whose great qualities, whose virtues, and whose amiable gifts, render them worthy of our love? No; upon the Samaritan or the Jew, upon whoever is in distress, upon any one who needs our help, upon every one, in short, whom God loves in His great and universal charity, without distinction.

Again, behold another simple-hearted, kind-featured old man, who is seated at the council-board of his king, suggesting the wisest and the best measures for the government of a vast kingdom, at its very height of prosperity, with statesmen and generals. Royalty itself listens with respect and veneration to every word he speaks. If you had gone forth early in the morning, you would have found him creeping through the silent city, covered with snow, and listening if he could hear the wail of a little one, abandoned by its unnatural parent; and you would have seen him take it into his arms, and carry it home with him, as though he had found a prize of matchless value. And if you will follow him in the evening, you will find him, not seated at the banquet-table of his sovereign, whose councils he has attended, but as gladly sitting on the same ignominious bench, with the galley-slave chained to the oar, and you may hear him whispering to him words of consolation, and bidding him be of good cheer, and reminding him that his Saviour was a prisoner for his sake, and encouraging him to love God, and, in Him, even those who were the cause of his misfortunes.

And what was this virtue which has made the venerable St. Vincent de Paul what he is in the love and estimation of the whole world? It was a knowledge of who was his neighbour; it was that charity which, springing from the love of God, made him feel that there was no exception to the law of its action; for, it embraced equally the true object of human justice, and the innocent victim of man's injustice; and which (though it may appear a fable, it is nevertheless a truth) extended from the infant and the culprit, even to the king. For it made the saint not shrink from giving up time to worldly occupations, which it may be supposed a devout ascetic, like him, might have thought at variance with his holier pursuits.

Such is the charity of the Church: and see what must have been the effect of such a feeling, since, from its beginning, it has been its very heart; what must have been its influence upon society, and upon those steps which have brought nations into their present condition! Can we imagine the state of ancient Rome, for instance, the city of palaces, bright with magnificence and grandeur on every side, where the wealth of the whole earth poured in, and was lavishly spent and displayed; where there were no limits to the enjoyment of luxury, and whither, consequently, for this is a necessary result, multitudes of poor must have flocked, armies of dependants must have worn out their lives; and yet, without a single charitable institution, or an hospital; without a term in its language for alms-deeds; without, in fact, the golden word charity, so familiar to our lips, yet which has no corresponding term in the rich vocabulary of ancient Rome? What became of those poor men and women, when they at last reached the years of infirmity, and when the failing vision, and the halting step, enabled them no longer to earn their bread? What became of that host of slaves, who had been pampered in luxury by their masters, so long as they were useful; but who were flung away when they could no longer minister to their pleasures and desires? What became of that mass of proletarianism, which must have festered in ancient Rome, where not a hand was stretched out to relieve or assist, and where the claims of different castes were unknown?

Oh! one shudders to think in what frightful ways they made their ends: how many snatched themselves, by their own act, from a life of misery; how many vanished under the compassionate assassination of their best friends; and how many, when pestilence, or other inflictions, visited that city, died in heaps, and were cast aside, and forgotten! Can we imagine a stronger contrast between modern times and ancient than this, that there should be now a feeling in society which makes it acknowledge the claims of poverty, of sickness, and distress, upon those who are themselves exempt from those evils? Sweep away at once all our institutions, and all our ideas and principles, relating to this important matter, and we should soon see the whole of our social fabric crumble, and sink as rapidly as did that vast empire. But this shows how the principle, laid down by our blessed Redeemer, had its action beyond that sphere that came within reach of each one's sensibilities, breaking down, in every instance, those distinctions which His answer was intended to remove.

But this would be a small part of that charity which He bequeathed to His Church. Turn your eyes once more towards that city to which I have just now alluded, and there, upon the brow of one of her venerable hills, you see standing yet the monastery, once the house, of the great St. Gregory. You see issuing forth from its portals, a procession of holy men, clad in the monastic habit, bearing on their countenances deep marks of the painful thought which their present work has excited in them. They are men who have left the world, because they feared it, who had scarcely for years ventured beyond the threshold of that religious house which had been their home. They knew nothing of foreign travel, or of foreign tongues, in the days when scarcely the more powerful, the more rich, ventured far beyond the limits of Roman civilization. And whither are those men going? and for what cause? They are going to an island in the northern seas, in which, it has been announced that there is a new race, a new people, who have taken possession of the land, and are still immersed in the darkness of heathenism. And what has excited this extraordinary desire to go, and visit this distant land? Some poor captives from that race have been bought in the slave-market of Rome, and the sight of them has excited the pity and the tender sympathies of the great and holy Gregory; and he has commanded his choicest disciples, his dearest children, to tear themselves from that city, from their homes, round which were circled all their affections, and beyond which they knew nothing, to seek, they knew not how, that distant land, and endeavour to convert its inhabitants to Christianity. And what again is this, but that same charity which was not engendered by acquaintance, by knowledge, by familiarity, but was felt towards strangers, aliens with whom there was no tie? And why? Because God had loved, and did love, the souls that were His, perishing; and because the Son of God had died for their sakes, as well as for those of Rome. Men felt this principle of charity, which broke down all social, and even natural distinctions between the families of men, urging them forward, not prompting them merely, but compelling them as a duty, to undertake such great and noble tasks. And this is the result of apostleship from the beginning till now. The boldest things which men have done, the greatest discoveries which have been attempted, have had this great principle of charity as their root, have emanated from it, and have only been one mode of manifesting it.

Then I ask, my brethren, why is this? Wherefore this desire, this yearning, this longing wish, to bring others, who are estranged from what the Church teaches, to a participation of its doctrines, and its holy institutions? Oh! my brethren, to explain this fully, it would be necessary to enter more deeply than time will permit, into a consideration of another and a most solemn truth; but I will briefly unfold it, for it will, perhaps, be a key, in the minds of many, to what too often is misunderstood, and misrepresented.

The Catholic, then, believes, that whatever gifts God has bestowed upon man, whatever blessings of a temporal character, whatever advantages of a mere accidental nature, whatever gifts of even a spiritual or intellectual kind, He may have given to individuals, to nations, or to the whole world, they are all as nothing compared with the gift of faith, the true, the saving faith. And hence the Catholic feels that, if the greatest of charities consists in bestowing upon man what is the most precious and valuable gift that can be secured to him, then the charity which knows no bounds, the charity of the good Samaritan, the charity of Jesus Christ our Lord, can in no way be manifested and practised so truly as this, in taking to those who know it not the word of truth, in communicating to nations in darkness the true faith, or in bringing those who are by circumstances estranged from it, into its full and complete participation. Hence, also, however great those charities may be, which, breaking down all social distinctions, minister to the poor, to the sick, to the captive, to the slave; these are all as nothing in the feeling of a Catholic heart, or of the Church of God—yea, truly, nothing in comparison to that charity, which immediately directs all its thoughts and energies to the soul that is to be saved, and does, in regard to the spiritual and immortal part of man, on which is really stamped God's image, that which those other, lesser, external, visible acts of charity perform in favour of the perishable body.

Then it is not wonderful that the Church at all periods should have considered this as the great exercise of its charity. Nay, I will go a step further, and ask, is it wonderful that the Catholic Church, with a principle in it like this, should at all times have been either fiercely attacked, or jealously regarded, for what is called its proselytising spirit, its desire, its earnest wish, its zealous efforts, to gather all, if possible, unto a unity of faith?

Oh! my brethren, if there be any doctrine upon earth that has been more sadly misunderstood and misrepresented in Catholic teaching, it is this, that salvation belongs to only one system of doctrine, or to only one Church. I mean when represented, for so it constantly is, as a narrow and uncharitable view. For, my brethren, that doctrine is the very mainspring of the most magnificent charity of the whole earth. No apostle would have gone forth to teach nations, and have faced prisons, racks, and death, if he had not believed in his soul that it was necessary that men should believe as he did, that they might be saved. For what motive less than this, could induce one to trample upon all that human nature takes delight in, and this for the sake of others? Can any one for a moment imagine, that we, or any others who act upon this Catholic principle, being ready even to die, if necessary, that all might be like ourselves except our bonds; is it credible that we would do all this for a foolish, vain, stupid, and unsatisfactory motive, which some think sufficient to account for it, a desire to domineer over the minds of men, or bring them into a captivity similar to our own? Whatever has been accomplished in the Church, from the time of the apostles until now, in the conversion of nations, one and all have had that conversion undertaken and accomplished solely as the result of this great conviction, that the true faith was the greatest of God's blessings upon man—that that faith it was of paramount importance, and even necessity, that all, if possible, should have it brought to them, that all who once had learned it should embrace it, and that all who had embraced it should preserve it.

This, and this alone, has led the Catholic Church to the accomplishment of the last great development of this lesson of our blessed Redeemer, that the neighbour whom we have to love, whom we have to love not merely with a barely speculative inward love, but whom we have to love with active, with zealous, and generous love, may be a stranger and a foreigner, and one living even on the most distant islands of ocean.

Then how much more are they neighbours, in every sense of the word, who, though at our side in the body, though living in the midst of us, as we in the midst of them, being one people, yet look upon us as aliens, on account of our creed, of that which should form our strongest bond of union; and consider us as not belonging to themselves, as almost out of race, because we hold doctrines which we deem far more precious than our very lives.

Yes, truly, my brethren, this will be reason enough, not merely now, but for ever, for the Church in this country to continue her untiring efforts; not satisfied, whatever may oppose her course, till she sees, if God reserves such a blessing for us, the whole of our native land bound together in one tie of charity and faith. For, see you not, that love men as we may, there is no bond so strait, so tight, and at the same time so tender, as that bond of charity which is intertwined likewise with community of faith; which unites not only hearts, but intellects also, in a common belief; which makes men partakers of the same spiritual consolations, breathers of the same divine life that is in the Church, closely knitted together, as parts of the same plant, or of the same body, to one root, or one head, our Lord Jesus Christ?

For this is the triumph of that charity which our Saviour enjoined, that it rests not until it establish likewise this additional and most precious bond, and brings all into perfect unity, by that which alone can constitute it completely, unity of faith and religion. And this shows that the charity which our blessed Redeemer inculcated in His reply, was a charity truly catholic in every sense of the term, a charity universal, that excludes none, a charity which binds us together by every indissoluble tie.

Therefore, I own that were I desired to name the blessing which of all others I would wish to this country, it would not be greater political influence, and dominion; it would not be an increase of its already exuberant wealth; it would not be the advancement of science and of literature, already so vastly developed; it would not be a still greater display and expansion of its innate forces, which astonish the world, in the creation of works requiring almost unbounded enterprise united with unlimited wealth. No; it would be none of these. I speak it boldly and without disguise, it would be that the Catholic faith should be the religion of this land.

For, I see here all the elements of human grandeur, wanting only the spiritual life added to them, which, quickening them with the divine principle, would make them truly magnificent, not only for this our earth, but infinitely more for the rewards of another and a better world. If, commensurately with this grace, there were also an exercise of that intense and truly sincere energy in matters of religion that is shown in all other pursuits ; and if men's minds were as active about the other world as they are about this earth, and, turning themselves to the study of spiritual things, were to be brought, as of consequence they must infallibly be, to earnestness of thought on the truths of salvation : then, indeed, we should see an example of what the world never before has contemplated, an example of what would be so great and so divine a work, that there would be nothing equal left for earth afterwards to attempt—a combination of all that is magnificent, and glorious, and noble upon earth, with all that is sacred, all that is honoured, all that is divine in heaven.

SERMON XX.

On the Celebration of a First Mass.*

JOHN, iv. 35, 36.

"Behold, I say to you, lift up your eyes, and see the countries, for they are white already to harvest. And he that reapeth receiveth wages, and gathereth fruit unto everlasting life."

ON a solemn occasion like the present, when the first-fruits of a ministry, to be dedicated to the salvation of souls, are consecrated on the altar of God, and when particularly this sacrifice of initiation ascends as a sweet odour before the Lord, under the auspices of that Saint who has always been venerated as the protector and patron of our country, I well know, my friends, how to calculate the tender and impressive emotions which you must feel. Each one will naturally transport himself, in his mind, into the situation of principal actor; he will figure to himself the awful moment, when, for the first time, his lips will pronounce the solemn form of consecration, and his hands, for the first time, bear the pure virginal flesh of his God made man; and he will anticipate, in fancy, the vivid faith, the profound adoration, and the glowing, rapturous love with which he will at that instant prostrate his heart at the feet of his present Redeemer.

* Delivered on St. George's Day, 1826.

God forbid, my friends, that I should have interrupted this solemn sacrifice, to check or cool such soothing and such salutary feelings. But, I am well aware, that they are not the only ones which occupy your minds. In that inaugural act of religion, you naturally behold the commencement of that career for which you will have passed so many years of preparation, and you know that you will, by it, be initiated into the state of life to which Providence has called you. Your thoughts turn to the period when you will be thus in possession of your wishes, and when no further prospect, except the zealous uninterrupted discharge of your missionary duties, will separate you from the grave. Your ardour is thus inflamed to rush into the midst of the combat; and that holy fire, which our Redeemer came down to kindle, catches in your breasts, and is an earnest of the success with which you will one day spread its sacred flames. These, indeed, are the solid, the useful feelings, which the function of to-day should suggest to all. To fan so hallowed a fire, shall be the end of the few words which I will venture to address to you this morning: and what motives can I employ more effectual to animate your ardour, than those which our Lord Himself suggested to His disciples? First, then, my friends, lift up your eyes and see the country in which you are called to labour—it is white already to harvest; and remember, secondly, that "he who reapeth receiveth wages, and gathereth fruit unto everlasting life."

It seems, my friends, the peculiar delight of divine Providence, to employ, for the accomplishment of its views, the very means which appear most calculated to thwart them. It leaves human malice and human blindness to design and arrange wants, according to their own perverse intentions; but what is their astonishment to see in the end, that they have only been forwarding the object which they had plotted to prevent? For three centuries, religious error has been endeavouring, first by force, and afterwards by art, to overthrow the Church of God. Year after year, it has given birth to some new monster; age after age, it has heedlessly plunged from one abyss into another, from heresy to indifference, and from indifference into infidelity. Every one of these dreadful steps seemed to remove it still further from the temple of Truth, which it first deserted. But no; every one, on the contrary, has facilitated its return, and brought it nearer, without the hope of recovery. The fearful precipitancy of its wanderings has alarmed the more sincere, and those who wish to preserve the small remnant of truth, have been obliged to plunge themselves into the opposite extreme of enthusiasm. These two powers of indifference and fanaticism, which so equally divide and convulse the reformed religion, have only one enemy in common. Both direct their strength against the true temple of the living God.

Their mode of attack, indeed, is different. The one, with insidious covered artifice, endeavours to undermine its foundations, by discrediting its revelations, and scoffing at the hopes on which they rest. The other, like Samson, though with an impotent frenzy, grasps the firm pillar of truth, which has been unshaken by the storms of ages, and endeavours to dash in pieces the sacred edifice, reckless of the consequence, that itself would be necessarily buried in the ruins. Against these two powers of darkness, therefore, our contest is to be principally directed; but, our struggle is far from difficult. For, while the attempts of both are fruitless when directed against the infallible promises of God, their mutual enmities are the triumphs of our cause. They are both fighting in our quarrel. The fanatic, to secure his religion, *must* prostrate the infidel before us; and he, in his turn, can never succeed in his aims, without overthrowing the vain attempts, and exposing the designing conduct, of the fanatic. This facilitates *our* labour. "For every kingdom divided against itself, shall be brought to desolation, and house upon house shall not stand. And if Satan also be divided against himself, how shall *his* kingdom stand?" (Luke, xi. 17, 18.) Oh! yes, let it be against us alone, that both unite their storms.

Let the force of such conflicting tempests beat on every side, let the waves of such opposite currents assail us all around—*our* house is founded on that rock, against which the strength of hell shall not prevail; and the sole effect which they *can* produce, is to shatter and overthrow those miserable edifices which they themselves have founded on the sand. Yes, the storms of this world, no less than the dew of heaven, must concur to ripen for us the harvest to which we are called.

But more; the spirit of the age is restless, and at the same time free. It searches for information with activity, and though its object be not perhaps to embrace the truth when found, there is, however, less of that prejudice in its pursuit, and less of that timidity upon its discovery, which characterized the periods that have preceded it. The first Reformers, to use their own expression, threw off the yoke of Rome, from a principle of religious liberty, and the same principle now induces sincere inquirers to return to her obedience. The intoxication of religious prejudice is passing fast away; and while all, when under its influence, were blind to the dangers into which they had rushed, many now, that the paroxysm is past, stand aghast at the precipices to which their wanderings have led them, and seem to regret the ill-fated moment which severed them from their unerring guide. Thus, then, are some of the most serious obstacles, which formerly impeded the labours of the missioner, gradually disappearing.

The country, indeed, is white to harvest. For, see how plentiful are the fruits already gathered, and yet, the labourers how few! Look on that handful of men, who, by their efforts, now sustain, and even propagate, religion in our country. Many have been the instructors or companions of our former years. They hold out to us a promise of what we shall do if we resemble them. Examine their minds, how devoted! their conduct, how irreproachable! They are men who have to suffer obloquy, and they murmur not; who have to struggle with privation, and they repine not. By them the fatigue of the body, the loss of health, the wear and tear of the mind, are valued at nought, because they are in the service of God. God, in return, has crowned such disinterested servants with success. They are, indeed, few, but their zeal and the circumstances of the times have abundantly compensated for deficiency in number. They have erected altars, where the name of Catholic was a term of execration; they have established their religion, where its exercise was but lately reckoned idolatrous; they are revered and courted by those men who, some years ago, would, perhaps, have punished them as traitors. How should their example animate our zeal, how should their success elevate our hopes! Ought we not to wish to rush to their succour, to lighten their labours, and to divide with them the spoils which they daily snatch from their enemies? Truly the harvest to which *we* are called is light and easy! Remember the days when the priest left this college to go, not to success and victory, but to torments and to death. Look back on that line of illustrious martyrs, who, within these very walls, prepared themselves for their missionary labours. They had to arm their minds, not against the cant of the sectary, but against the terrors of the judge; they had to steel their souls, not against the reproach of religious opponents, but against the weight of public ignominy and disgrace; they had to harden their bodies and their feelings, not only against the rigours of missionary duties, but against the knife of the executioner. Then, indeed, might the mind of our young seminarists have stood appalled at the prospect before them, and felt cold on entering their career. But no, they rejoiced like a giant to run their course; they boldly advanced to grapple with the united powers of earth and hell—they wrestled, and they conquered. Oh! these men, indeed, *sowed* in tears; and what they thus sowed, what they even watered with their blood, we are now called only to reap, and to reap in exultation. With such facilities and with such encouragement, who is the dastard that is willing to shun the labour? and yet more, who is so indifferent as not to long for its reward; for "he that reapeth receiveth wages, and gathereth fruit unto everlasting life"?

For lips unexperienced as mine to attempt to paint the rewards which, even in this life, must attend the fervent discharge of missionary duties, would be to presume too much upon myself, and to value too little your discernment and reflection. You are well convinced that God has promised a hundred-fold to all who despise the allurements of the world to labour in His cause; and how is this paid, if not by tempering every action with the approbation of a sincere conscience, and the conviction that what they do will finally receive its reward. Now what life can with such justice enjoy the recompense of inward approbation, or promise to itself an eternal reward, as that which we have determined to embrace? Its merit is not defined by duration: whether called at the third, the sixth, or even the ninth hour, our reward will be measured not by the length, but by the fervour, of our service.

It will not be estimated by success. However ineffectual our efforts, the zeal and exertions alone, which are in our hands, will be weighed for the recompense. It is not limited to great or splendid actions. All the pomp of learning, the most successful efforts of eloquence, together with the popularity, the esteem and veneration which they may draw upon their possessors, will be but as the dust of a balance, when put in competition with one act of solid sterling zeal, however secret or despised, with one poor soul regained from error, with one wandering sinner reclaimed from evil, with one falling just supported in his path. Oh! it is, indeed, often by the more despised and more hidden missionary duties, that most fruit is gathered unto everlasting life. What can appear more contemptible to human wisdom than to have to instil, with unwearied patience, the first principles of religious knowledge into the rugged and almost impenetrable mind of the struggling inhabitant of the cottage; to lisp with the half-famished infant of the labourer, the first forms of prayer to its Creator, without weariness, and without reluctance; and often to defend the truths of religion against the grossest ignorance and most inconvincible pertinacity? Yet, in the exercise of such tedious functions, the missioner is happy; he is laying up fruits unto eternal life. He remembers his Saviour condescending to invite and encourage children to approach Him; he consoles himself with the promise, that those who instruct others shall shine for ever like the stars of the firmament, and thus he boldly lays claim to the crown of an apostle. What can be more revolting to worldly pride than to be the servant of the poor, and listen with cheerfulness to their complaints? to follow misery to its abode, there to administer consolation to its sufferings? But, oh! can man come nearer to the example of our good Samaritan than by thus relieving distress, not casually found, but sought and pursued for the purpose of alleviation, and by infusing wine and oil into the bruised soul of the meek and unheeded poor? or can we more splendidly earn the kingdom prepared for those who succour Christ in the persons of His suffering little ones? What would be more appalling to earthly feelings than to attend the deathbed of the poor? There all the horrors of wretchedness, disease, and death, are centred so to harrow, if possible, the heart of the most callous. For, what can appear more repulsive than to hang over the couch of infection, inhaling its contagion at every pore, to administer comfort and strength, to a mind delirious with anguish, and to a frame racked by pain, exhausted by want, and to receive the last breath of beings near whom, one would think, a heart would sicken as loathsomely insupportable? Still, to the zealous priest, this is a scene of consolation and of triumph: he receiveth wages; he gathereth fruits unto everlasting life. He is transmitting one soul more to the bosom of its God. He is sending before him one more patron to represent his merits to the tribunal of his judge; he has provided another friend who will receive him into everlasting mansions.

But, my friends, it will be at the moment when the missioner himself is placed at that last dreadful hour, that he will chiefly receive his wages, and value the fruit which he has gathered. Then, the forms of all those whom his zeal has rescued from error, and of those whom his piety has saved, will appear to him like guardian angels, hovering round his bed, affording him comfort and protection. He will look back upon years full of merit before his Lord. He will examine his life; it has been spent in the service of God—what has he to fear? An account of his thoughts is on the point of being demanded. They have been occupied in meditating on the law of his divine Master. Of his words? They have been the words of eternal life, dealt out with diligence to his flock. Of his works? Oh! here is his consolation—they are already standing at the right hand of God. The sinner who would have perished but for his pious exertions, the unbeliever who would have died in error but for his unwearied instructions, the just who would have fallen from his way but for his strengthening admonitions—these rush in a body between his soul and the bar of divine justice; these demand that their pastor should be given to them, to be led in triumph to the mansion they have prepared for him. If he looks around him on earth, he sees nothing but objects of consolation: the altars which he has raised, the children whom he has instructed, the piety which he has disseminated in every rank, and which now raises its hands to heaven to implore its choicest graces on his head. Oh! my friends, that soul need not fear condemnation, which, upon its departure from the body, rises to heaven on the prayers of the poor, the sighs of the orphan, and the benedictions of the widow, and which is received and conducted to judgment by those whom it has already sent to glory. No, it is not to judgment that it goes, it is only to hear those sweet, consoling words: "Well done, thou good and faithful servant: enter thou into the joy of thy Lord." These are the wages, this is the fruit, to which he has aspired; these he has now obtained, and these he will enjoy for an eternity of bliss. Who amongst us does not envy such a lot; and yet who amongst us has it not in his own hands?

When St. Paul was at Troas, he saw in a vision "a man of Macedonia before him standing, and beseeching him, and saying, Pass over and help us." (Acts, xvi. 9.) Such a voice, my friends, this day calls to us, not from the shores of a foreign country, but from these of our native land. It is the voice of that spirit of religion which has for several ages fled. It resounds from the tombs of our Catholic ancestors, who once gained for their country the title of the Island of Saints, and whose ashes call upon us to regain the glorious name; it is re-echoed by that feeble remnant which is crying for the bread of life, and there is no one to break it to them. Shall such an appeal be unanswered on our parts? Shall not such a call rather inflame our hearts to prepare ourselves for the moment when we shall be called into action? Every day our prospect is enlivened, obstacles are vanishing, facilities are increasing; and may we hope in God to witness, before long, truth everywhere triumphant over error. "O Lord of Hosts, how long will thou not have mercy upon this country, against which thou hast been angry?" (Zac. i. 12.) "O God, why hast thou cast us off unto the end: why is thy wrath enkindled against the sheep of thy pasture?" (Ps. lxxiii. 1.) "Remember thy congregation which thou hast possessed from the beginning. The sceptre of Thy inheritance which Thou hast redeemed: Mount Sion in which thou hast dwelt." (Ib.) But no, "Thou shalt arise and have mercy upon it; for it is time to have mercy on it, for the time is come. For the stones thereof have pleased Thy servants, and Thou shalt have pity on the earth thereof." (Ps. ci. 14, 15.) Thou hast matured the harvest, do Thou give us strength to gather it, that for all eternity we may " rejoice before Thee, as they that rejoice in the harvest, as conquerors rejoice after taking a prey, when they divide the spoils." (Is. ix. 3.) Proceed, then, minister of God, proceed with the solemn sacrifice, which I fear I have too long interrupted: and in this propitious moment of grace, when thou offerest up on that altar the first-fruits of a life of zeal, do not forget, before God, the country which thou art called to reap, and those who aspire to be thy fellow-labourers in the harvest.

SERMON XXI.

On Fickleness and its Remedy.

MATT. xi. 7, 9.

"What went ye out into the desert to see? a reed shaken with the wind? .... But what went ye out to see? a prophet? yea, I tell you, and more than a prophet."

WHEN the Son of God condescends to pronounce the praises of man, it must be virtue of no ordinary class, and in no inferior degree, that forms His theme. There were many in His time who enjoyed great fame of holiness, towards whom the wonder and respect of the people were turned, as towards those who inherited the excellences, together with the authority, of their fathers. There were Pharisees, with prolonged fringes and phylacteries, proud of a strict observance of every tittle of the law, men of much prayer and severe fasts; there were Scribes, learned in the doctrines of the synagogue, who could discourse most eloquently of the righteousness which is according to the works of the law, and reprove unmercifully all transgressors of its injunctions; there were priests and elders, who zealously sighed after the restoration of their religion to its ancient independence and splendour. Yet, when was Jesus heard to open His lips in praise of any of these men, or to join His suffrage to the public commendation? Nay, clean the contrary. When missed He an opportunity of tearing off the mask of hypocrisy from before their faces, and laying the scourge of His reproof upon their backs? John, too, like them, had been followed by wondering crowds, and had been respected by the people as a holy man and a prophet; he likewise had fasted rigorously, and had unsparingly assailed the violators of God's commandments; and he no less had foretold the approach of that kingdom of heaven which they so earnestly desired. And *he* was, on the other hand, the only living man whom Jesus chose out to commend.

It was not, therefore, my brethren, for those outward works of striking austerity, which distinguished them no less than him from the rest of men, that John deserved and obtained from our Lord the sole panegyric He pronounced in His ministry. What was it, then, that made him worthy of so much honour? Ye have heard it in the words of my text. He was not a man clad in soft garments; he was not a reed shaken by the wind. "And is this all!" some will perhaps exclaim. "Was there no higher proof of John's extraordinary virtue than this? Might he not have been praised for his humility, or his zeal, or his charity, or the sinless course of his youth, or the unblemished chastity and mortification of his late life, or the intrepid witnessing, in bonds, of his present?" Assuredly he might. And who can for a moment doubt, that the praise of all those singular virtues was, in some sort, comprehended in the simple eulogy pronounced by Christ? For, opposed to the character of the waving reed, in John denied, appears that highest of all commendations, that he was a prophet, and more than a prophet; and that of those born of woman, there had not been a greater than John the Baptist.

Here, then, it would seem we have described to us the bane and its antidote—the evil and its cure. For, in fact, it is not too much to say, that by no characteristic is an imperfect virtue so strongly marked, as by its inconstancy and unsteadiness; and he who shall, indeed, raise himself above its weakness, and stand in contrast with those that bear it, may truly deserve the praise of being a prophet—yea, more than a prophet. Allow me to engage your attention to these two considerations.

In reading that painful series of reproaches, which form the great body of the prophetic errand to the house of Israel, one can hardly fail to be struck with the imputation of a two-fold perversity, one species whereof is seemingly at variance with the other. For, on the one hand, they are ever denounced as a generation obstinate and stiff-necked, bent towards evil with an incorrigible propensity; and, at the same time, as fickle and unsteady in every purpose—now, returning to God, in sackcloth and in ashes; then, once more listening to the first seduction, and giving their worship to Astaroth and Baal. Yet, in all this, is no contradiction. For these men belonged to that lowest and most degraded class of pretended followers of religion, in whom the occasional practice of duty and of virtue may well be considered a departure from the perversity of their habitual conduct, and an unsteadiness of purpose in their natural proneness to evil. Through their sojourn in the desert, they required a course of almost unceasing wonders to keep them even outwardly attached to the God who had freed them from Egypt: a temporary absence of Moses from the camp was enough to excite a mutinous call for the idolatry of that country; a casual scarcity of water was sufficient to rouse them to blasphemous murmuring against the Most High. And so, ever after, is their history but a repetition of similar unsteadiness in their fidelity to God; while, under the government of their judges, they are alternately the champions of His justice against the idolatrous tribes of Chanaan, and their slaves and fellow-worshippers—and this is their commoner lot; now they will have no ruler, but each tribe and house cares for itself; then they become clamorous for a master and king. And when they have obtained one to their cost, it is only that they may still more conspicuously display the fickleness of their character.

Fasting and weeping with Ezechias; rioting and revelling with Achaz; slaying false prophets with Elias; stoning Zacharias, the son of Jojada, to death in the very court of the temple; trembling at the menaces of Isaias, and despising the tears and counsels of Jeremias; purifying the temple only to defile it anew; consulting alternately the ephod and the idol of Accaron; (4 Kings, i.) such is the history of the people which God had chosen to be His peculiar care upon the earth. And when the Son of man came into His own, He was again provoked by them, even as He had been in the desert of Sin, by the inconstancy of their affections. The very men who, to-day, have followed Him into the wilderness, and forgot their homes and their daily bread, to feed upon the word of God, will, to-morrow, take up those stones, which would have made better children of Abraham than they, to cast at Him; the same miraculous exercise of His power is necessary, one time to avoid being, perforce, proclaimed king, and at another to escape being hurled over a precipice; the same crowd which, on the first day of the week, gives Him a triumph, on the fifth votes Him an execution; and they who, on the first, bore in their hands the palm-branch that symbolized His conquering might, on the last, thrust into His, the ignoble reed—the emblem of their own base inconstancy!

Well might Jesus, sickened by the heartless degeneracy to which the fickleness of His people had reduced them, proclaim him more than a prophet who was free from its reproach. Well might He, in dismissing the messengers of John, after having charged them to inform him how the blind and the lame were cured, and the dead rose again, add these humbling words: "And blessed is he that shall not be scandalized"—that is, offended—" with Me!" (v. 6.) Gracious God! and is this credible—that He, who might have asked for so much in return, should place His estimates so low? Might He not have exacted that the widow of Naim should ever have a room apart for Him in her house, as His prophet had at the Sunamitish woman's? and that the ruler and the centurion should stand His friends, and oppose their influence to the machinations of His enemies? Might He not have claimed, as His, every limb restored to health, and every sense re-endowed with activity; and demanded that the feet which, crippled, He had strengthened, should rush forward to His rescue, and the arms to which, withered, He had given life and nerve, should be stretched out to snatch Him from His foes? Ah! He knew too well the weakness of man's wavering, reed-like heart, to place upon it so heavy a load of gratitude; and He is content if any of those, who have sworn to Him eternal fidelity and love, in requital for so much kindness, shall refrain from being His enemy, and finding in Him cause of offence! And so, in truth, we may say, that after having, for three years, journeyed over the length and breadth of Palestine, and having, wherever He went, healed *all* their sick, He must have had, collected at Jerusalem, at His last passover, such an army of indebted followers, as might, had they raised their voices, have drowned the priestly yell for Barabbas, and might, by but lifting their hands, have overawed the Roman president into justice. But their fickle hearts had been turned aside, and they had forgotten their benefactor and their obligations.

Do you, my brethren, stand astonished at such inconstancy of good feeling in these men, and does your indignation burn at the baseness of their heart? Then look into your own, and see if this counterpart be not there! Do you discover fainter evidences of loving-kindness, and of a watchful care over you, than Israel received, in the wilderness or the promised land? Has a shorter arm rescued you, or from a bondage less severe than that of Pharaoh? Have you been baptized in waters less marvellously prepared than those of the Red Sea, or drunk of spiritual drink waters less precious than trickled down the figurative rock, or been fed with bread of angels that came down from heaven less than the manna? Have you been borne from the cradle, even till now, in any arms but those of your God, or has any one loved you more than He? He, moreover, hath done for you what, in the days of His flesh He did for His people: He hath cured your soul when sick, and restored it to life when dead in sin. And, in return, where has been the steadiness of your fidelity and virtue? You were young, and as yet innocent, and you seemed to flourish as a green plant set by running waters; your growth tended upwards towards heaven, and your healthy branches spread on every side. A perfumed breeze of pleasure came, soft and enervating; it played and dallied with you, and scarcely had you felt its touch but you bent beneath it; its poison reached your core, the sap of your virtuous energies was parched up; and when it had passed away, you found that you were but a hard, dry reed which the wind had shaken! You fancied yourself strong and powerful, as the cedars of God; you believed you had twined your roots round the clefted rock of divine revelation, and had lifted your head till it seemed to hold communion with the regions of heaven; you had defied the assaults of temptation to shake you from your proud standing. But the storm came, the winds blew and the rains fell; the hour of tribulation proved your hollowness; you crouched down, powerless, your virtue bent down, and you discovered yourself to be no better than a feeble reed which the wind had broken!

But will you say that never have you been thus rudely shaken and clean overthrown, but that those virtuous purposes, wherein ye began, in the same you have persevered till now? Truly, then, you are not of the race, whereof it is said that " all flesh is grass." Can we remember a month of steady perseverance in resolutions taken at its beginning, or a week of fervour without relaxation? How often have we recommenced, as we flattered ourselves, a virtuous life, and imagined that we had changed our hearts ; but, after a brief course, have fallen back into torpor ·or cold neglect? And what hath so quickly turned us aside, but a breath ? The sneer of a worldling hath baffled our resolves of prudence, the invitation of a friend has overthrown our plans of temperance, the prolongation of amusement has shortened our allotment of prayer, a trivial disappointment has blown away our patience, a hasty word has blighted our meekness, a silly shame has made us deny Christ ! Oh ! surely in the best of our purposes we are but as reeds shaken by the wind !

And even in the little, often fancied, good, which we do perform, how feeble and wayward we are ! One time we are in love with some peculiar practice of devotion, and then it is cast off for another. Now we are all alive to this scheme of charity, and after a time another becomes the favourite in its stead. One year the peculiar views and suggestions of popular guides, or fashionable theories, fill our minds, which the next will banish to make room for something new. By turns we are indulgent and rigorous: we retire from the world, and we mingle in its amusements ; we serve our God by caprice, and not by law ; we have a changeable idol of self-love, ever placed beside His altar, and it is often hard to say which we adore; and we may one day be surprised to find, that, however solid the foundation whereon we have built, there hath been much wood, or hay, or stubble laid upon it, and fashioned into some seemly form, which "the wind shall carry off, and the breeze shall take away." (Is. lii. 13.)

Nor would it be possible for me, in a congregation such as this, to withhold that evidence of the fickleness of man's heart, when left to its own guidance, in the best of purposes, which our common country supplies. Look over its broad and fertile expanse. See how the gorgeous vestures, cast over her by active industry, has almost concealed the noble features into which lavish Nature moulded it. See her wealth how princely, her arts of peace how magnificent, her prowess in war how irresistible! What intelligence in all her designs, what vigour in her performances, what power, to others denied, of maturing, by experience of ages, the wise thoughts of her forefathers! Yet, still in one thing wayward and fickle as a child, unsteady of purpose, and changeable in humour; listening, as one that hath sickly visions of hope, to every soothsayer that promises he will interpret them; stretching forth her arm, as one that has been wounded, to whoever offers to bind her sore; and multiplying her charmers and her physicians, till divided and sadly perplexed by the variety of their conflicting counsels. If to any people ever applied that description of St. Paul, that they are as little ones rocked and carried to and fro on every wind of doctrine, surely it must be to multitudes of hers. Among them the enthusiast may raise his voice, and thousands flock around him; among them the sophist may speak his delusive theories, and find willing listeners; the stern inculcator of a blighting severity, that nips every holy affection in the bud, will form his knot of gloomy adherents, and the publisher of a laxer morality will soon be surrounded by a host. And of these, the man who one day shall be an active partisan of one doctrine, shall the next be found in the ranks of its opponent, and he who lately followed after new forms and feelings, returns, after much wandering, to his earlier thoughts.

Yet the land itself bears testimony that it was not always so. While the ephemeral doctrines of each successive fancy cover it with new temples suited to their character, and therefore calculated for no long duration, but of their nature coeval only with the generation that raised then, and able to pass from the professors of one, to those of another, creed, there stand in their midst piles of awful and unchanging grandeur, which have seen cities fall and rebuilt around them, and partake of the immortality of those great principles which erected them. In the vast complication of their strength and their beauty, in the amplitude of their dimensions, and the marvellousness of their finish, we have proof of an inflexibility of purpose, a perseverance in virtuous work, which carried forward successive generations to the accomplishment of a single undertaking, and could give uniformity of idea and of execution to the efforts of ages. There was nought of the reed-like wavering in the religion of those men, any more than there is of reed-like frailty in their works; and in the massiveness of their splendid temples, we can surely read a stronger evidence that they hoped to spare posterity all further labour in this great work, and that they were jealous of that glory being shared by others, which they, like David, coveted for themselves.

And, oh! that our blessed Saviour's similitude could in our times be no further borne out! Oh! that following the impulse that moves him, each could be content to yield to its varying action, and not too often by fretting, in his restlessness, against all around him, kindle, as naturalists tell us has happened in their types, a conflagration of uncharitable and angry contention. Alas! poor heart of our native country, yet quivering, like that of the stricken deer, with the reed of religious perplexity that hath pierced it, when shalt thou be still? when shalt thou, no longer cloven with warring affections, send forth one healthy stream of love and unity, to invigorate our moral life? So soon as thou shalt put aside the unsteadiness of self-willed opinions, and learn the prophet's duty of an unvarying faith.

We have now seen the fickleness of man's heart in his moral guidance, and the world of evils which it produces; we have seen the inconstancy of his belief if left to his own devices: to a two-fold ill the Son of God hath appointed us a two-fold remedy, though we must reverse the order of application. Whoso would cure the latter, must be even as a prophet; he that would heal the former, must be more than a prophet.

What was the calling and office of a prophet? To be made partaker of the counsels of God, and communicate them to man. He was one chosen, by a peculiar mercy and favour, to soar to a sublimer sphere of knowledge than man ordinarily possessed, not by any power of his own intelligence or reason, but by the docility wherewith he received the revelations of heaven. It was a gift which raised the humblest minds to the level of the highest, which took Amos from among the shepherds of Thecua, and placed him side by side with Jeremias the priest. It absorbed, so to speak, individuality of powers and abilities, in the interior light of inward knowledge which it bestowed. It made the weakest heroes in the cause of truth, inflexible in insisting upon its claims, inexorable in vindicating its rights, zealous in making known its perfections, invariable in stating and inculcating its principles. And he who shall thus far copy the prophetic character, shall partake of its stability, and shall surely cease to be a reed shaken by the wind.

When the dispensation of grace entered by the New Law, the temporary and shifting character of the preceding one was changed for a fixed rule and a constant method. That which had been left to the direction of occasional messengers, was confided to an unfailing authority, and the expedients of the prophetic mission were supplied by an unvarying principle. Revelation, before partial, was now complete; and, if formerly provision had been necessary for ensuring its progressive development, it now was wanted to secure its integral preservation. And, whereas the prophet in the old covenant could only be cognizant with that portion of the divine will which had been made known down to his own time, while, on the other hand, the Christian is at once admitted to the full knowledge of revealed truth wherever God hath deposited it, so does our blessed Saviour, after having so highly commended John, the last and greatest of the prophets, adds, " yet he that is the lesser in the kingdom of heaven is greater than he."

There must, then, be some great and lasting institution wherein the fulness of that revelation is preserved: for, who shall presume to say, that the partial knowledge of divine truths, which his own unaided powers will enable him to acquire, can be at all comparable with what the

Baptist, inured from infancy to heavenly contemplation, had attained? But the poorest peasant, who is not left to conjecture or individual investigation, but is at once put in possession, single and indivisible, of the entire counsel of God, placed by Him in the keeping of an unfailing authority, may well hold himself more perfectly instructed in the system of divine revelation than the greatest of the prophetic race. He himself becomes as the prophet, having a clear and intimate conviction of all that he believes, a chain of evidence in his mind, which is linked at last to the teaching of God, clearly manifested, and imperishably preserved.

My brethren, if God love not wavering and inconstancy in man; if the reed, shaken by the wind, be not the characteristic He admires in His servants, far be it from us to attribute to His institution any system which allows no security, to those that follow it, against indecision and uncertainty. Let us all come to this conclusion, at least, that the true teaching of God's wisdom, providentially communicated, shall be there found, where the qualities of the prophetic character, just enumerated, shall be best discerned; where the feebleness of individual judgments shall merge in the evidence of unerring doctrine; where all seeing, reflected as in a common mirror, the same objects of faith, shall believe alike; where but one unvarying standard of truth shall be admitted, and where zeal and love shall bind the united hearts of men to doctrines unhesitatingly and gratefully accepted. It shall be a scheme that supplies, in every part, the prophetic institution, that shall be to the preservation of truth revealed as complete a safeguard as this was to its gradual manifestation; which shall even be more perfect, by filling up those breaks of continuity in teaching which the other necessarily contained, and be complete in duration as in extent, unfailing by perpetuity as by immortality. This great prophetic power is the living Church of Christ, His undivorceable spouse, His ever faithful witness; and all that live by its faith, partake of its ministry.

But, even so, what security have we against the fluctuations of our own hearts, and the fickleness of our moral affections? Ah! he that overcomes their weakness is far more than a prophet—he hath acquired the perfection of the new and better law. For even when those of old had been raised to the prophetic dignity, the frailty and insecurity of the heart of flesh did too often betray itself. The prophet who had been commissioned by God to denounce vengeance on the ten rebel tribes, and strictly charged not to loiter on the way, allowed himself to be seduced from his obedience by the false suggestions of a fellow-prophet, and was devoured, therefore, by a lion. Jonas, sent to Ninive, flies from the face of God, and would have perished, had not a strange miracle preserved him; then he preaches penance, and is sorry that his preaching has counteracted his prophecy; rejoices in the gourd which gave him shade, and peevishly desires to die because it withers. Not even, therefore, were prophets exempt from the inconstancy of the heart; and he must needs be more who, like John, has steadied it. On the peculiar perfections of his character, a future discourse shall, God willing, treat: let us, therefore, now look rather to ourselves. I say, then, that the man who walks, with invariable direction, in the path of God's commandments, who turns not to the right to seek a passing pleasure, nor to the left to shun a temporal evil; whose soul meditates by day and by night on the law of his God, and whose heart swerves not from the love of his Saviour, is such a man as should seem fitter to converse with angels than to sojourn among men. His conscience is at peace, and his anxieties are all stilled; his lot is cast into the bosom of his Maker, and his being is placed under the protection of the God of heaven. He stands upon the surface of this earth, but his affections cast thereinto no root, for his nourishment comes from the dews above. The summer plays upon him in warmth and smiles, and his leaves are not parched up, nor his sap diminished; the winter comes, and shakes him, and his fruit does not fall, neither is he broken. His cheerfulness never degenerates into boisterous mirth, nor yields place to melancholy broodings; his speech is neither arrogant nor undignified; his bearing is courteous, his feelings kind. The season of prayer ever finds him already recollected, and his occupations of life are followed with undivided energy. Every day increases his love for his God, and diminishes his attachments to earth; and hope and charity, triumphant over the pressing burthen of corrupt mortality, buoy up his soul towards that country where endless joys await him.

Is not such a one more than a prophet? And yet I have not spoke of gifts beyond the possession of ordinary men, of tongues, or prophecy, or discernment of spirits. This is but the virtue at which every Christian should aim; and the nearer he shall approach it, the further shall he be removed from that reproach of fickleness, which throws us back from day to day in the service of God, and destroys the fruit of all our good endeavours.

But remember, too, that if our affections easily lend themselves to be the sport of every varying influence that engages them, there is a whirlwind and a storm reserved for them, which plays not with what it visits, but tears and utterly roots up; a burning east-wind which parches and withers—the breath of an angry God, who, in the end, will have no more patience with our lightness and inconstancy. Provoked at our repeated relapses after repentance, at our violated promises, our broken pledges, our inconsistencies and our thoughtless levity, He shall visit us as He threatened Israel, saying: " And the Lord God shall strike Israel as a reed is shaken in the water, and he shall root up Israel out of this good land which He gave to their fathers." (3 Kings, xiv. 15.) But as a man who has to walk upon a narrow pass, with a precipice on either side, will fix his eye as steadily as possible at the point whereat he aims, and forbear casting it below or around him; so let us, settling our looks upon the heaven which we desire to reach, hasten forward on our slippery path, and steady our steps, and save them from a perilous fall, by the unity of our purpose, and by the constancy of our efforts, which the divine blessing will crown with eternal success.

SERMON XXII.

On Tribulation.

Rom. v. 3, 4.

"We glory in tribulations, knowing that tribulation worketh patience, and patience trial, and trial hope."

Did I deceive you, my brethren, when, on Sunday last, I endeavoured to represent to you the earth, and all that inhabit it, as bound, by ties of everlasting gratitude, to bless and praise God, for the multitude of His benefits, and the infinity of His mercies? Did I mislead you when, describing to you His dealings with us, as ever munificent and most gracious, I excluded from the picture the dark mass of evil which seems to oppress mankind, and counterbalance, at least, the more cheering prospect of its happiness which we surveyed? Look on your right hand and on your left, and tell me what you see. "Not," you will answer, "as the prophet's servant saw, after seven times returning to look out, one small cloud ascending from the sea, (3 Kings, xviii. 44) but the darkness of sorrow overshadowing the land. On the one side I see war ravaging the pleasant fields, and driving helpless thousands into distress; on the other, black pestilence, with its flaming scourge, lashing to despair the inhabitants of entire cities; on the sea, storms that overwhelm ships and their crews, and ruin the merchant's hopes; in the desert, the marauder; in the fertile fields, the oppressor; where men are few, want and feebleness; where they are many, dissensions and strife."

Has some avenging angel, such as slew the first-born of Egypt, visited us, that no house should be without its sorrow? Behold that palace of the rich; it is like unto Pharaoh's: all bewail the loss of some one most dear; and the daintiest fare remains untasted, and the lute and the viol untouched, and the most sumptuous ornaments lie unheeded, in the poignancy of unusual, and therefore severer woe! See the cottage of the poor; how quieter, because commoner, affliction fills it! where the slow and torturing anxieties of protracted and unfriended illness, eat into the hearts of many, themselves pining with hunger and distress! Then look into the mind of each individual man: where is the one that hath not his sorrow? Hath God blessed him with plenty and ease? Perhaps a racking ailment is lodged in his frame, and threatens speedy destruction, or inflicts a lasting pain. Is he struggling with misfortunes? Then is his sleep restless and his waking anxious; neither body nor mind can find repose. Hath he many children? The undutifulness of one, the sickliness of another, the future provision for all, agitate and distress his thoughts. Is he alone in the world? Then is he solitary and comfortless; if he fall, there is none to raise him up; if he suffer, he hath no consoler. Then, who shall recount the inward tribulations of men, the sinner's pangs and remorses, the sincere believer's anxious doubts, the willing spirit's returning trials, the watchful heart's unceasing temptations, the devout mind's perpetual distractions and dreariness, the loving soul's timid anxieties, nay, the perfectest saint's unabated struggles against the infirmity of the flesh? Add to these the sins and failings of others, the injustice of rulers, the caprice of masters, the infidelity of friends, the uncharitableness of equals, the negligences of inferiors, the world's slight, the disappointment of hopes, the gradual decay of old and well-secured fortunes, the instantaneous and irretrievable ruin of well-matured prospects,—and where have we left room for good upon this earth? where is the abode of happiness among the children of men? May we not say of it, as of wisdom, that "it is not found in the land of them that live in delights? The depth saith, it is not in me; and the sea saith, it is not with me." (Job, xxviii. 13, 14.)

Then may we answer of it in like manner: "God understandeth the way of it, and He knoweth the place thereof." (23.) And therefore hath He, through His Apostle, whose words I have taken for my text, declared it. And where, then, hath He placed it? In the very midst of those sorrows and tribulations which overspread the earth; in the most barren deserts He hath made it to flourish; from the darkest clouds He causes the brightest bow, ensign of hope and security, to be reflected. Yes, hope, the sweetest cheerer of our exile, the strongest staff to the broken spirit, the mildest balm to the bruised soul, the virtue which most of all can twine its roots inseparably round the heart of man, is traced, in an expressive genealogy, by the Apostle of the Gentiles, to tribulation and sorrow: "Tribulation worketh patience, and patience trial, and trial hope." If, therefore, we desire to study and learn this mysterious providence for man, whereby an almighty and all-wise disposer worketh out our greatest good, let us carefully attend to this beautiful and most orderly arrangement, and see how the first result of affliction is patience, that is, the humble endurance of men who know that it is their lot and their desert to suffer ; and how, afterwards, this ripens into trial, the consoling consciousness that tribulation is the refining furnace of virtue, whereby it is assayed and proved, and brought into perfect purity. And hence shall we learn how men may glory in tribulation, through the joy of its hope, the last but greatest in this family tree of virtue.

That God should have allowed evil to remain in this world, after man had introduced it by his fall, was only a necessary result of the new condition in which the world was placed after that event,—a law of that moral state, which left the weal or woe of each individual in his own hands, to be worked out by his own efforts. That God, on the other hand, should have made what was most humbling, most disagreeable, in man's lot the source of his greatest glory and happiness, was exactly what was to be expected from so good and benevolent a being. The curse which He pronounced upon the earth, and the consequent labour of man, the sorrows of woman, and the death of both, were, in truth, a punishment well deserved. And in these particular clauses of the sentence were included all the other evils that befall us, and that form our portion upon earth. For, if this was pronounced barren and ungrateful to man's toil, it was not merely of fruit and grain, but of all other return to our most painful cultivation. Its generosity was to yield but a tardy and sour crop of honour, to repay our ambitious activity ; its liberality was to give but a scanty interest for the anxieties and fatigues of seeking from it wealth and fortune ; its justice was to return but a lean growth of thankfulness for the expenditure of our time, our ablilities, our health, and lives in its service. All the evils, in short, of social life, whether external, from the treatment of men, or inward, from the distresses and uneasiness of the mind, were comprised in this award. The thorns and the thistles, thus foretold, as the requital of man's industry, were such as should not only prick his hand, but should wound his very soul ; and in the other clause, which fell principally on women, were comprehended all the evils incident to domestic life : its alternations of hope and disappointment, its separations and bereavements, its daily cares and frequent sorrows. Then comes the common doom of returning to the dust whence we were taken, which embraces all the ills resulting from our frail composition, the returns of lighter indispositions, the assaults of heavier maladies, the rackings of acuter pain, and the throbs of mortal agony.

These, therefore, are, collectively and singly, the punishment awarded to man as the due of his transgression ; yea, as but a residue of those more terrible calamities which redemption in part removed, and throughout mitigated. Now, it is not usual for men to find any ground of merit, or motive of reward, in the undergoing of a just sentence pronounced upon a criminal. We may pity the wretch who pulls, in fetters, at the oar, or labours at the public works; we may admire his cheerful submission and resignation to what he has deserved; nay, we may even go so far as to say, that he may thus earn an abbreviation of the term of his punishment, or some moderation of its severity. But who ever thought of telling such, that by the first year of their chastisement well endured, they should merit a title, and by the second great honours, and by the third dignity, and, in the end, the sublimest elevation to which man could aspire? Yet the goodness of God has reached this point, and acted precisely thus, with one important difference: that He does not make us wait so long, nor does He attach the splendid rewards He gives, to a severe course of such endurance, but at once promises the highest and noblest to our smallest and daily participation in the common lot. "For that which is at present momentary and light of our tribulation, worketh for us above measure exceedingly an eternal weight of glory." (2 Cor. iv. 17.) Surely, mercy and goodness could not well display themselves beyond this.

But if this consideration alone, of the gain to be drawn from afflictions, should suffice to make us embrace them with patience, yet are there other reflections that must serve to show us how just and reasonable this is. For, in the first place, it lies not with us whether we suffer or not, except only for such part as results from our own sinfulness, or passions, or imprudence. Could we shake off but one scruple's weight from the burthen imposed upon us by Almighty hands, could our writhing and clamour milden for an instant the pain which a merciful sentence inflicts, then peace be to the outbreakings of human indocility, and the repinings of our feeble hearts. But if, on the contrary, fretfulness is in itself a pain, and, moreover, hath a fault; if murmuring is heavy to the ears of others, and removes their sympathy, and, besides, deserves punishment; if impatience increases the sensibility of the mind, and is, in addition, guilt: what gain we by indulging in these useless, nay, hurtful, expressions of a peevish humour, and, at the same time, laying upon our souls iniquity, and calling down upon our heads additional and better-deserved chastisement? But, on the other hand, do we desire to lighten our load of sorrow? Oh! there is a buoyancy and strength in the meek and patient spirit, that bears it as the appointment of God. Like the branches of the palm, so significant of victory, that seem to develop an elastic power in proportion to the weight that is laid upon them, it puts on new strength under every pressure of additional affliction. Patience is as a case of armour round the heart, which deadens the blows inflicted on it; while impatience not only strips off that covering, but lays the very quick, in all its tenderness and delicacy of nerve, bare to the wounding knife.

But, in the second place, so true is it that suffering is the natural portion of man, for which, from his first ability to reason, he must prepare himself, that God has been pleased, in some sort, to make it the badge of His servants, of those in whom He desired to present us models and specimens of the purest and noblest of human kind. His patriarchs, one after the other, were so formed and trained. Abraham, the great headspring of all his benedictions to earth, is early torn from all the sympathies of country and home, and led by the hand of a kind but concealed and darksome providence, to be for the rest of his life a wanderer in a distant land : he is exposed to the distresses of famine and war, to the oppressions of the kings of Egypt and Chanaan, and the dissensions of his own family. Long is he made to sigh for a promised son; then is commanded to immolate him : and so at length concludes a life of trial in perpetual exile. Isaac, the most favoured of the race, is afflicted by the enmities of his twin-sons, and the evil conduct of Esau, and has long to endure privation of sight. Jacob, throughout, is the child of affliction : first persecuted by his brother, then a slave to the capricious Laban, distressed by the quarrels and crimes of his numerous offspring, plunged into years of bitter mourning for Joseph slain, as he thought, by a wild beast, robbed of Benjamin, the child of his old age; so that he could say, at the close of a long life, that his days had been "few and evil." What shall we say of Moses, the deliverer of his people ? Who more harrassed by unmerited persecution and afflictions of spirit ? How was he obliged, after a delicate education in the household of Pharaoh, to flee from Egypt into the desert, for having avenged one of his own countrymen ! How much endured he, in witnessing their oppression ! What anxiety did it cost him to achieve their deliverance ! What torments of mind, and what fatigues of body, during forty years, did he suffer, to bear with their murmurings and their hardness of heart, and with the bickerings of his own brother and sister ! And, after all, to die without attaining the great object of all his labours and desires, the seeing his people introduced into the promised land! Who knoweth not the sufferings and sorrows of all others that God loved of old, of Samuel and David, of Elias and Daniel, of

Job and Tobias? "Take, then, my brethren," saith St. James, "for an example of suffering evil, of labour and patience, the prophets, who spoke in the name of the Lord. Behold, we account them blessed who have endured. You have heard of the patience of Job, and you have seen the end of the Lord, and that the Lord is compassionate and merciful." (Jas. v. 10, 11.) Can we expect or desire to be treated better than those men, the chosen ones of God? Shall we complain, when we see them, instruments of His most glorious works, channels of His richest blessings, depositaries of His most splendid promises, doomed to lives of sorrow and suffering, and ourselves only transiently and most leniently afflicted?

Nay, methinks we may with truth assert, that only once did the providence of God make proof of an opposite course, and exhibit to the world a favourite of His choice, daintily nursed, and borne through a long and prosperous life, without a temporal care, courted and honoured, reigning in uninterrupted peace, and yet commanding the tributary wealth of nations, the wisest as the most fortunate of men. That man was Solomon; and painful was the issue of this brilliant experiment. He allowed himself to be seduced into idolatry, after having drunk too deeply of pleasure.

For this, my brethren, is a further, and more important consideration than the other two, that we are sinners ourselves, and have deserved afflictions, nay, that they are necessary for us. That which was due to us, and allotted to us, as the portion of our fallen and degraded nature, we have appropriated to ourselves by special transgressions, and have had awarded to us by a particular sentence.

Come, let us be sincere with ourselves. Sin is an evil which merits punishment: we believe it, and we own it. We call to God, in the language of His word, entreating Him not to repay us according to our iniquities; we beg that He will not punish us in His anger and fury; but, in penitential tones, we add that we are ready for scourges, and willing to submit to the chastening of His hand. For we make no secret that we acknowledge ourselves grievous sinners. Well, He takes us at our word; He delivers us from that endless and insufferable torment which we have deserved; He sends us sickness, or reverse of fortune, or the loss of some one dear, or melancholy spirits, or disappointment of hopes, or some other grief; and we complain, and are dissatisfied; we trouble our fellow-sufferers with our pitiful expressions, as though no one on earth endured so much or so unreasonably as we; and we consume and gnaw our own hearts with bitter fretfulness! How astonished and indignant must saints and angels be at such insincerity and hollowness of our protestations, and at such unbecoming levity of speech! Tell me, have you ever in spirit acted the parable of the prodigal? Have you, in a sincere and contrite heart, returned to your Father's home after sin; and did you exclaim that you were no longer worthy of the name of son, but asked only a menial's place? And did you mean that which you said? If, then, though received like a son by a most loving Father, still your fidelity and truth were put somewhat to a test, and you were made to taste something of the bitterness of sin, that so you might be weaned from its deceitful lures; is it just or decent that you should fall to complaining, and not rather trust your kind, indulgent parent, that He has so justly appreciated the sincerity of your protestations, as to give you the opportunity of proving it, by cheerfully submitting to the humiliations and chastisements you have deserved? And all this time there is no proportion between what we have merited and what is inflicted, between the grievousness of sin and the lightness of its punishment. Beautifully has the Church embodied these sentiments in a prayer, which she hath hung on tablets round the tomb of the apostles; almost every clause of which expresses our unsteadiness between forgetfulness of God if He strike and afflict us not, and complaints and impatience of His visitations when He does.

And this proves at once, that afflictions are not only our just due, but are necessary for us. For, sinners as we are, we should be too often in danger of forgetting ourselves in a fatal oblivion, if we were not aroused by them. While all goes well with the sinner, while the world smiles upon him, while his schemes are successful, what shall awake the conscience from its heavy lethargy? Nothing, but some visitation of God's justice. It is a case where nought will do but cutting deeply, and searing with fire, to excite sensibility. Nay, if blessing can attach to God's enemies, blessed may we say is the sinner who knows not rest of heart or ease of body, rather than the one who sins without a warning or a check. Yes, it is, in truth, a fearful thing for a man to have the Almighty his declared enemy; to be visited by Him only by calamities and remorses when waking, and by hideous dreams when sleeping; to be given up during life to the tormentors, till the last farthing be paid on the rack of conscience, and under the whips and scorpions of persecuting misfortunes. It is a fearful thing for one to be thus kept in mind, while he continues to sin, that there is a just God, and an avenger beyond all partialities, and a judge above all bribes; one who neither sleepeth nor forgetteth; one whose right hand can bring back from the extremities of the earth, and can bury in the depths of hell. It is fearful, too, to be kept continually in the prospect of a miserable death, whether it be one of surprise without the time, or of stupidity without the sense, or of obduracy without the grace, or of circumstances without the opportunity, of making a penitent end. But in all this there is matter, however small, of hope. While God visits us at all, it is a sign that He thinks of us. The present life is not the time for punishment, devoid of mercy. While the debtor is on his way to prison, he may agree with his adversary, and escape the messenger's hands. While the sick man feels pain, there is vitality and activity in his constitution, and he may recover. And therefore, I think, it must be a much more fearful thing for the sinner to be forgotten of God, and never to feel a sting in his bosom, or to see a cloud over his pleasures. It must be a terrible thing to have one's perdition sealed; to have the process already closed, both depositions and sentence, and laid up in God's chancery, as an irreversible doom; and so him who is its object troubled no further, but allowed the full choice of his pleasures; as one permits to a man between sentence and execution his choice of viands, in full certainty that when his hour hath tolled, the terrible law will take its course! How smoothly glides along the boat upon the wide, unruffled, though most rapid stream, that hurries it onward to the precipice, over which its waters break in thunders! How calm, and undisturbed by the smallest ripple, slumbers its unreflecting steersman! Oh! for one rock in the midst of the too smooth channel, against which it may be dashed and whirled round, to shake him from this infatuated sleep! It is the only hope that remains for him! Woe to him, if, to the end, his course be pleasant! That end will pay it all!

Thus far, then, we have seen, my brethren, how tribulation begetteth patience, that is, how, in sorrow and affliction, is exercised that submission of the will to the decrees of God, which makes us receive them as coming from His hand, as a portion of our state in this place of our banishment, and as the punishment due to our manifold transgressions. Such is the lowest degree of virtue regarding tribulations which the Christian is called to practise. Such was the virtue which all men might have attained who loved God, before His Son came down to perfect patience, and give it that higher dignity which results from conformity to His sufferings. For, while even the holiest of men must feel that they have to suffer, both because the original sentence hath so appointed, and because they acknowledge themselves, before God, to have so deserved; yet do they find nobler and higher motives than these, motives which impel them, not merely to a patient endurance, but to an ardent desire of suffering with and for Christ. The word of God hath compared affliction to a furnace or crucible, wherein virtue is perfected, as gold and silver are in the fire. After years of endeavours in the path of perfection, some dross will be found to adhere to the soul, some little earthly tendencies, or, at least, attachments; some love of vanity, some lurking pride or selfish desires, which have long escaped observation, and afterwards defied all efforts.

When God wishes to purge His servants of even slighter imperfections, He visits them with sorrows, sometimes more severe than what would be employed to chastise the most profligate vice. He has removed sovereigns from thrones, which they had honoured by their virtues and charity, and sent them, outcasts, to beg the alms of their own subjects; He has allowed the foulest calumny to blacken, before the entire world, the character of the most innocent and spotless; He has wrung the hearts of the most devoted to His love with frightful anguish, till they almost reached the borders of despair. And by the searching trials of these visitations, He has probed their reins, and peered under every fold of their hearts, till the most concealed defilement was scoured away, and the soul burnished to beauty and splendour. But what a tribute is here to the wisdom and mercy of God, and what noble homage thence results to Him! For where would have been the wisdom and the power, where the glory or the magnificence, to have made men happy only where they have what they desire, and loudly thankful when all things succeed according to their wishes? Do not the very heathens and publicans do this? It is only a wonder that the sounds of praise and hymns of gratitude ever cease ascending, day or night, from the houses of the prosperous and rich, or from the fertile fields. But it was a splendid design, and splendidly executed, and only by God to have been designed and executed, to make songs of jubilee ascend from dungeons, to raise up thanksgivings from the bed on which one lies, racked with exquisite tortures; to make benedictions be invoked on His name from the dunghill, whereon a leper, once rich and powerful, is obliged to sit. "The Lord hath given, and the Lord hath taken away: blessed be the name of the Lord." Such is the greeting with which the accumulation of every possible calamity, short of death, is welcomed by the patient Job. For, in his history, God hath recorded for us the noblest example of that process whereby men, acceptable to Him, are brought unto perfection.

But is it not presumptuous in us to propose to ourselves so high a degree of virtue, as this willing and rejoicing suffering, this glorying in tribulation, in bonds, and in death, which formed the crowns of the apostles' and martyrs' patience; while we must be so far from imagining that we are in a condition for such refining, being yet wholly involved in the corruption of our base nature? Certainly it would be great presumption in us to imagine that we are worthy of such distinction; but there is nothing to prevent, but rather much to encourage, our aspiring to those higher and purer motives of patience, which animated them to courage and resignation. These were summed up in one short phrase: Christ has suffered, let us suffer with Him. "If doing well," saith St. Peter, "you suffer patiently, this is thanksworthy before God. For unto this are you called, because Christ also suffered for us, leaving you an example that you should follow His steps." (1 Pet. ii. 20, 21.)

Where, think you, that the closest friendships in the world's history were likely to be knit, and the sincerest interchange of affection to be established? Would it be between those who, at the gayest banquets, reclined on the same couch, and drank from one goblet? Would it be among the pupils of one philosopher, who sat upon the same form, to hear the same doctrines, and believe alike? Would it be between those who fought in the same chariot, against the same enemy, and parried each the blows aimed at the other, and had but one fate common to them both? No; but rather between those who had been stretched for hours upon the same rack, and had drunk together the same cup which their Lord had drained before them; between those who, standing bound in one chain, and each trying to relieve the other as much as possible of its weight, listened, with indivisible joy, to a common doom, to lay down their lives for Christ; between those who set out together to conquer death, dragged on one hurdle through crowds of spectators, to mount one funeral pile, or bend their necks to the same sword. There is, there can be, no community of hearts, no purity of love, no perfection of charity, like that which suffering together in a holy cause can beget. See, then, at once, the grandeur of that divine idea, which allows our sorrows and sufferings to unite themselves with those of the incarnate Son of God, admits an assimilation between the two, and allows us to claim all the glory, all the dignity, and all the merit of so sublime an alliance. Who wonders, then, that Andrew looked forward, through the toils and perils of his apostleship, to the cross, as to the goal of his labours; that coming within sight of it prepared to receive him, he should have reverently saluted it upon his bended knees, as about to bring him into close conformity with the outward form and exemplar of his dying Master.

And hence, how endearing and how loving of Him, to have given afflictions and trials this very name, inviting all who suffer, to take up their cross and follow Him! It is as mothers, wishing to allure their little ones to take some bitter but wholesome potion, will studiously conceal its name under some other more tempting, and ask them to drink it for their sakes. And so would not Jesus command us to bear our calumny, or our oppression, or our sickness, or our grief, or our calamity, lest the rudeness of the very name should make horror creep through our breasts; but lovingly exhorts us to be like Himself, and take up the cross, which will authorise us to follow Him. Who will refuse such an invitation? Who will not be ashamed to be without one? Nay, by I know not what still more inviting image, it would seem as though our cross were confounded with His own, and we, as the happy Simon of Cyrene, only helped Him to bear it! For on that which pressed His shoulders was written, yea, written in characters of blood, every sorrow, every distress, every suffering which nature or malice could inflict, from calumny to wounds, from spoliation to death; and each of us has but a small portion of the burthen shared out to him to carry. And shall we not welcome it with joy, saying, with the Apostle we have named, "O good cross, long desired, and now prepared for a soul that covets thee, secure and joyful I come to thee"?

And do you wish to see that sinners may aspire, with confidence, to this conformity of sufferings with Jesus, even where they only pay the forfeit of their transgressions? Look at him who is crucified at His right hand: he ascended his cross a thief, infamous before God and man; his sentence was just, and he knew it. He suffers no more than his fellow, with whom he is, probably, equally guilty. But the latter throws away the salvavation within his reach, and undergoes his sentence but as a human penalty. Not so the other, who, fixing his eyes upon Jesus crucified before him, learns from Him how he should suffer. Never was disciple in such a short time perfected. Never did sculptor more closely imitate the model before him. See how he catches at once His spirit, and makes it his own. He submits to the tortures of his punishment with humble acknowledgments that he has deserved them, but with earnest hope that, consecrated and blessed by His sufferings who hangs beside him, they shall open to him the gates of paradise. See how he copies the unresisting meekness, the calm looks, the patient attitude of the innocent Sufferer; how every word that he hears, is a new lesson which he practises during the short life now allowed him. Such is the conformity which we, sinners, and worthy of severest punishment, may aspire to; and our tribulations shall lead to hope.

But if we want a model of still closer conformity, and that where not the outward man is brought into similitude with the suffering of Jesus, but His image is impressed upon the inward soul, at the foot, rather than at the side, of the cross, you shall see one that seems summoned forth on purpose, to show how much the human soul can possibly bear, with calm resignation, when it is commanded from above. It is the only one on earth who could call her Son God; and of that Son she is to be now deprived, and Him she must look upon in all the extremes of disgrace, of abandonment, and anguish. Her maternal feelings, so singularly blended with a deeper reverence, and those sentiments of adoration which His divine character inspire, are now centred upon the sorrowful spectacle of His sufferings; and, by a force of natural sympathy, no less than of love divine, every wound and every gash has stamped her heart with a corresponding pang, deepened by every recollection of first joy, and the sense of future desolation. Sum up the afflictions which can separately crush the tenderer heart of woman, and see if one is wanting. Yet does no complaint escape those lips—no thought of repining alloy the purity of unparalleled anguish! There you have the most perfect model of conformity in the soul with the suffering of Jesus; in griefs and in resignation the likest to His that man can display.

Let your own hearts decide for yourselves. Do you, after this, desire to be exempt from suffering? Do you hope that God will leave you without trials? His mercy forbid it: for surely you would not wish to live and to die without an opportunity of copying Him in His blessed passion, and of enjoying that fellowship which no other situation or relationship can give, and which even His blessed Mother was expected to attain. And from tribulation thus endured, hope—blessed hope—shall spring; when, lifting up your eyes to heaven, you shall see the reward that awaiteth you. For, if we suffer with Christ, we shall be glorified with Him. Amidst the desolation of spirit which your afflictions shall cause you, you shall, in this thought, find comfort and security. We read, in the book of Judges, how Gideon, wishing to overthrow the numerous enemy with a small force, gave to each of his men an earthen pitcher, wherein was concealed a burning light, so that when, by clashing together, the brittle vessels were broken, the brightness of the lights would burst forth. (Jud. vii. 20.) And so to something of this sort, does St. Paul compare this light of hope and faith in Christ crucified, which is shut up in our hearts, which is as a treasure hidden in an earthen vessel, and then shines forth in splendour, when this, its frail receptacle, is shattered. " For God, who commanded the light to shine out of darkness, hath shined in our hearts, to give the light of the knowledge of the glory of God, in the face of Christ Jesus. But we have this treasure in earthen vessels. . . . In all things we suffer tribulation and are not distressed ; . . . we suffer persecution but are not forsaken." (2 Cor. iv. 6–9.) For, in conclusion, let us never forget that all tribulation comes from the hand of a most merciful and loving God, who will not lose sight of a moment's patient suffering, or allow a sigh to escape, or a tear to fall, for His sake, without its reward.

SERMON XXIII.

Conclusion of a Course.

Eccles. xii. 13.

"Fear God, and keep His commandments; for this is the whole of man."

WE are now, my brethren, approaching the conclusion of our religious instruction. Next Sunday will be occupied by the consideration of those mysteries which the approaching season is instituted to commemorate, and by the attention to those holy sentiments which they ought to excite. That will, indeed, be the most appropriate termination to any series of discourses; for, the death and passion of our dear Redeemer, must be the most noble object of Christian meditation, and the one best calculated to add weight, and give efficacy, to those truths which derive their saving virtue from His blood, and receive their seal of authority from His death. But that these may make their full impression on the mind, there are other topics which should be well weighed, there are other considerations which should be allowed a fair and impartial attention, and should naturally result from a course of instructions on religious subjects.

These instructions, my dear brethren, have obviously one tendency; they are all directed to expound what the law of God commands us to believe and to practise in order to reach those rewards which He has prepared for His faithful servants. They are directed to suggest such motives as may induce us to fulfil these commands; to encourage those who are already on the path to persevere in it, to bring back those who have wandered, to impart strength to the weak, and resolution to the wavering and undecided. We cannot, then, better conclude instructions tending to these objects, than by proposing at one view the duties which have been separately inculcated, together with the motives which should induce us seriously to study them, and to put them in practice.

It is a deliberation which the mind must make. After having had proposed the belief, and the practices which God exacts; after having had impressed upon it the dangers of a life at variance with the Gospel, and the blessings that follow compliance with its injunctions; after having, in fine, reflected on the obligation of virtue and the prohibition of evil; whether it wills it or no, it *must* make, at least, a virtual choice between the one and the other. It must, at least in practice, resolve to embrace either the good, with the rewards that attend it, or the evil, with the curses and punishments allotted to it.

It was thus that the great Jewish legislator acted. At the conclusion of his mission, he repeated in a compendious form the laws which God had imposed upon the people, enumerated the blessings received from Him, which should act as incitements to observe them, and expatiated upon the rewards and punishments which awaited their compliance or rejection. After this solemn rehearsal, he thus addressed them: "Consider that I have set before thee this day life and good, and on the other hand, death and evil; that thou mayest love the Lord thy God, and walk in His way, and keep His commandments, and thou mayest live, and He may bless thee. But if thy heart be turned away, so that thou wilt not hear, I foretell thee this day that thou shalt perish. I call heaven and earth to witness this day, that I have set before you life and death, blessing and cursing. Choose, therefore, life, that both thou and thy seed may live, and that thou mayest love the Lord thy God, and obey His voice, and adhere to Him, for He is thy life" (Deut. xxx. 15-19).

A voice as strong and as clear as this is addressed by the Almighty to each man, every time that the great truths and commands of religion are proposed to him by the mouth of His ministers; a choice as formal and as awful is made by every mind, when, after hearing them so proposed, it accepts or rejects them. Let us, then, see this day what are the objects upon which we are to deliberate, and what the importance of making a correct decision. And if we want one short impressive motive, to determine our choice, and lead to a satisfactory conclusion, where can we find one more weighty than is suggested by the wisest of mortals, in the words of my text. After expatiating on the vanity and folly of every pursuit which human weakness, or human passions, are accustomed to deem most valuable and happy, he sums up in a few words the result of his deliberations and instructions: " Let us all hear together the conclusion of the discourse. Fear God and keep his commandments ; for this is the whole of man. And all things that are done, God will bring unto judgment, for every hidden thing, whether it be good or evil."

The first thing, on which all must make a salutary decision, and for which God will bring us to judgment, is correctness of faith and religious principle. There can be no doubt that, besides the grand work of our redemption, the Son of God came amongst us to manifest to the world religious truths, of which till then it had been ignorant. It has been a favourite theory that this communication regarded chiefly the moral law; that the principles of belief were not meant to be so strictly defined; that it will be expected of all that their *lives* be virtuous, but that as to their *creeds*, every latitude is to be allowed; for, as God looks only to the good intentions and dispositions of the heart, and well knows that the understanding is a weak and erring faculty, which frequently wanders in its best-intentioned search after truth, it seems inconsistent with His amiable and loving goodness, that He should exact exactness of belief on every point from so fallacious a guide, or precise justice of decision in so unenlightened a tribunal. It would be, contrary to his own principles, expecting to gather grapes from thorns, and figs from thistles.

Yet, if Christ did communicate any truths addressed purely to our belief, it must have been with the intention that all men should accept them. The idea that He should have manifested them to the world, without an earnest desire to have them universally adopted is self-repugnant. But then the truth which came from Him *can* be only one; whatever is at variance with this must be false; and falsehood cannot possibly be pleasing to Him. The Jews, when He came among them, were in possession of a code of doctrines delivered by the

Almighty : to these they clung with sincerity, and were justified in doing so. But when Christ preached His additional articles to them, did He treat their rejection of these as an affair of no consequence? Did He ever say, "As to belief, act as you please ; it is a matter of comparative indifference. Only attend to my moral law—practise its precepts, lead good, virtuous lives ; and whether you attach yourselves to one society or to another, God, who only looks at the heart, will be perfectly satisfied by your moral conduct, and you shall be saved?" Oh, no ; instead of this gentle, comfortable doctrine, He tells them, that to the heaven where He was going, they could not follow Him ; not because they neglected the moral law, but because they did not believe His doctrines. "I go My way, and you shall die in your sins ; whither I go, you cannot come. For if you believe not that I am He, you shall die in your sins." (Jo. viii.)

Did He say to His apostles : "Go proclaim My religion through the world. With regard to articles of belief, leave every one to choose for himself. Only insist upon My moral code ; for, those alone who neglect this shall incur My indignation." In place of this lax and consoling commission, how differently does He send them forth? In terms which we almost fear to use, He thus gives them His last injunctions : "Go ye into the whole world, and preach the Gospel to every creature. He that believeth and is baptised, shall be saved ; but he that believeth not, shall be condemned" (Mar. xvi. 16). After these clear denunciations from the mouth of Jesus Christ Himself, can any one, for a moment, entertain a suspicion that

He was indifferent as to what is believed, so long as men's actions are moral? The doctrine of the Master is no less that of the disciples. Why is Paul so anxious that the Ephesians should not be moved by every wind of doctrine, if it mattered not what doctrines they believed? Why does he, in writing to the Galatians, pronounce an anathema against any one who should preach a doctrine different from his own, even should he be an angel from heaven? Why does he so earnestly exhort Timothy to be zealous for preserving the doctrines which he had received, and even careful to transmit them in the very form of sound words in which they had been given to him; or inculcate on Titus that one of the principal qualities of a bishop is his "embracing that faithful word which is according to doctrine, that he may be able to exhort in sound doctrine," when he should rather have left all doctrines to their own choice? With what right, in fine, did St. Peter assert, that many wrested the Epistles of St. Paul to their own ruin, by interpreting them according to their private opinion, if every one is justified in following what interpretation he pleases, and all in doing so are equally acceptable in the sight of God.

The apostles should, one would think, have confined themselves to the teaching of the moral law, if this alone was to be valued in the dread judgments of the Almighty. But, in fact, as the code of belief, and that of morals, come equally from the same Lawgiver, is it not an equal offence against Him, whichever we violate? Why should the weakness of the understanding be made a plea for this liberty of creed? Might not the libertine as much complain, that God should expect him to preserve virtue in a mind, which His own Scriptures acknowledge is prone to evil from its youth? That He should exact unbroken perfection in vessels which His apostle owns to be frail and easily shattered? That He should, in fine, demand immunity from sin and all offence, in a world wherein He Himself has declared it *necessary* that scandals should come? The heart is no less weak than the mind; their tendency is to evil and error, in consequence of our original transgression; both are bound, therefore, to strive after what is right. When every effort has been made for this purpose, God will certainly be satisfied. He will not impute to us the wanderings of either, when acting under the influence of sincere conscientious principles. But as a systematic rule, He cannot love truth equally with error, any more than he can love equally virtue and vice; and therefore every one must be fully and conscientiously convinced of the correctness of his belief, to escape the just judgment of God.

The remark which I have just made at once clears this doctrine of all harshness and uncharitableness. With those who in all simplicity of heart have sought out the truth, and are convinced that they have found it, who would be ready to embrace any doctrine, however repugnant to their ideas or feelings, which they might discover to come from God, and who, with the sincerity of the distressed father in the Gospel cry out in their hearts, "Lord I believe, do thou help my unbelief,"—with such as these the Almighty must be fully pleased. But with those who neglect to search after the truth, from malice, from interest, or from prejudice, or having found it do not embrace it, with these certainly it is not harsh to say, that the God of truth cannot be satisfied. Far be it from any one to "judge another man's servant; to his own master he must stand or fall." The inward motives, and dispositions on which all depends, can be ascertained and valued by Him alone who searches the reins and hearts. Hence it is, that we presume not to condemn any person, whatever his spoken creed may be. Nay, we hope in God and His charity, that he follows it in singleness and sincerity of heart; and that even those who, so unrelentingly, charge us with the worst crimes in religion, with superstition and idolatry, do so from the best of mistaken motives, and think, as Christ told His disciples their enemies would, that in doing so they are rendering a service to God.

The truth of all that I have said is strikingly illustrated in the conduct of our Redeemer. Never were men more slightly separated from the acknowledged truth, than were the Samaritans in His time. Besides the Jews, they were perhaps the only nation that believed in, and adored, one only God as a spiritual and perfect Being; and as appears from the expressions of the Samaritan woman, in St. John, like the Jews expected a Redeemer and Messias. Not one grossly erroneous article of faith or morals can be substantiated against them; they, perhaps, only differed in not receiving all the same books as inspired which the Jews did, a difference not reckoned essential in modern liberty of faith. Indeed, their only crime was schism in its most mild and mitigated form. They had a rival temple; yet even in this, their priesthood descended from Aaron, and their worship was in strict conformity to the Mosaic ritual.

In addition to these extenuating circumstances, they seem to have had much in their favour. Their charity and hospitality were chosen by our Saviour to be the model proposed in one of His most beautiful parables; their docility was such, that, though at declared enmity with the Jews, in two days He made a considerable number of disciples among them. In a word, so prepared were they for the sublimer truths of the gospel, that, with a docility not equalled among their neighbours, they instantly yielded to it on the preaching of Philip, and that with such unanimity, that it could be said, "that, in consequence, there was great joy in that city" (Acts, xviii.).

With a woman of this nation, Jesus entered into conversation at a well, and, notwithstanding that her life had evidently been far from virtuous, He treated her with all His usual affability and kindness. Though He concealed His real character, she took Him for a prophet, and put the question to Him, which of the two religions was the true one. My friends, what is His answer? Does He reply that the distinctions of outward religion are of no value, but exhort her to reform her life, and attend to the practice of virtue as the only requisite for salvation? Slight as were the dissenting principles of these sectaries, amiable and charitable as may have been their manners, ripe as they were for Christianity, affable and conciliating as His interview had hitherto been; upon this question being put, He makes no allowances, no compromise, but answers her clearly and positively: "Salvation is of the Jews." The woman still seeks a subterfuge; she hints at the difficulty of deciding, and defers the painful inquiry by appealing to the future Messias who would be qualified to give a definitive judgment. But that the principle which He had laid down might want no sanction, that the woman might have no further plea for her errors, He instantly throws off His disguise, and replies: "I am He who am speaking with thee." (John, iv.). Thus did this benign and charitable Saviour express Himself on this important question. He hesitated not to pronounce that no deviation from the true religion, however slight, could be excused.

If, then, God requires from us to believe a particular creed, and will demand an account of every departure from it which is any way our own fault, of what importance must a correct decision be upon such a momentous point? For, the instant a doubt occurs to a person upon the truth of the principles which he has been taught, or an insufficiency appears in any of their proofs; the moment the arguments on the other side present themselves to Him with real force, or seem deserving of His inquiry: if an examination of them is neglected, or if, through fear, or any other motive, these reasons to doubt are at once rejected, such a person becomes instantly responsible for the errors in which he may be involved; they are no longer mere frailties in the judgment, they are malicious wanderings of the will; for he shows that he cares not whether he be in the right or in the wrong. He sees reasons to suspect that he may not be in the proper path, and yet walks on in it, without inquiry; can he be supposed to be anxious that it should lead him right, or that he has a wish to reach his destination? But, in addition to this duty of inquiry, comes the still more weighty and difficult obligation, of embracing the truth the moment it is discovered. For, if any human interest or attachment, any ambition or fear of what the world will say, prevent us from adopting it, it is clear that the sincerity which could alone excuse our error is at an end, and leaves it in its unpalliated deformity before the eyes of God. From all these reflections it clearly results, that according to the doctrine of Christ and His apostles, an account of the correctness of our belief will be demanded of us, an account of great responsibility, in which the slightest flaw in our sincerity, the smallest departure from full concientious conviction, the least fault from prejudices or passions will prove a weighty charge against us. The conclusion is obvious; it becomes the duty of every individual to assure himself of the foundation of his faith, to ascertain whether the grounds on which he believes are those which God requires; whether they will stand the test of the most rigid examination, and remain after this, rooted in his mind unconnected with the slightest doubt. On the correctness of your belief, then, God will call you to judgment, and upon this, consequently, you must now make your first election of good or evil.

The next great point on which we are bound to make a correct decision, as preparatory to that which God will one day make upon us, is the full observance of His moral laws. You may be in possession of the most accurate and certain doctrines; but if you persevere not to the end of your lives in the practice of solid Christian virtue, your faith will be of no value in the sight of God. " Not every one that saith to me, Lord, Lord, shall enter into the kingdom of heaven, but he that doth the will of My Father, he shall enter into the kingdom of heaven." It is here that with peculiar emphasis I may repeat to you the words of Moses. " I call heaven and earth to witness that I have this day set before you life and death, a blessing and a cursing. Choose, therefore, life, that both thou and thy seed may live, and that thou mayest love the Lord thy God, and obey His voice and adhere to Him, for He is thy life." The decision which you have to make is between a life of virtue and a life of evil; in other words between a life of real pleasure and a life of pain, between a life of true happiness and a life of misery. Paint to your imaginations an existence, according to what the passions might suggest would be the most happy possibility, independent of virtue. Give it riches, give it honours, give it friends, give it every indulgence. Suppose even, if you please, that its goods shall be independent of the instability of fortune and the caprice of men, that its friends shall never prove faithless, that its enjoyments shall be uninterrupted.

You may fancy that all these, united, must raise their owner above the feelings of our nature, and make his condition one of pure enjoyment and delight. But if possessed of all these, would your lot be equal to that of Solomon, who, besides what I have enumerated, wore the honours of a sovereign in the peace of a conqueror, with a reputation for wisdom over all the earth. Yet what was the result of his attempts to obtain, by earthly enjoyments, a perfect felicity? These are his words: " I said in my heart, I will go and abound with delights, and enjoy good things; and I saw that all this was vanity. . . . I heaped together for myself silver and gold, and the wealth of kings and princes; and I surpassed in riches all that were before me in Jerusalem; my wisdom also remained with me; and whatsoever my eyes desired I refused them not, and I withheld not my heart from enjoying every pleasure. And when I turned myself to all the works which my hands had wrought, I saw in all things vanity and vexation of spirit." . . . . (Eccles. ii.) Yes, my friends, he saw in them vanity and vexation of spirit, because they still left the body subject to all its natural sufferings, and the mind open to every pang of anxiety and sorrow: he saw in them vanity, because a few years of enjoyment wore out their novelty, and made them pall the heart with a sickly pleasure which it would have gladly changed; he saw in them vexation of spirit, because they themselves were ever a source of uneasiness, and apprehension; and oh! that he may have reflected on them in the same spirit at the conclusion of life. He would then, doubtless, have pronounced them something infinitely worse than vanity and vexation; for they had proved sufficient to seduce his heart from God, and plunge him, though the wisest among mortals, into the most brutish and degrading excesses of idolatry. If such be the experience of one who had it in his power to ward off every breath that could for a moment ruffle his scheme of perfect happiness, what must it be with those exposed to a thousand external causes of uneasiness, whose pleasures depend upon the will or the conduct of others, of whom a trifling accident may disconcert the plans, or totally destroy the prospects?

How very different from these, and how perfectly independent of all the goods or evils of this world, are the enjoyments of a virtuous life. Look at Joseph, whether the favourite of his father, or a slave to Potiphar; whether a prisoner in the common dungeon, or the second man in the kingdom of Egypt; his happiness throughout is uniform; he appears in all these various situations equally noble, equally superior to his outward condition. He forfeits none of his dignity in chains, accused of a most odious crime; he loses none of his sweetness by elevation nearly to the throne; because virtue is the characteristic which everywhere distinguishes him, and makes him equal to every situation. Consider the life of your Redeemer. How perfectly independent were His enjoyments of all that the world could give or take away. His temper was never ruffled, His mind was never disturbed; though He had not a place wherein to lay His head, He never was otherwise than cheerful; because His only wish was to execute the will of God, and to do good wherever it was in His power. But, my brethren you are not called to decide between a life of virtue and a life of pleasure in the severe manner in which *He* selected the former; for, wretched as a life of mere pleasure is, independent of virtue, all those enjoyments which it attempts to possess are real and solid, the moment they are combined with a Christian life. You have not to reject the goods and pleasures of life, when God invites you to choose the way of His commandments; you have only to add to them what will convert them into blessings. Can any request be more moderate? Can anyone be reasonable who refuses to comply with it?

For, if the experience of Solomon proves, that only vanity and affliction of spirit are to be expected from the most exalted state of human felicity, when itself is the final object of our desires, we know equally well, from the example of a thousand saints, whether in scripture or in history, that by making a virtuous and holy use of the advantages of our situation, we may attain a true and solid happiness here on earth. When, then, God desires you, in the words of Moses, to choose this day life, by loving and adhering to Him, he only requires you to choose that path which will ensure a blessing to you and to yours, "that thou and thy seed may live;" He only exhorts you to select that course which will secure you, much more than any precaution of human prudence, against every reverse, making your state superior to the vicissitudes of this life; He only invites you to prefer that system which will preserve you, far better than all the intoxication of pleasure, from uneasiness and disturbance of mind, will keep the soul undefiled by sores that corrode it, and exclude from it all that can sting it with remorse; so as to enable you to look forward to an eternal reward, in recompense of present happiness. If this be an invitation worthy of a good and loving God, the manner in which these blessings are to be attained is no less in conformity with His kind and tender mercies. It is not by a career of painful or sublime virtue. It is only by a regular and conscientious discharge of the obvious duties of your respective situations, which for the most part must be discharged in some way, from worldly motives; and which it costs little more to discharge well. Thus, the respects of society require you to be guarded and well-regulated in your outward conduct—be so from obedience to the law of God, and it instantly becomes the modesty of the gospel. The necessity of preserving character obliges you to distribute alms. Distribute but the same quantity through the love of God, and you have laid up a treasure in heaven. Your situation imposes on you a duty of giving your children some education; give them a virtuous one, and you shall be called great in His kingdom. In compliance with the very prejudices of the world, you must attend the worship of the Church, and perform acts of devotion; do so attentively, do so devoutly, do so fervently, and you will draw on yourself blessings, and secure to yourself the friendship of God. Add to these practices the internal works of virtue, the love of a God whom it requires an effort not to love; keep a guard over your mind, which will ensure you a perpetual tranquility; and you have nearly the whole system of virtue, by choosing which you will have procured for yourselves a life of true consolations here, and stored up for all eternity the fulness of delights.

Yes, "fear God and keep his commandments, for truly this is the whole of man." And if this consideration be not sufficient, remember "that all things that are done, God will bring to judgment, whether it be good or evil." Perhaps, while in youth and health, while in pleasant and active occupation, this reflection may not make its full impression; but in the words of the wise man, the years draw nigh " of which thou shalt say, they please me not." In a few weeks we shall all separate and disperse, never more to meet, each in pursuit of his own peculiar recreation or occupation. We shall all seek different paths, and journey towards different objects, but sooner or later we shall all reach the same destination. You may vary and adorn as you please the walk which you prefer, to beguile its toils and to cheat the eye; the tomb—the tomb alone, and its trophies, can decorate its termination. For the day will come—and oh! my brethren, may years of happiness yet keep that day distant from you all—but still that day *will* come, when, in looking back over a life however prolonged, its joys and pleasures will appear reduced to a few moments of masked folly and dissipation, as brief, as empty, and as completely vanished, as the days of carnival which you so lately passed; its pains and its sufferings will appear to have flown with the same rapidity as those few weeks of penance and mortification which are hastening to a conclusion. All the value of life and its goods will then appear concentrated in one consideration—the virtue or the vice which has accompanied them. Wealth and distinction cannot exempt you from that day and its reflections; though revelling in the possession of every luxury and all the magnificence in a degree equal to Nabuchodonosor's in his new and sumptuous palace, a voice from a watchman and a Holy One shall come down from heaven, and pierce your souls as it did his. "Cut down the tree and chop off the branches thereof" (Dan. iv.); or as to the rich and proud man in the gospel: "Thou fool, this night thy soul is required at thy hand, and whose shall those things be which thou hast laid up?"

That, my brethren, will be the moment when you will be able fairly to judge of the importance of virtue, and the worthlessness of everything else without it, when riches or influence will not be able to purchase for you one hour of life, or one moment of tranquillity. For, what consolation will it afford you to think that you *have* enjoyed yourself, till, perhaps, you have by it broken your constitution, and brought on your present sufferings? What pleasure will it impart to you to reflect that you are still surrounded by wealth which you cannot enjoy, and which has already ceased to be your own? And, oh! above all, what hope will it procure you, to see that you are going to render an awful account of life, to a terrible and just judge, without having lived it well?

But if, in that hour, your eye rests upon a life of virtue, how differently will you feel! You will smile to see, that without having deprived yourself of one true pleasure, you have been preparing a store of happiness for eternity. How valuable will the sufferings of your lot then seem, when they are found equivalent, in the just balance of God, to an eternal weight of glory! How fruitful will your devotions appear, when, for every prayer well said, you see blessings granted, infinitely greater than you had presumed to hope! How well spent will every little charity seem, when you find that the Almighty has written Himself your debtor for it, and is going to refund you a thousand times the amount! Amidst those reflections, you will gradually sink into calm repose, esteemed by those who knew you, loved by all who were in contact with you. Then you will sing with Job: "I shall die in my nest, and shall multiply my days as the palm. My root has been opened out all day upon the waters, and the dew has laid all night upon my branch." (Job, xxix. 18.) You will feel that your life is only going to be continued and perfected in heaven, in practice of that same virtue which you have here followed; your heart, long and gradually detached from the world, will feel no violence in slipping from its last faint ties; your soul, which has tended towards God, is only going to summon its energy, to effect that union which it has so longed for; and closes its last look round earth with the same equanimity, with the same peace, with the same joy, with which it will, in another instant, open it again, to gaze upon the revealed glories of the Deity.

You have thus, placed before you, the two great points on which God will bring all to judgment—accuracy of faith and soundness of morals. Your decision upon them will be the rule by which *His* will be guided. Perhaps, the conclusion to which you shall now come, may be final. Perhaps, as you this day make up your minds, you will persevere, whether for good or for evil. The grace and inspirations of God come not at our good pleasure; if we once reject them, they may never more return. "Because," says He, "I called and you refused, you have despised all My counsel, and have neglected My reprehensions, I, also, will laugh at your destruction, and shall mock when that which you feared shall come upon you. Because they have hated instruction, and received not the fear of the Lord." (Prov. i. 24.) Among the graces and inspirations most free from delusion, and most impressive, the principal is, the word of God. The great sin of the Jewish people always was, that God had sent His servants the prophets, rising early in the morning, and admonishing them, and they refused to hear them. If, then, you have heard the word of the Lord, harden not your hearts as they did, lest He swear also to you in His wrath, that you shall not enter into His rest. Throw open your best feelings to this heavenly seed, and let it produce a hundred-fold. Resolve this day to embrace the truth wherever you may find it, and to search diligently for it; resolve to practise all virtue, and to fulfil every commandment.

Yes; to Thee, eternal fountain of all good, I turn to obtain weight for these reflections, and efficacy for these wishes. If, to use the words of Thy apostles, "my speech and my preaching be not in the persuasive words of human wisdom," (1 Cor. ii. 4) remember that it is Thy word which I have endeavoured to dispense. Fulfil, then, Thy promise; for Thou hast said: "As the rain and the snow come down from heaven, and return no more thither, but soak the earth, and water it, and make it to spring: so shall My word be . . . . It shall not return to Me void; but it shall do whatsoever I please, and shall prosper in the things for which I sent it." (Is. lv. 10, 11.) Prosper it now; may my worthless accents, fertilized by Thy grace, fall upon a good soil, and produce abundant fruit; may no prejudice, may no seduction of the world, prevent any from embracing and practising Thy holy law. Receive on behalf of all present that prayer which Thy well-beloved Son poured out for them, saying: "And not for them only do I pray, but for those also who, through their word, shall believe in Me; that they may all be one, as Thou Father in Me, and I in Thee, that they also may be one in us." (John, xvii. 20.) Oh, yes! may we all be *one*, in the profession of the same saving faith which He taught; may we all be *one*, in the practice of the same holy law which He delivered; and then may we all be still more perfectly *one*, in the eternal kingdom of charity and peace!

THE END.

www.ingramcontent.com/pod-product-compliance
Lightning Source LLC
Chambersburg PA
CBHW020543300426
44111CB00008B/778